Sources of
West Indian History

compiled by
F. R. AUGIER
and
SHIRLEY C. GORDON

LONGMAN CARIBBEAN

LONGMAN CARIBBEAN LIMITED

Trinidad and Jamaica

LONGMAN GROUP LIMITED
Longman House, Burnt Mill,
Harlow, Essex CM20 2JE, England
and Associated Companies throughout the World

First published 1962
Latest Impression 1983

ISBN 0 582 76303 7

Printed in Hong Kong by
Wilture Enterprises (International) Ltd

Contents

Acknowledgments

WE are grateful to the following for permission to include copyright material:

The Daily Chronicle Ltd., British Guiana, for material from past issues of the paper; the author for material from his pamphlet *Federation— Jamaica's Folly* by W. A. Domingo; Faber & Faber Ltd. for material from Olivier: *Jamaica the Blessed Island*; the Hutchinson Publishing Group for material from *A Colonial Governor's Notebook* by Sir Reginald St. Johnston; Edward Stanford Ltd. for material from *Economic Resources of the West Indies* by Sir D. Morris; the Trinidad Publishing Co. Ltd. for material from past issues of the *Trinidad Guardian*.

Unpublished Crown Copyright material in the Public Record Office has been reproduced by permission of the Controller of Her Majesty's Stationery Office.

Foreword to First Edition

THIS book is primarily intended for use in the senior forms of secondary schools.

It is not a history in itself but a collection of various accounts written about many of the events which have taken place in the West Indies. Some of the writers participated in the events which they described. Others wrote of conditions which they themselves had observed. Such writings are an important source of information for the historian, and in this book you can explore historical sources, and use them to enlarge on, and question, the statements of the textbooks.

These accounts have been selected from a variety of documents. Some of them are from official papers such as the despatches between governors and the British Government, debates and laws of the West Indian legislatures, and reports of officials. Others are from private papers, such as letters, journals and diaries. Selections have also been made from books published at the time of the events or conditions they discuss, from contemporary newspapers, and from public petitions.

The extracts selected have been grouped under seven heads. The period for two of them, *Government and Politics* and *Economic Life*, is from the settlement to the recent past. The first chapter, *People of the Caribbean*, stops in the mid-nineteenth century. The dates of four of the topics are those of their subjects. Their titles are *Religion and Education before Emancipation*, *Slavery and its Abolition*, *Emancipation and Apprenticeship* and *Social Conditions since Emancipation*.

Many different kinds of people wrote these accounts and it is important to consider who the writer is when you are trying to assess what he is saying. He may be biased about the subject he is discussing, and you must judge whether other people would have reported the matter in the same way. Sometimes two accounts of the same events have been printed, to let you learn about such events from different witnesses.

To use a source profitably it is necessary to ask as many questions of it as you can. For instance, who wrote or said it? Why did he write it? You can see that there will be differences in what is said according to the answer to the second question. You will not expect the same kind of document, for example, from an official laboriously writing his compulsory annual report as from an indignant citizen writing a spontaneous letter of complaint to a newspaper; their intentions are quite different even when they are discussing the same matter. The accounts printed in this book have been affected by indignation, by national and racial prejudices, by religious beliefs, by economic interests, by ignorance. Most men get indignant at some time and most men are prejudiced, so you must expect to find their opinions influencing what they have written. So when you ask the question: What happened according to this account? you must also ask: What did the writer think about it? Why did he think that?

Questioning the source is one of the most important activities of the historian. This selection of accounts from West Indian history allows you to practise that part of the historian's activity in learning about the past.

SHIRLEY C. GORDON

F. R. AUGIER

May 1961

For this third impression a number of changes have been made to the text. The two chapters *Government and Politics* and *Attempts at Unification* have been rearranged and combined in a new chapter entitled *Government and Politics*. This new chapter has been brought entirely up to date, and includes extracts from official papers, reports and speeches since 1962. Several new extracts have been added in other parts of the book.

February 1969

1

People of the Caribbean

1. Europeans found many American Indian communities throughout the continent as they explored it. Here are some impressions after encounters in the Caribbean area.

a. Arawak Indians

Journal of Columbus, 1492

All that I saw were young men, none of them more than thirty years old, very well made, of very handsome bodies and very good faces; the hair coarse almost as the hair of a horse's tail and short; the hair they wear over their eyebrows, except for a hank behind that they wear long and never cut. Some of them paint themselves black (and they are of the colour of the Canary Islanders, neither black nor white), and some paint themselves white, and others red, and others with what they have. Some paint their faces, others the whole body, others the eyes only, others only the nose. They bear no arms, nor know thereof; for I showed them swords and they grasped them by the blade and cut themselves through ignorance; they have no iron. Their darts are a kind of rod without iron, and some have at the end a fish's tooth and others, other things. They are generally fairly tall and good looking, well made. I saw some who had marks of wounds on their bodies, and made signs to them to ask what it was, and they showed me how people of other islands which are near came there and wished to capture them, and they defended themselves. And I believed and now believe that people do come here from the mainland to take them as slaves. They ought to be good servants and of good skill, for I see that they repeat very quickly all that is said to them; and I believe that they would easily be made Christians, because it seemed to me that they belonged to no religion.

b. Carib Indians

Letter from Dr. Chanca, physician to Columbus's fleet on his second voyage,
1494

The habits of these Caribbees are brutal. There are three islands: the one called Turuqueira (Marigalante); the other, which was the first that we saw, is called Ceyre (Dominica); the third is called Ayay (Guadeloupe): there is a resemblance amongst all these, as if they were of one race, and they do no injury to each other; but each and all of them wage war against the other neighbouring islands, and for the purpose of attacking them, make voyages of a hundred and fifty leagues at sea, with their numerous canoes, which are a small kind of craft with one mast. Their arms are arrows, in the place of iron weapons, and as they have no iron, some of them point their arrows with tortoise-shell, and others make their arrow heads of fish spines, which are naturally barbed like coarse saws: these prove dangerous weapons to a naked people like the Indians, and may inflict severe injury, but to men of our nation are not very formidable.

c. Caribs continue warfare

Berkel, *Travels in South America*, 1670–1689

When a campaign is decided on, the General or Supreme Captain sends to tell all the village and households who have to be collected a stick in which there are as many notches as there are days remaining before they are to come to the place of meeting: they cut one of these notches out every day, until the time appointed, and they can all know by it, that the time has arrived. . . . They put to sea with painted canoes or boats which are made out of one piece from a tree, which is hollowed out like a trough, and is so large that altogether two or three tons of goods can be carried in them. Their weapons are bows with poisoned arrows and short staves of speckled wood. Some carry for their protection bucklers or shields which are handsomely made and cut with figures. They keep no order in fighting, and unless they recognise a marked advantage likewise make no attempt except by night. The men whom they manage to capture they put to death with the greatest cruelty that bloodthirsty people can think of towards enemies who have fallen into their hands. The children and women they make slaves of, and sell for knick-knacks. They once upon a time attacked the French in Surinam, and tried it also upon the English when they first came there: but they were so treated by the latter that they still repent their folly.

2. Spaniards settled in Hispaniola and on the mainland. They attacked, killed or enslaved the Indians.

Las Casas, *An Account of the First Voyages and Discoveries made by the Spaniards in America*, 1540

(*a*) An infinite number of people have left Spain to dwell in these countries. They generally touch at Hispaniola, which is a very fertile and large island, and is become very famous. The extent of it is about 600 leagues; it is surrounded with a multitude of small islands and abounds so with inhabitants, that there's no country in the world more populous. The continent, which is above 250 leagues distant from it, is of a vast extent; a great part of which has been already discovered, and fresh discoveries are made every day; and such great numbers of people inhabit all these countries, that it seems as if providence had amassed together the greatest part of mankind in this part of the world.

(*b*) We shall make it evidently appear to your Majesty, that the Spaniards in about eight and thirty or forty years have unjustly put to death above twelve millions of your subjects; and what an incredible damage must your Majesty have further sustained by these massacres, as they have hindered all these people from multiplying. . . . And how unjust soever those wars have been which they have made upon the Indians, if the poor creatures put themselves in a posture of defence, they cruelly cut their throats without any distinction of quality, sex or age; such as escaped their fury they reserved for slaves, many of whom they condemn to the gold or silver mines, others they yoke together like beasts to make them carry vast burdens. They don't much concern themselves whether the Indians live or die, provided they reap some advantage by their labour.

3

(c) Sometimes three or four towns or villages are given up to the disposal of a certain number of Spaniards, and the inhabitants distributed among them. . . . They employ them in all sorts of service, as to manure the ground, to work in the mines, and to carry burdens in journeys of 50 or 60 leagues. And their masters so constantly exact the hard tasks of work they set them, that the poor wretches have not time to attend the instructions of the divine word, and to learn the rules of Christianity. These people, though free, have been made slaves, and the greatest part of them destroyed.

3. Spain excluded other Europeans from her colonies. To share in the wealth of the Indies the others tried both trading and fighting.

a. Hawkins seeks to trade in slaves

Petition of John Hawkins, 16 April 1565

Very Magnificent Sir: I, John Hawkins, . . . state that:

Whereas by order of Elizabeth, Queen of England, my mistress, whose fleet this is, I cleared on a certain voyage, and was by contrary weather driven to these coasts where, since I have found a convenient harbour, it behoves me to repair and refurnish my ships to continue said voyage;

And whereas to do this I have need to sell the slaves and merchandise I carry; . . . I therefore petition your honour to grant me licence to sell my cargo. I stand ready to pay His Majesty the duties usual in this land and to sell the said merchandise at acceptable prices. . . .

And whereas I do not desire to offend or occasion difficulties, . . . I petition your honour to grant me the licence requested under which to sell to the Spanish in order that I may purchase of them. If this petition be not granted, I shall seek my own solution, for I cannot leave this port, nor will I leave, without supplying my said necessities, for even were I willing to do so, yet am I unable, for I cannot prevail with my people;

Therefore, since between Spain and England there is no enmity nor war, and this fleet belongs to the queen, . . . let your honour not anger me nor move me to aught that I should not do, as will be inevitable if your honour refuse me the licence I ask.

b. French corsairs prowl the Main

An Official of Nombre de Dios to the Spanish King, 30 June 1569

News arrived that numerous corsairs are scattered from Santa Marta, the mouth of the Rio Grande, and the Baru Islands to this place. They must have come in the wake of the fleet, for they took one of its ships which was left unloading at Cabo de la Vela. . . . In it there was a heavy cargo of merchandise, and religious and other passengers, to a number which makes its loss a great pity. . . .

Shortly before this fleet arrived . . . five French corsairs . . . in one of the frigates they had taken . . . were wrecked in a storm on the reef outside this harbour, and were made prisoners here. Having been taken to Panama . . . they said they were natives of Normandy, and had sailed from the port of Havre. . . .

They said that another large vessel they met at Baru and the San Bernardo Islands, which carried more than a hundred men, had sailed from Rouen, . . . and that the men of this large vessel took and sacked the town of Tolu, in the province of Cartagena, and on the coast of New Spain captured a ship laden with sugar (which vessel they took along with them), and five or six frigates of the coastwise trade of Tierra Firme; and that together they had sailed close by this port of Nombre de Dios, to see if they could take it, and continued to the Chagre River. . . . These cursed corsairs are so rife along this coast, especially since the last fleet, . . . and so unprotected this port that this town is in extreme danger of being taken and burned by them.

c. Drake captures Cartagena on his 'Indies Voyage', 1586

Commander of the Spanish galleys at Cartagena to the Spanish King, 5 April 1586

On Ash Wednesday at midday the corsair Francis Drake appeared before this city with 27 sail, large and small. He had ten large ships of 600 tons, and ten or eleven others from 150 to 200 tons. The rest were pinnaces.

From windward this city of Cartagena had been warned a month before that the corsair intended to attack us. Therefore during this time trenches and ditches and very good defensive works were built, especially in that quarter we feared most. . . .

There we had a masonry wall and a ditch which I dug. In this work there were four pieces of artillery and 300 harquebuses and 100 pikes and 200 Indian bowmen. Here, too, were both galleys, bows to shore, with ten pieces of artillery and 150 harquebuses. It seemed impossible for the enemy to enter the city this way.

Yet here, on Thursday, an hour before day broke, he attacked us with 500 to 600 men in such manner that we were almost man to man in numbers, and we had the trenches and ditches and artillery. The galleys fired their artillery and killed about 100 men, and from the trenches we gave them two rounds. They let us have another two.

I saw that the enemy had halted and did not dare to come up. I came out of the trench, sword in hand, crying 'Victory!' The enemy trumpets began to sound retreat. When I was outside the works, already surrounded by enemies, I turned to see whether our men were coming after me and observed that, instead of following up the advantage, they had turned their backs and were fleeing at full speed. When the enemy saw this he shouted, rallied, and went after ours. . . .

So I went and got together some 300 harquebuses and returned by the bridge to face the enemy; and when I began to skirmish they again left me alone, and so the city was lost because it was Your Majesty's luck to have in it the most cowardly subjects there can be in the whole world. . . .

The corsair entrenched himself in the city and burned the buildings outside his trenches, which were some 250. For those which remained within his trenches, although they were half demolished, these people have been pusillanimous enough to give him 110,000 ducats to keep him from burning them. . . . The Franciscan monastery, which stood outside the trenches, was ransomed for 700 ducats and they would not let me defend it, saying that if I did the enemy would burn their houses.

The corsair came in on Ash Wednesday and today, which is the last day of Lent, he is in the harbour, aboard his vessels. . . . I do not know when he will leave.

4. Other Europeans settled land the Spaniards had not occupied.

a. A Dutch settlement in Guiana

The Description of Guiana (17th century)

The sixth colony was undertaken by Captain Groenewegen a Dutchman who had served the Spaniard in Orinoco. But understanding a Company of Merchants of Zealand had undertaken a voyage to Guiana, and attempted a settlement there, he deserted the Spanish service, and tendered himself to his own country; which was accepted and he despatched from Zealand Anno 1616 with two ships and a galliot, and was the first man that took firm footing on Guiana by the good liking of the natives, whose humours the gent. perfectly understood. He erected a fort on a small island 30 leagues up the River Essequibo, which looked into two great branches of that great river. All this time the colony flourished. . . . He was a great friend of all new colonies of Christians of what nation soever. And Barbados oweth its first assistance both for food and trade to this man's special kindness Anno 1627 at what time they were in a miserable condition.

b. The English in St. Kitts

Relation of the First Settlement of St. Kitts and Nevis, John Hylton, storekeeper and chief gunner of Nevis, 1675

A gentleman of London, one Captain Thomas Warner, who was a good soldier and a man of extraordinary agility of body of a good wit and one who was truly honest and friendly to all men, who having made a trading voyage for the Amazons, at his return came by the Caribbee Islands, where he became acquainted with several Indian kings, inhabiting these islands, among the rest with one King Tegreman, king of St. Christophers. He well viewing the island thought it would be a very convenient place for the planting of tobacco, which ever was a rich commodity. Being arrived at London, he made some of his friends acquainted herewith, who in hopes of

7

great benefit became parts with him and did disburse their monies towards the setting forth a ship and men for the design of tobacco, which was in the year of our Lord 1623. And being arrived at St. Christophers with divers gentlemen and others, he brought with him the licence of King Tegreman. They did settle themselves betwixt the two rivers near to the king's house, ... and began to build their houses, and also a fort of palisadoes with flankers, and loopholes for their defence.

c. And in Barbados

Brief Description of the Island of Barbados (17th century)

The English first planted a colony here, Anno Domini 1627. There are supposed to be 30,000 people in this island, masters or freemen, Christian servants, and slaves, which must needs speak it a well settled and planted place, considering the small extent of it. For the merry planter, ... he is never idle; if it rains he topes securely under his roof, if fair he plants and works in the field. ...

It is the custom for a Christian servant to serve four years, and then enjoy his freedom; and (which he hath dearly earned) £10 sterling or the value of it in goods if his master be so honest as to pay; the negroes and Indians (of which latter there are but few here) they and their generation are slaves to their owners to perpetuity.

d. The French in St. Kitts

Du Tertre, *Histoire Générale des Antilles*, 1667-71

As he (D'Esnambuc) needed certain rich people of quality, to establish a company, ... he made every effort through some of his friends to inform Cardinal de Richelieu of the fertility of all the Antilles and the great riches that could be derived from them. This remarkable Minister who was always seeking means of reviving the glory of France, ... listened to him many times with pleasure, and promised to discuss the matter with the king. Finally having been informed in detail of the advantages that France could derive from these distant islands, if trade was established there, His Eminence decided to form a company, which might meet the expense of a first expedition and provide the funds necessary to convey men who would be sent to St. Christopher's; he discussed it with those nearest to him and with others concerned with finance: all of them backed his enthusiasm and . . . many even took shares in the company themselves.

e. *The French in St. Kitts nearly starve to death*

Du Tertre, *Histoire Générale des Antilles*, 1667–71

M. d'Esnambuc, considering that the Company would not wish to advance the help necessary to save the colony, and would not send assistance so that they could defend themselves from the insults of the English, to which they would be exposed daily just as much as to the raids of the Spaniards, with the frequent passing of their fleets to Peru, decided with his settlers to abandon everything; with this in view they did not re-plant food crops; everyone worked only at cultivating tobacco to make a good crop of that before returning to France; they were so discouraged by all their misfortunes, that some even uprooted their food crops to have more ground for planting tobacco.

But completely changing their minds six months later, they began to want the food crops, and suffered more than ever; and the famine was so great that they would all have perished, if divine providence had not brought back the Dutch captain who had traded with them the year before; he sold them flour, wine, meat, shirts, materials, and generally all that they needed, with credit for six months, satisfying himself for the time being with the tobacco which he found in the island; . . . and it is true to say that without this help that our colonies have received from the Dutch they would never have survived.

f. *The Danes in St. Croix*

Governor of Leewards to the Council of Trade and Plantations, March 1734

It is affirmed here the French have actually yielded or sold their pretended right to the Island of St. Cruz to the Danes, and that these are going amain

9

to settle it. . . . The Danes adding this island to the settlements they already have among us, gives me no alarm that anything of danger can ever be hereafter apprehended from them in case of a war with them. No, my Lords, they have always hurt us more by being at peace with us than at war. A war would soon rid us of such neighbours. But whilst we are at war with our most dangerous enemy the French these neutral friends at St. Thomas have always had their ports open to the French privateers, this was always a safe retreat to leeward for their privateers and their English prizes.

5. European nations fought each other for colonies and trade in the Caribbean area.

a. The English take Jamaica from the Spanish

Narrative of General Venables, 1655

Loving Brother, These are to let you know that we are at the Island of Jamaica, which is a very good island, very fruitful of cattle. At present we are possessed of the town and of their houses, and the people are fled into the mountains not daring to fight us, so that now we are spreading our army into the country to quarter and to prevent the enemy from getting provision, so also to plant for our own relief; for our shipping not coming to us hath put us to great loss and hardship, so that all the loss we had at Hispaniola was occasioned thereby, which was for want of arms, provisions, and of guides, but that you will hear all and more than all by some that came back from us; some of which I suppose came only to see golden mountains and to plunder, not expecting to meet with so many difficulties as we met with, which was much occasioned by some misinformation that my Lord Protector had of the great supplies of men and provisions that we should have at the island. Which was much to their and our hurt, for they did for us what they were able, and for the men we had from thence, for the most part they proved good for little. . . .

But blessed be God those that are in chief place are godly, and we have godly teachers among us, so that I hope God will carry on His work among us, and I hope that the Lord Protector will be careful to send better men, I mean both better soldiers and as many godly men as may be, for certainly we had a great many of bad commanders as well as bad soldiers. How they got in I know not, but Barbados did discover many of them, and God will discover them I hope more and more, and weed them out from among us.

b. The English plan to attack Martinique, Guadeloupe, Hispaniola

(i) *Proposal from the Committee for Plantation Affairs*, June 1691

The Plan. Proposal for destroying the French Plantations in America. There are at present in the West Indies five or six frigates. It is proposed to send a squadron of eight more ships and three fireships at once, so as to leave the Downs on the 1st of August, these ships or the merchantmen with them to carry 400 recruits for Bolton's regiment and two regiments more. The whole would rendezvous at Barbados, take what militia can be spared from thence and proceed to Martinique, some of the ships meanwhile always cruising before the Cul de Sac to cut off French supplies from Europe. The troops would keep on landing and destroying the island, to harass the people and drive them to withdraw. . . . Martinique having been destroyed, the expedition could proceed to Guadeloupe and the other islands to destroy the plantations and forts and transport the inhabitants to Europe or the Main. . . . When the service is performed some of the frigates might go with our regiment to Jamaica and picking up as many militia and volunteers as possible, attack Petit Guavos, Tortudas, and the French settlements on or near Hispaniola, the Governor of Jamaica being duly advised of the design. The Spaniards should be invited to co-operate.

(ii) *Memo. of the Agents of the Leewards to the Board of Trade and Plantations*, 26 July 1692

The Purpose. Martinique and Guadeloupe are now practically the only islands from which the French obtain sugar. The loss of them would not only be a great blow to them but a great security to us. . . . Martinique taken, Guadeloupe may be next attacked, and Hispaniola afterwards.

c. Spanish attacks on English ships

Governor of the Leewards to the Duke of Newcastle, March 1735

The Spaniards from Puerto Rico have begun an open war with H.M. subjects in these islands, with the advantage of carrying off all they meet from close under the shore of St. Christophers, nor are our homeward bound ships out of danger though I have once already, and now again have fitted out a sloop of my own, and at my own expense, to open for them if possible a free navigation. We have not one of H.M. ships of war at present in the Government that I know of.

d. Battle of the Saints

Admiral Rodney to Vice-Admiral Parker, 14 April 1782

On board *Formidable*, between Guadeloupe and Montserrat.

Sir, I am this moment favoured with your letter of the 20th of March and have the pleasure to acquaint you that after having a partial engagement with the French fleet on the 9th in which sixteen of my rear having been becalmed under Dominique could not join the action, on the 12th I had the good fortune to bring them to a general action, which lasted from 7 o'clock in the morning 'till half past six in the afternoon without one moment's intermission. Count de Grasse with the *Ville de Paris* and four other ships of the Line are in our possession. Jamaica was certainly their object. I am hastening with my whole fleet to succour Jamaica and wish you could join me with such ships and frigates as are ready off the east end that we may keep the enemy at a distance and prevent their hostile attack.

I send a list of the French ships that are taken; the remainder of their fleet are in so shattered a condition that it must be a very considerable time before they can possibly be repaired. Their loss in men is inconceivable as their whole army consisting of 5,400 men were on board the ships of war, with their whole train of artillery.

6. Some islands were declared neutral.

a. St. Lucia, St. Vincent, Dominica to be occupied neither by French nor English

H.M. Instructions to the Governor of Barbados, November 1730

Whereas the French for some years have claimed a right to the Island of St. Lucia, and do insist that the right to the Islands of St. Vincent and Dominica under your Government, is in the Caribs now inhabiting the same, although we have an undoubted right to all the said Islands, yet we have thought fit to agree with the French Court, that until Our right shall be determined, the said Islands shall be entirely evacuated by both nations; It is therefore Our will and pleasure and you are accordingly to signify the same to such of Our subjects as shall be found inhabiting any of Our said islands, that they do forthwith quit the same until the right to these islands shall be determined as aforesaid. . . . But it is Our will and pleasure that you do not execute this Our order, until the French Governor of Martinique shall have received the like directions from the French Court, and shall jointly with you put the same in execution without any exception. And you are to use your best endeavours that no ships of our subjects or of any other nation do frequent the said islands during the time aforesaid, except only for wood and water.

b. St. Martin and St. Bartholomew to be shared peacefully by French and Dutch

Governor of Leewards to Council of Trade and Plantations, 1734

The Dutch and French, our next neighbours, have concluded a treaty of neutrality for the islands of St. Martin and St. Bartholomew, that inevitably in case of a war cuts off all communication between Montserat, Nevis and St. Christopher, and Great Britain and Ireland for ships bound hence and thither. . . . M. Champigny has foisted a neutrality for St. Bartholomew . . . so that with the careenage of that island, where there is a fine small harbour, within 2 hours sail of St. Christopher, and with cover for French privateers at St. Martin not above 3 hours' sail from St. Christopher, a vessel can't sail from Montserat, Nevis or St. Christopher for Great Britain or Ireland, without being liable to be taken by the French privateers which have these snug waiting places given them by the Dutch, but not to be touched by the English. This treaty may produce irretrievable ruin to the foresaid sugar colony, especially if it is considered the further use which the French will make of St. Thomas and another intended Danish settlement at St. Cruz, in case of a rupture. As the fondness between the French, Dutch and Danes in those parts, is of such a threatening nature, I doubt not but their Lordships will contribute to defeat the bad purposes thereof.

7. Styles of life of free men in the West Indies.

a. Buccaneers, a problem for administrators

French Official to Colbert, 1664

There are 700 or 800 Frenchmen scattered along the coasts of the Island of Hispaniola in inaccessible places, surrounded by mountains or great rocks of the sea, by which alone they can pass from place to place in their little boats. They are three, or four, or six, or ten together, separated from one another by six, eight or fifteen leagues according as they find convenient places. They live like savages without recognising anyone's authority and without any chief, and they commit a thousand brigandages. They have robbed many Dutch and English vessels, which has caused much disorder. They live on the meat of wild swine and cattle and make a little tobacco which they barter for arms, provisions and clothes. So it is very necessary for His Majesty to give an order to cause these people to leave the said island of Hispaniola and betake themselves in two months to Tortuga, which they would do without doubt if it were fortified. And it would bring in a great revenue to the King if all captains of merchant ships and other vessels were forbidden to buy or sell anything to these Frenchmen along the coasts of Hispaniola, but rather here.

b. *A Surinam planter on his estate*

Stedman, *A Five Years' Expedition Against the Revolted Slaves in Surinam*, 1772–74

A planter in Surinam when he lives on his estate (which is but seldom), gets out of his hammock ... about six o'clock in the morning, when he makes his appearance under the piazza of his house; where his coffee is ready waiting for him, which he generally takes with his pipe, instead of toast and butter; and there he is attended by half a dozen of the finest young slaves, both male and female ... to serve him. ... He is next accosted by his overseer, who regularly every morning attends at his levée, and having made his bows at several yards distance, with the most profound respect informs his Greatness what work was done the day before; what negroes deserted, died, fell sick, recovered, were bought or born; and, above all things, which of them neglected their work, affected sickness, or had been drunk or absent; the prisoners are generally present, being secured by the negro-drivers, and instantly tied up to the beams of the piazza, or a tree, without so much as being heard in their own defence; when the flogging begins, with men, women, or children, without exception. ...

His worship now saunters out in his morning dress; having loitered about his estate, or sometimes ridden on horseback to his fields, he returns about eight o'clock. ... Should this prince not mean to stir from his estate, he goes to breakfast about ten o'clock, for which a table is spread in the large hall, provided with a bacon ham, hung-beef, fowls, or pigeons broiled; plantains and sweet cassavas roasted; bread, butter, cheese, with which he drinks strong beer, and a glass of Madeira, Rhenish or Moselle wine, while the cringing overseer sits at the farther end, keeping his proper distance, both being served by the most beautiful slaves. ...

After this he takes a book, plays at chess or billiards, entertains himself with music, till the heat of the day forces him to return into his cotton hammock to enjoy his meridian nap. ...

About three o'clock he awakes, when, having washed and perfumed

15

himself, he sits down to dinner, attended as at breakfast by his deputy governor and sable slaves, where nothing is wanting that the world can afford in a western climate, of meat, fowls, venison, fish, vegetables, fruit, and the most exquisite wines are often squandered in profusion; after this a cup of strong coffee and a liqueur finish the repast. At six o'clock he is again waited on by his overseer, attended as in the morning by negro-drivers and prisoners, when the flogging once more having continued for some time, and the necessary orders being given for the next day's work, the assembly is dismissed, and the evening spent with weak punch, sangaree, cards and tobacco. His worship generally begins to yawn about ten or eleven o'clock, when he withdraws, and is undressed by his sooty pages. . . .

These are the planters who are the pest of the colony. . . . Exceptions, however, take place in every circumstance of life; and I have known many planters in Surinam as good men as I ever would desire to be acquainted with.

c. Some other Europeans

Edwards, *History of the West Indies*, 1793

Let it not be imagined that . . . any considerable part . . . expatriate themselves in the fond idea of living luxuriously without labour. . . . At present among the numbers whom accident or choice conducts to the British West Indies, the juniors in the learned professions of law, physic and divinity, constitute no inconsiderable body. These men ought to be, and generally speaking, really are, persons of education and morals. Few places afford greater encouragement to the first and second of these employments; and as ability is fostered and called forth by exercise, no part of the British dominions has, in my opinion, produced abler men in either (in proportion to their number) than these islands. . . . The British Navy and Army likewise contribute considerably to the augmentation of the white inhabitants. Individuals in both these professions . . . become peaceful citizens and industrious planters. Next to these may be reckoned the mercantile part of the inhabitants, such as factors, storekeepers, book-keepers, and clerks; who are followed by tradesmen and artificers of various kinds, such as millwrights, carpenters, masons, coppersmiths, and others; most of whom, either through accident or necessity, after some years residence, become adventurers in the soil. Then come the husbandmen, or cultivators of the land, professedly such; who are commonly distinguished by the appellation of managers, overseers, and plantation book-keepers; and they constitute a numerous body of people, composed of men of all countries and characters; for, unfortunately, every enterprising genius, who has either learnt no particular trade, or has been brought up to one which is useless in these regions, fancies himself capable of speedily acquiring all the various knowledge of the sugar planter, and the right management and government of his fellow creatures, the Negroes; though in truth a more weighty charge in itself, and more important in its consequences, can scarcely fall to the lot of man.

d. *How Negroes became free during slavery*

Will of Duncan Campbell, 19 August 1811

I give and bequeath the following money legacies to be paid to the respective legatees in Jamaica currency viz., unto each of my quadroon reputed daughters Mary Ann Campbell and Christiana Campbell £100, unto my reputed quadroon son Duncan Campbell £200 and each of my three reputed mulatto daughters by Esther, belonging to Retrieve Estate Old Works, named Susanna Campbell, Jane Campbell and Ann Campbell £100, and unto my reputed mulatto son William Campbell by the same mother £300; and the last named 4 mulatto children I will shall be immediately manumised. Unto my negro woman Hanny Clarke as a reward for her due attendance on me £70 and unto her youngest child known by the name of Eliza Campbell Clarke £30 and unto my old and faithful servant John Campbell £30 and his freedom.

e. Special laws are made to restrict the actions of free Negroes

An Act for the Better Government of Slaves and Free Negroes, Antigua, 1702

And be it enacted that all free Negroes, Mulattoes, or Indians, not having land, shall be obliged in thirty days after the date hereof to choose some master or mistress to live with, who shall be owned by them, and with whom they shall live, and take abode, to the intent that their lives and conversations may be known, to be called to their respective duties.

And if any free person, not being white, shall presume to strike a white servant, he shall be by order of the next Justice (on proof of his striking) severely whipped, at the discretion of the said Justice.

And that all persons who are not whites, and are fit to go out to trades, shall be bound apprentice to any person that will receive them for seven years (unless they choose a master or mistress to be bound to) by the next Justice, who is immediately to cause them to be bound in ten days after such information, to any willing to receive them, on penalty of forfeiting ten pounds.

And be it enacted . . . that for the future no free Negro shall be owner or possessor of more than eight acres of land, and in no case shall be deemed and accounted a freeholder; always provided, that if any Negro ever be possessor of more than eight acres of land in his own right, he may within six months make sale of the overplus of the said land, and, for want of sale of the said land in the aforesaid time, the said overplus above eight acres to be forfeited to the Queen.

f. Right of inheritance limited for free Negroes and mulattoes in Jamaica

An Act to Prevent the Inconveniences arising from Exorbitant Grants . . . made by White Persons to Negroes, . . . and to limit such grants, 1751

Whereas divers large estates, consisting of lands, slaves, cattle, stock, money, and securities for money, have from time to time been left by white persons to mulattoes, and other the offspring of mulattoes, not being their own issue born in lawful wedlock: And whereas such bequests tend greatly to destroy the distinction requisite, and absolutely necessary, to be kept up in this island, between white persons and negroes, their issue and offspring, and may in progress of time be the means of decreasing the number of white inhabitants in this island: And whereas it is the policy of every good government to restrain individuals from disposing of property, to the particular prejudice and detriment of their heirs and relations, and to the injury and damage of the community in general . . . be it therefore enacted . . . that, from and after the first day of January, which will be in the year of Our Lord 1752, no lands, negro, mulatto, or other slaves, cattle, stock, money, or other real or personal estate in this island whatsoever, shall be given, granted to, or declared to be in trust for, or to the use of, or devised by any white person to any negro whatever, or to any mulatto, or other person not being their own issue born in lawful wedlock, and being the issue of a negro.

That nothing in this act contained shall extend to any gift or grants hereafter to be made, for any full, valuable, and adequate considerations, really and bona fide paid by such negro, mulatto or other person not born in lawful wedlock . . . out of their own proper monies and effects; so as the whole of all such gifts, . . . shall not in the whole exceed the value of the sum of £2000 in realty.

8. The numbers of free white men resident in the islands decreased for various reasons. In the extracts which follow some of them are given. While the numbers of whites went down, the black slave population grew. Attempts made to maintain a safe proportion of white to black were not successful. Here are some of the ways proposed.

a. Encourage new settlers with land and credit

Governor of Jamaica to the Council of Trade and Plantations, December 1730

By all accounts the inhabitants are of late considerably decreased, it having been some years ago computed there were 10,000 white men, women and children, the return now made is only 7,648. I take this in a great measure to proceed from our decay in trade and want of due encouragement by law for white men and their families to come and settle. And it is a general mistaken notion that there is not land sufficient to give them upon their arrival, there being still enough ungranted and uncultivated for many hundreds of families.

The French upon Hispaniola have an admirable method of improving and cultivating their colony. The King by his order obliges every merchant ship trading thither to carry a proportionable number of white people according to their tonnage, freight free. Upon their arrival the Government allots them a proportionable quantity of acres suitable to the number of their family, gives them credit for a number of negroes and utensils for manuring their ground, with sufficient provisions until the land given them can produce the same. For which the poor people give bond to the King to pay the value of the negroes, utensils and provisions so soon as the lands so given them shall produce the same. So that in this case your Lordships will observe there only wants first an original fund, because the annual income afterwards will be sufficient to support the same. By this means the colony is mightily settled and improved. This and suchlike proposals have been often mentioned to our Legislature here but alas without success. There has been always some private view or other that have obstructed proposals of that kind.

b. Stop employing Negroes as tradesmen

Governor of St. Kitts, 1734

The number of men capable of bearing arms does not exceed 200 men. The decrease of white men in the island I apprehend to be owing to several causes. Epidemical distempers have destroyed numbers; dry weather, want of provisions, and inability to pay their taxes have obliged others to go off. Land has been at so high a price from the smallness of the quantity in the said island that the settlers of ten or twenty acres who formerly raised only provisions have been tempted to sell their possessions to the sugar planters and have thereupon quitted the island. . . . Another and very great cause of the decrease of white inhabitants, is the employing negro tradesmen, such as carpenters, coopers, millwrights, masons. . . . A very likely means of bringing a considerable number of white men, would be to remedy this evil not by an immediate act against employing such negro tradesmen, which would be too great a hardship upon the inhabitants, considering the value of such negroes, and the other great inconveniences that would arise from obliging the inhabitants all at once to provide themselves with white workmen, a thing almost impracticable, but by preventing the breeding up any more negroes to any such trades for the future.

c. Compel slave owners to hire white servants in proportion to their slaves

Council of Trade and Plantations to Governor of Jamaica, May 1734

As the want of a number of white people in Jamaica proportioned to the number of blacks or other slaves there has apparently been the chief occasion of misfortunes, we are surprised to find, when the island seems never to have been in greater want of white men, that by the last acts passed there to provide a certain number of white people, . . . one white person to every thirty slaves or 150 horses or cattle, is allowed to excuse a deficiency and even that to be commuted by paying six pounds ten shillings quarterly, except the absentees who are charged with a deficiency for want of a white person to every twenty slaves or 100 horses or cattle. Whereas by former acts, particularly one passed in 1703, to encourage the importation of white men, . . . every master of slaves is required to have one white man for the first ten slaves, two white men for the first twenty, and one white man for every twenty slaves after the first. Amongst other means which may be conducive to the improvement and security of the island, . . . encouragements for the importation of white servants should be renewed and increased . . . and a portion of land allotted to every white servant at the expiration of their indentured time.

d. Population at the end of the eighteenth century

Edwards, *History of the West Indies*, 1793

The present state (1791) of the population in the British West Indies appears . . . to be as follows, viz.:

	WHITES	BLACKS
Jamaica	30,000	250,000
Barbados	16,167	62,115
Grenada	1,000	23,926
St. Vincent . . .	1,450	11,853
Dominica	1,236	14,967
Antigua , . . .	2,590	37,808
Montserrat . . .	1,300	10,000
Nevis	1,000	8,420
St. Christophers . . .	1,900	20,435
Virgin Islands . .	1,200	9,000
Bahamas	2,000	2,241
Bermuda	5,462	4,919
Total . .	65,305	455,684

There is likewise in each of the islands a considerable number of persons of mixed blood, and Native Blacks of free condition. In Jamaica they are reckoned . . . at ten thousand; and I . . . believe they do not fall short of the same number in all the other islands collectively taken. The whole inhabitants therefore may properly be divided into four great classes. 1. European Whites; 2. Creole or Native Whites; 3. Creoles of mixed blood, and free Native Blacks; 4. Negroes in a state of slavery.

9. After emancipation West Indian planters tried to recruit estate labourers from many countries. Here are expressions of various attitudes towards the migrants and to the system of indentured labour under which they worked.

a. *Trinidad makes provisions to encourage emigration and offers encouragement to immigrants*

Trinidad Ordinance, 24 November 1838

1. That from and after the promulgation of this Ordinance, it shall and may be lawful for the Governor of this Colony ... to issue and pay from the Colonial Treasury in respect of every Labourer accustomed and inured to Agricultural Labour in a Tropical Climate, who shall come into this Island for the purpose of settling therein, such sums of money as shall be sufficient for the purpose of defraying the expenses of the passage and maintenance on board of such Labourer, and of the Wife and Child or Children of such Labourer, with reference to the place from which such Labourer shall have come; ...

2. ... That it shall be lawful for the Governor ... to nominate and appoint an Agent for the purpose of facilitating Immigration into this Colony in every such place as shall be from time to time selected by the Governor by and with the advice and consent of the Council of Government, and to pay ... out of the Colonial Treasury ... to every such Agent, the following sums of money, that is to say, for every such Labourer ... the sum of Ten Shillings Sterling.

6. ... That for the purpose of facilitating the location of such Labourers. such Agent-General shall receive applications from all Persons who shall be desirous of employing such Labourers, stating the number of Labourers required by such Employer, the employment in which the place where and the terms on which such Person is desirous of employing such Labourer, and shall enter the same in a Book of Registry, which shall be open for the inspection of all such Labourers on their arrival, and of all other persons, at all fit and proper times.

b. *Madeirans and Indians to British Guiana*

Premium, *Eight Years in British Guiana*, July 1846

The tide of immigration has now set in. God prosper it! for it is our only remaining chance, of which everyone is aware, and the Governor is harassed by importunate demands for coolies. Determined to leave no stone unturned, I have embarked deeply in this species of speculation. Besides one hundred Indians, who are now located on the *Fortune*, I expect fifty Portuguese from Madeira in a month. To accommodate these strangers, I have been under the necessity of building a new range of cottages, of suitable dimensions, and the cost has dipped deep into my remaining funds. The law, very properly, requires that those dwellings shall be inspected by the stipendiary magistrate, before the people enter them, and that a certificate of their ample accommodation, and also of the proper drainage and other local circumstances, implying a salubrious locality, shall be granted by that functionary before the Governor awards the immigrants to the estate. And no planter can obtain them unless he employs regularly a medical attendant, properly qualified, by diploma, and there is a hospital, with the proper nurses and attendants kept up for them. I was fortunate in getting mine, scarcely any of my neighbours having yet been so lucky.

c. Chinese to Trinidad

Agent-General for Immigration, Trinidad, 1863

Of the (Chinese) immigrants introduced by the *Wanata* in July of the preceding year it is impossible to speak with any satisfaction. . . . They have died and absconded in great numbers, and the remainder, with few exceptions, are unable to earn anything like comfortable wages. As the colony must no doubt look to China in future for much of its contract labour, it will be well to view this emigration by the light of such experience as we already possess. In 1853 a considerable number of Chinese, about 1,100, were introduced here. They were imported in three ships, of which the first, named the *Australia*, arrived on the 4th of March. Having left Amoy about the close of 1852, she disembarked upwards of 400 men, nearly all in good order. Although at first troublesome from misunderstandings on the score of work or wages, which were neither easily avoided nor arranged on account of a total absence of interpreters, yet these people generally turned out well, because they were able-bodied peasants, and landed here early enough in the year to become seasoned during the dry weather to the climate and customs of the country. The second ship, the *Clarendon*, arrived from Canton on the 23rd of April with an equal selected body of men—rather late in the season perhaps, but still early enough for the lot to become somewhat settled before the rains commenced. This is a *sine qua non* to all safe immigration hither; for even the native labourers from the other islands undergo a more or less sharp seasoning if they migrate to Trinidad late in the year. . . . The last ship of 1853 was the *Lady Flora Hastings* from the Province of Fokeen. Her immigrants were inferior to those by the other two ships, and many were confirmed opium smokers. They . . . proved a source of continual annoyance to the estates that received them, and, before six months passed, suffered so severely from dysentery and sores, as to form a subject of inquiry by the Local Government.

d. What has British Guiana gained from the immigrant workers?

Dalton, *History of British Guiana*, 1855

During the years 1846 and 1847 as many as 7000 or 8000 have been introduced into this colony, and, apart from the expense, what has been the result? Owing to them and the Portuguese, pauperism has been introduced into a land where, before their arrival, it was unknown. . . . As regards coolies, they have likewise suffered from diseases, consequent on the change of the climate . . . and from their want of cleanliness; they have become, along with the Portuguese, almost the only occupants of the public and private hospitals. But the more careful and intelligent among them have had every reason to be satisfied with the advantages of their new position.

e. What has Trinidad gained from the immigrant workers?

De Verteuil, *Trinidad*, 1858

Immigrant Asiatics at present form the great body of our available agricultural population, and are almost the sole resident labourers on sugar or cacao estates. The Coolies are a mild and industrious race, not so robust as the African, but more steady and obedient, and do not seem to entertain any dislike to agriculture. They are highly intelligent, and saving, but they seem to learn and speak foreign languages with difficulty. The African is far their superior in that respect. They are, in general, filthy in their habits, and it is not rare to find, in crowded hovels, men, women, and children indiscriminately herding with their domestic animals; many, however, have already adopted a better mode of living.

The Coolies of the Mahometan faith have been found, on the whole, more intelligent, active, industrious, and orderly than those of the Gentoo and other castes of India. Many of the former can read and write, whereas few of the latter can. These Asiatics still adhere to their own peculiar habits and creeds; they even continue, with rare exceptions, to wear their country costume, and but few have become converts to Christianity: this may be attributed partly to the little interest manifested towards their conversion and partly to the unfortunate arrangement which insures their return to India after a term of five years' service. They are thus naturally led to retain most of those habits which they expect to resume in full force on revisiting their native land. As to the Chinese, they are few in number— about 500—and but recently arrived in the colony. Of them, as far as observation goes, it may be said that they are stubborn, obstinate, and prone to suicide; but they are well acquainted with the tillage of the soil, and are steady workers; in fact, those who have become acclimatised may be considered as the best labourers in the colony.

f. A claim that the immigrant benefits vastly

Sewell, *Ordeal of Free Labour*, 1861

It has been stated that the British coolie immigration is cruelly conducted, but I can affirm that the very reverse is the case. . . . Upon arriving here they have no thought or care about the future. They are immediately provided for . . . and their wages are five times more than they could earn at home. The physical appearance of a crowd of coolie immigrants returning to

India attests the beneficent results to themselves of an industrial residence in Trinidad. Instead of being a set of naked, half-starved, gibbering savages, ready to eat any dead, putrid animal, fish, flesh, or fowl that lay in their path, they are clothed, sleek and well fed, strong and able-bodied, speaking English with tolerable accuracy, and looking the intelligent people that they really are. I have seen them arrive and I have seen them depart, and speak from actual observation. After they are landed from the ship, not only families, but people from the same district are kept together; their wants are immediately cared for, and, the prospects of work and wages being certain, their condition is far more comfortable and encouraging than that of the mass of Irish immigrants who arrive every week in the city of New York. So jealously does the imperial government watch over the interests of the coolies that no more than 350 or 360 can be carried in a first-class ship. They are not more crowded than steerage passengers in an ocean steamer—not half so crowded as a regiment in a troopship going to the East—and the mortality among them, considering their wretched and impoverished condition when placed on board, is inconsiderable. During the voyage from Madras this year the deaths among the coolies have amounted to three-quarters per cent.

g. The immigrant is abused by 'sirdars'

Dalton, *History of British Guiana*, 1855

The coolies in general are gregarious in their habits; a number of them fed and lived together. . . . They recognised as their leaders some few persons whom they called 'sirdars', and the influence which these had over them was incredible. The sirdar chose their place of residence and at his will removed them to another. He received the money they earned, and arranged the rate of wages, expenses, etc. He compelled them to obey him by hard words, and often by blows. In many instances they were sadly cheated and deceived by these 'sirdars', who led them in droves like cattle over the country, and thus assisted, if it did not originate, their unsteadiness of work and conduct. Hence has arisen the dissatisfaction and disappointment sometimes expressed towards them as a class of immigrants, and although in many places they have worked well, and by their numbers have not failed to be of service, yet on the whole the scheme of coolie immigration cannot be considered to have succeeded so well as had been anticipated.

h. The immigrant is abused under indenture and changes in the system are suggested after estate riots in British Guiana

Des Voeux Letter to the Secretary of State, 25 December 1869

Knowing . . . that there is a very wide-spread discontent and disaffection existing throughout the immigrant population, both Indians and Chinese . . . and believing . . . that these ill feelings, which have already vented themselves in disturbance, will . . . unless checked by remedial measures, result in far more serious calamities, . . . I trust that I need no other apology for communicating with you on a subject unconnected with my present duties.

To superficial observation it would seem that persons who have been rescued from a state said to be bordering on destitution in their own country, who are provided with free houseroom, regular work, and wages when they are in health, and in sickness have the advantages of a hospital, the attendance of a medical man and medicines free of expense, who have moreover a magistrate always at hand to hear their complaints, and a department of officers with the especial duty of securing their good treatment, can have no ground for dissatisfaction. A closer scrutiny, however, would detract much from the apparent value of these advantages, and would show that some of them at least are more nominal than real. . . .

I am confident that it is a common practice of medical men to discharge immigrants from treatment before they are completely cured; and to this may be attributed a large proportion of the cases of so-called idleness which are brought before magistrates. By the strict letter of the law an indentured immigrant is bound to do his daily task of work, if he is not in hospital; and though the magistrate has a discretionary power of declining to convict, if he believes the accused is physically unable to work, it is difficult for him on account of the accomplished malingering propensities of the Coolies, to decide in other than extreme cases against the expressed opinion of the doctor.

The consequence of this . . . is that of the great numbers of immigrants who are weekly committed to gaol for breaches of contract, a very considerable proportion are convicted of neglect to do what they were physically incapable of doing; and . . . I know that a sense of the injustice of such convictions is a very potent cause of the prevailing discontent. . . .

The remedy is to make the estates' medical men Government officers, payable either out of the Immigration Fund, or by a tax directly levied for this purpose on the proprietors. . . .

The independence of the Stipendary Magistrates is of even greater importance to the immigrants than that of the doctors. But, at present, these officers are almost equally, though not as directly, subject to planting influence; and their decisions in consequence are, I believe, the chief cause of the prevailing discontent. . . .

Your Lordship will readily understand that . . . in the courts of such magistrates an immigrant is by no means certain of obtaining his rights, and I do not hesitate to assert . . . from personal observation, that they do not; and that they are thus often reduced to a position, which in some respects is not far removed from slavery. The most trifling offences too often subject them to loss of wages and exorbitant fines, or the alternative of certain punishment in gaol and they are governed, not by kindness and good treatment, but through fear of the severity of the law.

. . . I would suggest the creation of a new and superior class (of magistrates), with sole jurisdiction in all cases both civil and criminal between employers and employed, both indentured and free, and in cases of trespass. They should be required to reside in town, and to hold a Court at each police station not more than once a month. They should moreover be invested with a power of summarily punishing illegal stoppage of wages and also false arrests, and imprisonment both in its authors and its agents: the ordinary redress of a civil action being practically out of the reach of ninety-nine labourers out of a hundred. . . .

Under the present law an employer is bound to pay to his indentured labourers the same price for their work as is paid to free labourers. It is, however, notorious that this obligation is as a rule evaded, and sometimes openly broken. . . .

These evils . . . can only be remedied by the appointment of Government officers whose duty it would be to make unexpected visits to estates, and whenever occasion might require, for the purpose of personally inspecting work assigned and the payment offered to immigrants, and of ascertaining the true facts in any doubtful case where these labourers were concerned, so that there might be always forthcoming, when necessary, independent and disinterested evidence as a guide to the magistrate in his decision.

2

Economic Life

1. There were animals and plants in the West Indies which the Indian inhabitants used. The European settlers introduced new varieties of both from Europe and the Mediterranean.

a. Indians and European seamen exchange goods

Voyage of Robert Dudley, 1594–95

I caused my master to shape his course directly for the Isle of Trinidad, ... and the first of February came to an anchor under a point thereof called Ouripan. About 3 leagues to the eastwards of this place we found a mine of marcasites, which glitter like gold; but all is not gold that glittereth, for so we found the same nothing worth, though the Indians did assure us it was *caluori*, which signifieth gold with them. These people did often resort unto my ship, and brought us hens, hogs, plantains, potatoes, pines, tobacco, and many other pretty commodities, which they exchanged with us for hatchets, knives, hooks, bells and glass buttons.

b. Fruit, trees and cattle introduced from Spain

Oviedo, On the West Indies, 1577

Such fruits as are brought out of Spain, into this island, prosper marvellously and wax ripe all times of the year, as herbs of all sorts very good and pleasant to be eaten; also many pomegranates of the best kind, oranges both sweet and sour; likewise many fair lemons and cedars, and a great quantity of all such as are of sharp, sour and bitter taste. There are also fig trees, which bring forth fruit all the whole year. Likewise those kind of date trees that bear dates, and divers other trees and plants, which were brought out of Spain thither. Beasts do also increase in like abundance, and especially the herds of kine are so augmented both in quantity and number, that there are now many patrons of cattle that have more than 2,000 heads of neet, and some three or four thousand and some more.

2. The earliest settlers in the West Indies experimented with the cultivation of various food crops for trade with Europe and the Spanish colonies on the mainland.

a. The foundation of Spanish Town, Jamaica

Letter of King of Spain, 1534

That as Francisco de Garay built in the town a stone house in the style of a fort, he has moved the town for us to the south side of the island, because there is great disposition to settle there as the land is plentiful in bread and beef, and is healthy and that all who reside there have a healthy and easy life because it is a land of very good water, without mountains or ranges of hills, and has very good ports, suitable for navigation to the provinces of Santa Marta, Cartagena, the mainland and Peru and Honduras, because no ship in this trade comes to the north coast but all load on the south because all the inhabitants of the said town are beginning to cultivate on the south coast, and that he has built a mill and they think of going there to live so as to have some comfort and be certain of food. For which reason and others that he has stated he has requested and begged us for the favour to order a licence to be issued that the said town may be built close to a sugar mill which has been commenced, where there may be thirty or forty inhabitants to settle, and that the thirty should be married Portuguese farmers and labouring people so that cultivation and stock rearing may be more quickly done for the use and advantage of the persons who might go to settle, and decree thereon as it may be our pleasure.

b. The crops of the earliest settlers

(i) John Hilton, *Relation of the First Settlement of St. Christophers and Nevis,* 1675

Tobacco. Captain Hilton and others having cleared ground, built houses and followed planting, it came to pass that the Indians betimes in the morning came upon them and did fire their houses and slew divers of his men. He with some others of his household, making their escape into the woods, got to the leeward of the rest of the English, where he did settle another plantation and with the company he had, made what tobaccos he could. And with that tobacco made his return for Ireland and from thence to England, being accompanied with some gentlemen planters of St. Christophers to their desired port London. And having sold their tobaccos for 20s. per lb. they resolved to settle Nevis Island by means of one Mr. Tho. Littleton, merchant, who set them forth with all things necessary.

(ii) Ligon, *History of Barbados*, 1657

Other crops. At the time we came first there we found both potatoes, maize and bonavists, planted between the boughs, the trees lying along upon the ground; so far short was the ground then of being cleared. Yet, we found indigo planted, and so well ordered, as it sold in London at very good rates; and their cotton wool and fustick wood proved very good and staple commodities. So that having these four sorts of goods to traffic with, some ships were invited (in hope of gain by trade) to come and visit them, bringing for exchange, such commodities as they wanted, working tools, iron, steel, cloths, shirts, and drawers, hose, and shoes, and hats, and more hands. So that beginning to taste the sweets of this trade, they set themselves hard to work, and lived in much better condition.

c. Trade with the Dutch

Letter from a Barbadian settler, 9 August 1651

I could heartily wish it you had sent a small cargo for yourself in any of the Dutch ships; it would have been excellent business. The Dutch sell their commodities after the rate at a penny for a pound of sugar. Broad and brimmed white or black hats yield here 120 lb. of sugar and 140 lb. and some 160 lb. Brown thread is at 36, or 40 lb. of sugar a pound; thread stockings of 36 pence will yield 40 lb. of sugar a pair; men's shoes 16 lb.; new fashioned shoes 25 or 30 lb. the pair; pins at great rates and much desired; a man may have for them what he desireth; an Anchor of Brandewyn 300 lb. of sugar, tufted Holland at 16 or 20 lb. of sugar; a yard of good whited osenbridge linen at 6 or 7 lb. of sugar; Holland of 12 pence, if fine, will yield 12 or 14 lb. of sugar a yard; and all commodities are accordingly. But these above said commodities are at present good, and make speedy returns: cards are in great request, if good, and will yield 5 lb. of sugar a pair. I could wish it you had so much of these commodities as come to two or three hundred pounds sterling.

d. Jamaica established as a plantation island by the English

(i) *Declaration of Lord Windsor, Governor of Jamaica, at Barbados*, 11 July 1662

Barbadian colonists encouraged to migrate. Forasmuch as His Majesty has given permission to all free persons to transport themselves with their families and goods, except only coin and bullion, from any of his dominions to the island of Jamaica; and the President and Council of Barbados, having ordered the same to be put into execution, desire to know the conditions, ways, and means, Lord Windsor hereby declares (1) that all persons now ready to transport themselves to Jamaica shall have the benefit of the present fleet, and upon their arrival shall receive allotments of land without delay; (2) that those who are desirous to entertain themselves as servants for a year or more shall have their lands set out notwithstanding; (3) that all handicrafts or tradesmen shall have all encouragement; (4) that none shall be imposed upon in point of religion provided that they conform themselves obediently to the civil government; (5) justice shall be duly administered agreeably to the laws of England, or such laws, not repugnant thereto, as shall be enacted by consent of the freemen of the island; (6) that free commerce with foreigners shall be allowed.

(ii) *Instructions to Colonel Modiford*, 1663

Instructions to a new governor. According to this you are to set on foot and encourage all ways and means which may promote and benefit the trade and commerce of that our island with all neighbouring plantations, colonies, and countries, inviting from thence as many planters as you can, for whom you shall, as you see cause, send vessels for their transportation; particularly you shall make it your care to correspond with any of the Spanish dominions, . . . offering to furnish them with all things convenient for them within your power. . . .

You shall take, or order to be taken, an account of all the considerable harbours and landing places, and erect in them such necessary fortifications as shall appear fit for the security or profit of the island, and this to be done at the public charge there. . . .

You are to give all possible encouragement and invitation to merchants, and such as shall bring trade and assistance to our said island, or any way contribute to its advantage. . . . And that we on our part may do what in us lies for their ease, we are content to allow that no goods, imported into or exported from the island to any other parts, have any custom laid on them for 21 years from the date thereof, nor that even those commodities from that island which shall be brought hither be burthened here with any impost or custom here for 5 years to come after the date thereof.

3. The early slave trade.

a. *A request for Negro slaves to relieve the Indians*

Jeronimite Fathers in Hispaniola to Spanish King, c. 1516

Especially that leave be given to them to bring over heathen negroes, of the kind of which we have already experience. Wherefore here it is agreed that Your Highness should command us to grant licences to send armed ships from this island to fetch them from the Cape Verde Islands, or Guinea, or that it may be done by some other persons to bring them here. Your Highness may believe that if this is permitted it will be very advantageous for the future of the settlers of these islands, and for the royal revenue; as also for the Indians your vassals, who will be cared for and eased in their work, and can better cultivate their souls' welfare, and will increase in numbers.

b. Other European nations develop the trade

A Spanish account of Hawkins's second slave voyage, 1565

I have used all diligence to obtain information about Hawkins's voyage, and find that after he left Galicia, where he touched, he went to Guinea and traded with the Portuguese slavers. He obtained a number of negroes and sent men on shore to obtain more. He took some but lost nine soldiers killed, amongst whom were some Portuguese. They say he must have had 400 blacks, but in the accounts he gives he says there were only 370, and with these and a good stock of goods, cloths, linens, and the like, he went straight to Dominica, and thence to Deseada, where he took water, fuel, and other necessities for the voyage to the mainland. He then went to a place called Barbarrota, and on his arrival the governor came with troops to know who they were. He was told they were Englishmen who wished to trade, and replied that they could not trade there, as Your Majesty had prohibited it on pain of death. The captain answered that he had a large number of men with him, and he was unable to restrain them from landing and doing damage if they were not allowed to traffic, and he thereupon entered into a private arrangement with the governor that he would send some men ashore next day who would make for the settlement and threaten damage, and the governor would then appear and give them leave to trade in order to prevent injury. This was done, and 200 troops, with some pieces of artillery, were landed, and firing was commenced, when the governor came out and a pretence of fighting was made, but soon ceased, and they were allowed to trade for the sake of peace. The people on shore bought a quantity of cloths, linens, and other things, and 140 slaves, and the expedition then sailed to another island, called Quiros Sall (Curacao), where they say they only found two Spaniards, who had a large quantity of skins. They bought 1,500 skins of them, and the meat they required for their use. They sailed thence to Rio de la Hacha, where the same took place with the governor as had passed at Barbarrota. There they sold the rest of the slaves and a large part of their merchandise.

c. Necessity for Negro slaves argued

Minutes of the Council of the Indies, 1684

It was certain that the Indies could not be maintained without negroes, because the lack of Indians has made it necessary that they be supplemented by making use of these people both for the labour of the estates, and for service in the families, as it is impossible to obtain Spaniards or Creoles who are willing to do this kind of work.

d. European companies for the slave trade in bitter rivalry

Company of Royal Adventurers to the King, 1663

The trade of Africa is so necessary to England that the very being of the plantations depends upon the supply of negro servants for their works. This trade was at the time of his Majesty's restoration managed by particular adventurers, who were so far from any possible design of having forts or asserting the honour of the nation that they were a constant prey to the Hollanders and were quite tired out of the trade by their great and frequent losses. . . .

The Company . . . sent out this last year above £160,000 in cargoes, have plentifully supplied the coast to the great satisfaction of the natives, furnished all the plantations with negro servants, set up new manufactures at home and improved the old, vented a great many native commodities, employed above 40 ships, and doubt not they shall import very considerable quantities of gold and silver, as they have repaired others, and have no European rivals but the Hollanders; but as to them, experience of the past gives just cause to apprehend what is intended for the future.

For the Dutch have endeavoured to drive the English Company from the coast, have followed their ships from port to port, and hindered them coming nigh the shore to trade, they have persuaded the negroes to destroy their servants and to take their forts, have seized their boats and goods, violently taken possession of Cape Coast, and shot at his Majesty's Royal flag. To complete the former indignities, one Valckenburgh, Director-General of the West India Company in Africa, has sent a protest to their factors, in which he challenges the whole trade of Guinea as their property, by right of conquest from the Portuguese. . . .

In a word, notwithstanding a stock so considerable, and the many good ships of force and the land forces they have sent, had it not been for the countenance of some of his Majesty's ships, to give the (English) Company a respect in the eyes of the natives and preserve their forts, the (English) Company had ere this been stripped of their possessions and interest in Africa.

4. By the middle of the seventeenth century sugar had been chosen as the most profitable crop for cultivation. To produce it on a large scale estates were developed and Negro slaves were the only reliable source of labour to work them.

a. Sugar found more profitable than tobacco

Ligon, *History of Barbados*, 1657

And their supplies from England coming so slow, and uncertainly, they were often driven to great extremities: and the tobacco that grew there, so earthy and worthless, as it could give them little or no return from England, or elsewhere; so that for a while they lingered on in a lamentable condition. . . .

But when the canes had been planted three or four years, they found that to be the main plant, to improve the value of the whole island: and so bent all their endeavours to advance their knowledge in the planting, and making sugar: which knowledge, though they studied hard, was long learning.

b. Sugar experiment described

Ligon, *History of Barbados*, 1657

At the time we landed on this island, which was in the beginning of September, 1647, we were informed, partly by those planters we found there, and partly by our own observations, that the great work of sugar-making, was but newly practised by the inhabitants there. Some of the most industrious men, having gotten plants from Pernambuco, a place in Brazil, and made trial of them at the Barbados; and finding them to grow, they planted more and more, as they grew and multiplied on the place, till they had such a considerable number, as they were worth the while to set up a very small *ingenio*, and so make trial that sugar could be made upon that soil. But, the secrets of the work being not well understood, the sugars they made were very inconsiderable, and little worth, for two or three years.

c. Negro slave labour for sugar plantations

Letter of George Downing to his cousin, 26 August 1645

If you go to Barbados, you shall see a flourishing island, and many able men. I believe they have bought this year no less than a thousand Negroes, and the more they buy, the better able they are to buy, for in a year and half they will earn (with God's blessing) as much as they cost. . . .

A man that will settle there must look to procure servants, which if you could get out of England, for 6, or 8, or 9 years time, only paying their passages, or at the most but some small above, it would do very well, for so thereby you shall be able to do something upon a plantation, and in short time be able, with good husbandry, to procure Negroes (the life of this place) out of the increase of your own plantation.

d. An estate's accounts

Ligon, *History of Barbados*, 1657

	£.	s.	d.
We will allow yearly to issue out of profits that arise upon the plantation	500.	00.	00.
As also for the moderate decays of our Negroes, horses, and cattle, notwithstanding all our recruits by breeding all these kinds	500.	00.	00.
For foreign provisions of victuals for our servants and some of our slaves, we will allow yearly	100.	00.	00.

	£.	s.	d.
For wages to our principal overseer yearly	50.	00.	00.
The charge of clothing the five subordinate overseers yearly	27.	05.	00.
Clothing the remaining 14 men-servants yearly	58.	16.	00.
Clothing four women servants that attend in the house	19.	4.	00.
The remaining six women servants that do the common work abroad in the fields	21.	06.	00.
The charge of thirty rug gowns for these thirty servants	37.	10.	00.
The clothing of fifty men Negroes	15.	00.	00.
The clothing of fifty women Negroes	20.	00.	00.
Sum total of the expenses is	1,349.	01.	00.
Sum total of the yearly profits of the plantation	8,866.	00.	00.
So the clear profit of this plantation of 500 acres of land amounts to yearly	7,516.	19.	00.

e. An estate described

Ligon, *History of Barbados*, 1657

Met there with Major William Hilliard, an eminent planter of the island and a councillor, who had been long there, and was now desirous to suck in some of the sweet air of England: and glad to find a man likely to perform with him took him home to his house, and began to treat with him, for half the plantation upon which he lived; which had in it 500 acres of land, with a fair dwelling house, an *ingenio* placed in a room of 400 foot square; a boiling house, filling room; cisterns, and still-house; with a carding house, of 100 foot long, and 40 foot broad; with stables, smith's forge, and rooms to lay provisions, of corn, and bonavist; houses for Negroes and Indian slaves, with 96 Negroes, and three Indian women with their children; 28 Christians, 45 cattle for work, 8 milch cows, a dozen horses and mares, 6 assinigoes.

After a month's treaty, the bargain was concluded, and Colonel Modiford was to pay for the moiety of this plantation, £7,000; to be paid £1,000, in hand, the rest £2,000 a time, at six and six months, and Colonel Modiford to receive the profit of half the plantation as it rose, keeping the account together, both of the expense and profit.

In this plantation of 500 acres of land, there was employed for sugar somewhat more than 200 acres; above 80 acres for pasture, 120 for wood, 20 for tobacco, 5 for ginger, as many for cotton wool, and 70 acres for provisions: viz. corn, potatoes; plantains, cassava and bonavist; some few acres of which for fruit: viz. pines, plantains, melons, bananas, guavas, water melons, oranges, lem ons, limes, etc. most of these only for the table

f. Fortunes expected

Ligon, *History of Barbados*, 1657

Colonel James Drax, whose beginning upon that island, was founded upon a stock not exceeding £300 sterling, has raised his fortune to such a height, as I have heard him say, that he would not look towards England, with a purpose to remain there, the rest of his life, till he were able to purchase an estate, of ten thousand pound land yearly; which he hoped in a few years to accomplish, with what he was then owner of; and all by this plant of sugar. Colonel Thomas Modiford, has often told me, that he had taken a resolution to himself, not to set his face for England, till he made his voyage, and employment there, worth him a hundred thousand pounds sterling; and all by this sugar plant. And these were men of as piercing sights, and profound judgements, as any I have known in that way of management.

5. European governments made laws for their colonies and themselves to secure the maximum benefit from their colonial trade. The English Government forbade the growing of tobacco in England, forbade the colonists to trade with foreigners, protected colonial produce in the English market, and reserved the carrying trade to their own nationals.

a. Cultivation of tobacco and its trade regulated

Act of the Privy Council, 24 May 1625

And for the better encouragement of all English planters to go on cheerfully in the advancing of any the English plantations their Lordships have likewise thought fit and ordered, that these instructions following be strictly observed and put in execution, viz.

That all tobacco whatsoever, which shall not be of the growth of the English plantations, be utterly prohibited to be imported into this kingdom.

That no tobacco be suffered to be planted within this kingdom.

That all tobacco of the growth of any English plantation whatsoever be brought into this kingdom.

b. Control of trade from the colonies

Warrant of the Privy Council, 6 April 1632

Whereas we have been informed that divers ships and vessels coming from St. Christophers and Barbados, the Caribbee islands in the West Indies, Virginia, Bermuda, and other English plantations in those parts, do go into foreign countries with their goods and merchandise to his Majesty's great loss, and prejudice in his customs. These are therefore to pray and require you the Lords Commissioners for the Admiralty to take effectual order, that all the aforesaid ships and vessels (when they come upon the coast of England or shall at any time be met with, by any of his Majesty's ships at sea) may come for the Port of London, or some other of the ports of this kingdom, and there duly to enter and unlade their goods, that his Majesty may not be defrauded of his custom by the evil disposition of any person, or the undue courses aforesaid.

c. Protection of English colonial tobacco in England

Warrant of the Privy Council, 24 February 1632

His Majesty having taken into his princely care, the estate of the plantations of his subjects in Virginia, Summer Islands, St. Christophers, Caribbee Islands, and other places (for the present) subsisting by tobacco, although with apparent hopes of better and more useful commodities, from thence shortly to be had, and considering that much of that tobacco is but of a mean condition, is graciously pleased to mitigate and abate a great part of the duties.

And therefore his Majesty's pleasure is, that all tobacco of the growth of Virginia and the Summer Islands . . . which henceforth shall be brought into the kingdom . . . by any of his Majesty's natural born subjects, shall pay 2d per lb. subsidy and 2d per lb. impost, or increase of subsidy, and all tobacco from St. Christopher, the Caribbee Islands and other plantations, 3d per lb. subsidy and 3d per lb. impost. . . .

And his Majesty's pleasure further is, that all Spanish tobacco, as of any other country, or place (being not of the plantations of his Majesty's own subjects) from henceforth brought into this kingdom, shall stand charged . . . to pay six pence for each pound of pudding or roll tobacco, and four pence for every pound of leaf tobacco; and to stand and remain charged with payment of impost, as Spanish tobacco hitherto hath continued (viz.) to pay eighteen pence for each pound weight thereof.

d. Carrying trade reserved for the English

Navigation Act, 1660

For the increase of shipping and encouragement of the navigation of this nation, wherein . . . the wealth, safety and strength of this kingdom is so much concerned, be it enacted . . . that from and after the first day of December one thousand six hundred and sixty . . . no goods or commodities whatsoever shall be imported into or exported out of any lands, islands, plantations or territories to his Majesty belonging . . . in Asia, Africa or America, . . . but in such ships or vessels as do truly and without fraud belong only to the people of England . . . or are of the build of and belonging to any of the said lands, islands, plantations, or territories as the proprietors and right owners thereof, and whereof the master and three-fourths of the mariners at least are English, under the penalty of the forfeiture and loss of all the goods and commodities which shall be imported into, or exported out of, any of the aforesaid places in any other ship or vessel.

e. Trade with the Spanish colonists allowed

King of England to the Governor of Barbados, February 1663

His Majesty being certainly informed that the Spanish planters of the West Indies lately attempted to trade with Barbados for a supply of negro slaves, but were given to understand that they could not lawfully do so, hereby grants licence to Spanish subjects in America to purchase from the Caribbee Islands and Jamaica supplies of negro slaves, and such other European commodities as their own plantations may want, on payment of customs for the same, for every negro five pieces of eight, at the rate of four shillings sterling for every piece of eight.

6. The reaction of the colonists to the Laws of Trade and Navigation.

a. The small tobacco planters of Nevis are forced to leave

Petition of Council and Assembly of Nevis to Governor, 29 April 1664

The Council and Assembly of Nevis to Francis Lord Willoughby, Governor of Barbados and the rest of the Caribbees . . . complain that whereas they formerly enjoyed freedom of trade with all nations, in amity with his Majesty, they are now debarred from same, by the self-driving interest 'of some not well affected to our well being'. Many of the meaner sort were wholly employed in the manufacture of tobacco, whereupon they lived comfortably, but now that supplies come only from English ports where tobacco is no commodity, and not being able to produce sugar, they are forced daily to desert the island. Beg his Excellency to intercede with his Majesty for their re-enjoyment of their former freedom of trade, so they may transport their goods to any country in amity with England, whereby they conceive his Majesty's revenue by customs may be much augmented, and his Majesty's poor subjects encouraged to continue their stations.

b. *Barbadian petition for free trade, especially in slaves*

(i) *Petition of the Representatives of Barbados to the King*, 5 September 1667

And now that they may not fail in their duty to let his Majesty know how they may be best secured and encouraged against their watchful enemy, they pray:—

> That whereas free trade is the best means of living to any colony, of which these islands having for some years been debarred, the planters have been so impoverished and the enemy's trade so advanced, that the English to maintain a livelihood have been forced to fish with the French nets; that they may have free trade with the coast of Guinea for negroes, or else that the Royal (African) Company be obliged to supply them at the price mentioned in their first printed declaration (though that too, like the canker of usury, will soon be the bane of a laborious planter). . . .
>
> For export of commodities to any place in amity with England, in English bottoms, on paying customs either in Barbados or in England.

(ii) *Answer of the Royal African Company to the petition of the representatives of Barbados*, 23 January 1668

That open markets and free trade are best for those that desire them is certain, and so it is to buy cheap and sell dear, and most of all to have commodities for nothing, and if all his Majesty's dominions and plantations were made only for Barbados, it might be expedient; but since it is conceived that his Majesty will have regard to what may preserve the trade of the nation, and not only to what will gratify Barbados, they think their desire of free trade will prove as impracticable and pernicious to themselves as destructive to all other public interests.

(iii) *The Privy Council replies*, 8 November 1676.

We have considered and examined the said petition and annexed paper of grievances.

As to the . . . want of sufficient supply of negroes from the Royal African Company we did send to the Sub-Governor and Deputy Governor of that Company for an account of that matter; . . . the said Colonel Thornbury agent for the island of Barbados likewise attending and being present, who . . . agreed that the island had been well supplied for this twelve months past, and that when there was an interruption, it was occasioned by the stop of trade in the late Dutch war.

But that which is the main matter for a dispensation of the Acts of Navigation and Trade. We need not lay before your Majesty of what evil consequence it is, that any of your subjects should presume to petition your Majesty against Acts of Parliament (which are the laws they must live under) and call them grievances, and acts upon which the whole frame of the trade and navigation of this kingdom doth turn, and indeed would be destroyed by such a dispensation, which nevertheless, if it were in any wise to be borne with or granted, as surely it is not being of that weight, we humbly conceive it only fit to be done by your Majesty in Parliament, the whole nation being concerned in it.

7. The development of the English colonies by the end of the seventeenth century.

a. The colonies described

(i) *An account of the present state and condition of . . . Jamaica*, 1 January 1676

Jamaica. Most of the ships trading from Europe come directly from London, and are between 80 and 100 tons, and some few of greater burden. Their lading is dry goods, servants, liquors, brandy, and all manner of ironwork, etc., for planters; many touch at the Madeiras and bring wine, and return with the commodities of the island, hides, and logwood cut at Cape Capoche, which has exceedingly contributed to the lading of ships and keeping up the trade. Some ships come from Ireland with provisions and servants, and return with sugar, tobacco, and logwood. Several merchants at Port Royal have correspondents at Bristol, Chester, Plymouth,

Southampton, who supply servants, coarse cloths, provisions, ironwork. . . .

Between Barbados and this place two or three vessels are constantly passing, and every day some people remove hither; from the other Caribbee islands no vessels come unless driven down by storms. There may be about 60 or 70 vessels belonging to the island, and wholly employed in fetching logwood and salt, turtling and striking manatee, or fishing in the bays of Cuba; others go to Tirisee, and the Lagunas of Yucatan; some sloops trade with the French for hides, meat, and tobacco; some have little designs with the Spaniards, and others with Curaçao. These small vessels built in the island pay no tonnage, or any duties and take out their let passes but once a year, or every six months; it being much to the interest of the island to encourage them, for they employ abundance of men, bring trade to the island, and constantly give advice, so that no enemy can surprise the island.

(ii) *Richard Blome's account of Barbados*, 1672

Barbados. The commodities that this isle produceth are sugars (which, though not so white as those of Brazil, yet better when refined, being of a fairer grain), indigo, cotton, wood, ginger, logwood, fustick and lignum-vitae. And these commodities, especially sugar, indigo, cotton and ginger, are here in such great abundance that about 200 sail of ships and vessels, both great and small, have yearly their loading, which, after imported in the several ports of England and Ireland, is again in great quantities exported to foreign parts to our great enrichment, and the rather for that they are not permitted to trade with any other nation but the English and such of his Majesty's subjects in New England, Virginia and Bermudas.

(iii) *Governor Codrington to the Lords of Trade and Plantations*, 13 July 1691

Shortage of currency in the Leewards. In the Leeward Islands there is very little money, and trade is driven mostly by truck. The merchants keep their books, and accounts in sugar or other produce and in that form state all debts due to or from them. I know how beneficial it would be to have our trade settled by money, as in England and in all the colonies but this . . . People who want clothing, etc., buy it with sugar, and those who are in circumstances to furnish themselves in England ship their produce home. At Barbados it is true that there is a money trade, and that produce can be sold, though at a less price than it would fetch in England. . . .

Pieces-of-eight if of full weight (which not one in a hundred is) are worth 4/4½d., but generally are worth from 3/6d. to 4/-. In Barbados, they pass for 5/-; in the Leeward Islands for 6/-. . . .

If a mixed metal coin of the interim value of a penny and of the size of a sole mark were struck, to be used only in the American plantations and to pass as forty-eight to the piece-of-eight, it would be a great convenience to the colonies and of some advantage to the king. . . . I do not think that there would be any complaint of the king's profit, since at present we use foreign coin at a higher rate than its intrinsic value.

b. The colonies in competition

(i) *Memorial of merchants and traders of the Leeward Islands to the Lords of Trade and Plantations*, 17 October 1690

The other Leewards with St. Kitts. St. Christophers has been recaptured, and an intimation has lately reached us from thence that many English intend shortly to settle thereon. Such settlement would be of very fatal consequence not only to St. Christophers but to all the British Caribbees; for the former inhabitants, who are now dispersed in various islands, would not only return themselves, but many of the people from other islands would go and settle with them, whereby they would be exposed to great peril in case of a French attack. If St. Christophers were allowed to lie waste for a time and were held only by a company or two at the fort there would be no temptation to the French to retake it. We beg the king's orders that the settlement of St. Christophers may be suspended till the close of the war.

(ii) *Governor of the Leewards to the Council of Trade and Plantations,*
18 August 1701

Barbados with the Leewards. Mr. Grey wrote me the people of Barbados would give these islands no assistance, and had addressed to him
not to spare the frigate. . . . It seems a little odd that Barbados could not
spare 200 men, when her militia was at least 10,000 strong. . . . I am very
well satisfied that Barbados has no inclination to serve or save these
islands, nor have one of these islands to help another, because if a sugar
island be lost, so much the less of the commodity is made, and consequently
the price is raised.

8. The African slave trade was made an integral part of England's overseas trade. A regular triangular trade developed between Africa, the Americas and England. European slave trading
companies tried to get a monopoly in the slave trade. The
monopoly of the Royal African Company was disliked by
English colonists but upheld by the English Government.
Jamaica merchants had an opportunity to take part in an illicit
slave trade to the Spanish colonies until 1713; then the *asiento*
to supply slaves to the Spanish colonists was ceded to England.

a. The triangular trade

Evidence to the House of Commons, 16 February 1735

Mr. John Hardman, merchant, said, that he lives at Liverpool, and
trades considerably to Guinea, and the British plantations; and freights
the ships, which he sends to those parts, with all sorts of English woollen
manufactures . . . and that with these goods, negroes are purchased; and
the rest of the freight is of cloths . . . and also iron hoes, etc., and toys fit
for the British plantations in the West Indies; for which, in return, he
receives the produce of those islands, and particularly cotton, which is
taken in last, and is one-fourth part of the loading of most of the ships
which come from thence, and is chiefly made use of in the manufacturing
of fustians.

b. Royal African Company complain of interlopers

Petition of the Royal African Company, 9 September 1680

Whereas his Majesty was graciously pleased to grant to them, the sole trade of the coast of Guinea, many of his Majesty's subjects as well from hence as from his Majesty's plantations and other parts, in contempt of his Majesty's said charter and proclamation have of late and still do presume to send out ships to trade in those parts more abundantly than ever heretofore.

Several have come lately to the island of Barbados and landed their blacks and merchandise and gone away again without entering their ships or taking out their despatches in defiance of the government and contrary to the Act of Trade and Navigation and a particular act of the country requiring it.

Whereby the company stock will be so much impaired as they shall not be able to carry on their trade and support the charge of about £15,000 per annum for the necessary maintenance of their forts and garrisons.

c. Government of Jamaica object to monopolies in the slave trade

Address of the Governor, Council and Assembly of Jamaica to the Queen, 2 June 1711

Understanding that your Majesty has at this time under your Royal consideration the trade to Africa, upon the establishment of which our estates in this your Majesty's island and the welfare of this your colony do entirely depend, and being assured your Majesty will always have a tender regard to the prosperity of all your good subjects, we presume to acquaint your Majesty that we have for many years past found very great advantages from an open and free trade to Africa, which we are under apprehension would not only be lost to us from an exclusive trade, but that we should thereby be involved in insuperable difficulties.

Besides all other inconveniences of monopolies we humbly conceive it will be plain to your Majesty what extreme hardships we are likely to suffer, if it be in the power of a few men to rate our commodities as they think fit, to furnish our markets or suffer us to want, as shall best suit their private gain; to engross entirely to themselves and their factors the Spanish trade which alone can be carried on by a supply of negroes; and in all other particulars to render our interest in great measure dependent on their own.

And whether this will not have an ill consequence upon the trade of Great Britain in discouraging the exportation of its woollen manufactures and lessening the importation of bullion as well as of the commodities of the growth of your Majesty's plantations, we humbly submit to your Majesty's wisdom.

d. Jamaica and Barbados to have factories for slaves in transit for Spanish colonies

Privy Council, 6 February 1690

His Majesty assents to, and gives orders in accordance with, a memorial of the Spanish Ambassador, Don Pedro de Ronquillo, representing that Don Nicolas Porcio having made a contract or *asiento* with his Catholic Majesty for furnishing negro slaves in his said Majesty's plantations in America, and in order thereunto his Chief Agent Sir James del Castillo hath contracted with the Royal African Company here, and other English merchants, for all or the major part of the negroes he shall want for that purpose, from which trade this kingdom and the American plantations belonging to it will receive very great advantage, and therefore . . . desiring his Majesty will be pleased to give effectual orders to his Governors in the American colonies, and particularly to those of Jamaica and Barbados (where the chief Spanish factories will reside) that they protect and receive all such persons and ships, as shall be sent for the said trade by virtue of his Catholic Majesty's orders, and permit and countenance that trade in the same manner as had been done in the late reigns and governments.

e. Illicit trade with Spanish America

The Voyages and Travels of Capt. Nathaniel Uring

In the beginning of the year 1711, I went over in a sloop, well-manned and armed, to trade on the coast of New Spain; and we carried with us a great quantity of dry goods, and about 150 Negroes. We first touched at Portobello, and being war-time, we used to go to the Grout within Monkey-Key, which is a very good harbour, and is about four or five miles from the harbour and town of Portobello.

As soon as we arrived there, our custom was to send one of our people, who could speak Spanish, into the town with letters to the merchants, to give them notice of our arrival; and they appointed the time and place, where and when our canoe should wait for them, to bring them on board, in order to traffic with us. . . .

We lay at this place trading six weeks, in which time the Spanish merchants at Panama had notice of our being there, and they came over the Isthmus to trade with us. These merchants frequently travelled in the habits of peasants, and had their mules with them, on which they brought their money in jars, which they filled up with meal; and if any of the king's officers met them, nothing appeared but meal, and pretended they were poor people going to Portobello to buy some trifles; but for the most part went through the woods, and not in the road, in order to prevent their being discovered by the Royal officers. . . .

While we lay at the Grout the first voyage, a Spaniard agreed with us for seventy slaves, and a good quantity of dry goods, which we delivered between Chagre and Porto Nova (Colon Bay); the signal agreed upon being made from the Castle of Chagre, we anchored about two miles from it, and sent our canoe on shore, where we found the Spaniards with several asses and mules laden with gold and silver, which we carried on board. . . .

But being not able to dispose of all our cargo there, we set sail for Cartagena. . . . When we arrived at the Brew, which is the place where we lay to trade with the merchants of Cartagena, we gave notice of it to some of the people of that island, who sent word into the city of our being there: several merchants came from thence to trade with us, and when we had sold what we could we returned to Jamaica. . . . I was several voyages to the Spanish coast, trading in this manner.

f. The English get the asiento

Asiento, 1713

To procure a mutual and reciprocal advantage to the sovereigns and subjects of both Crowns, her British Majesty does offer and undertake for the persons whom she shall name and appoint that they shall oblige and charge themselves with the bringing into the West Indies of America, belonging to his Catholic Majesty, in the space of the said thirty years, to commence on the 1st day of May 1713, and determine on the like day which will be in the year 1743, viz., 144,000 negroes, *Piezas de India*, of both sexes and of all ages, at the rate of 4,800 negroes, *Piezas de India*, in each of the said thirty years, with this condition, that the persons who shall go to the West Indies to take care of the concerns of the *asiento* shall avoid giving any offence, for in such case they shall be prosecuted and punished in the same manner as they would have been in Spain, if the like misdemeanours had been committed there.

That for each negro, *Pieza de India*, of the regular standard of seven quarters, not being old or defective, according to what has been practised and established hitherto in the Indies, the Asientists shall pay 33 pieces of eight and one third of a piece of eight. . . .

His Catholic Majesty, considering the losses which former Asientists have sustained, and upon this express condition, that the said company shall not carry on nor attempt any unlawful trade, directly or indirectly, . . . has been pleased . . . to allow to the company of this *asiento* a ship of five hundred tons yearly during the thirty years of its continuance, to trade therewith to the Indies, in which his Catholic Majesty is to partake a fourth part of the gain, as in the *asiento*; besides which fourth his Catholic Majesty is to receive five per cent out of the net gain of the other three parts which belong to England, upon this express condition, that they may not sell the goods and merchandises which each of these ships shall carry but only at the time of the fair; and if any of these ships shall arrive in the Indies before the *flotas* and galleons, the factors of the *asiento* shall be obliged to land the goods and merchandise with which they shall be laden, and put them into warehouses that shall be locked with two keys, one of which to remain with the Royal officers and the other with the factors of the company, to the end the said goods and merchandise may be sold during the continuance of the said fair only; and they are to be free of all duties in the Indies.

9. American trade with foreign colonies was regarded by some in England as detrimental to the trade of the British sugar colonies and was forbidden by Act of Parliament. The Americans ignored the law.

a. A merchant describes the American trade with the French islands and its effect on the British islands

Report of William Frazier, 22 March 1730

Mr. Wm. Frazier said, that in November and December, 1729, he went from Barbados to Martinique, and St. Lucia, for his health, and saw about 30 New England and Rhode Island vessels there, loading with molasses, and some rum, for Boston; was personally acquainted with several of the masters of those vessels, being a rum and lumber merchant himself at Barbados; and that the masters of those vessels informed him, that, if they brought in 60 horses alive, they paid nothing for their permission to trade, horses and lumber being absolutely necessary for the French, as well as English, sugar plantations: that those vessels loaded chiefly with molasses, in return for the horses and lumber; which molasses they distil into rum at Boston, where there are near 50 distilling-houses, and thereby lower the value of rum, made in the sugar plantations, about £25 per cent., by sending the same to Maryland, Virginia, North and South Carolina, to the New-foundland fishery, and also some to Guinea. . . .

That the French colonies have of late very much increased, by being supplied with horses and lumber, and other plantation necessaries, from New England, and other northern colonies, and also by the consumption of their molasses, which formerly they had no vent for.

That the sugar colonies are in a declining state, upon account of this trade, especially Barbados, plantation necessaries being sold there £25 or £30 per cent. dearer, and the produce of the English sugar plantations £25 or £30 per cent. cheaper.

b. American trade with the French islands should be forbidden

Speech in the House of Commons, 23 February 1731

Sir, . . . the affair in hand is the dispute between the English and the French commerce: we are now to determine, whether we ought to encourage a French trade, which tends to the ruin of our own sugar-colonies. . . . Now, Sir, I think that the French are our greatest rivals in the sugar-trade; and that the French have been enabled to become our rivals in the sugar-trade, only by the trade carried on between them and our northern colonies; the great vent they thereby have for their rum and molasses, and the easy access they thereby have to lumber, horses, and all other necessaries for their sugar-plantations, which are naturally much more fruitful than ours, enable them to sell their sugars and rum at a much lower price than it is possible for our sugar-planters to sell at; it is therefore apparent that our sugar-plantations must be undone or we must fall upon ways and means of preventing the French from selling their sugars so cheap as they do: those ways and means are easy; they are every day in our power; put a stop to the trade that is carried on between our own colonies upon the continent and the French sugar-islands, and you must at once a great deal enhance the price of all French sugars; the charges of making their sugars will then be a great deal more, and their rum and molasses will yield them nothing; they must lay all charges upon the returns of their sugars, and therefore it will not be possible to sell them so cheap as they are sold at present. By this method our own sugar-colonies will be greatly encouraged, and the French may be totally undone; whereas if we leave matters in the present situation, the French sugar-colonies will be increasing every day, and in a little time our own will be quite destroyed.

c. Americans violate the Act

Petition of merchants of London, British sugar planters, merchants ... trading in his Majesty's sugar colonies, 7 March 1750

The British traders in North America forgetting all ties of duty to his Majesty, the interest of their mother country, and the reverence due to its laws, have, as though they thought themselves independent of Great Britain, for some years past, carried on a very large and extensive trade, not only with the foreign colonies in America, but also with the French and Dutch in Europe, directly in violation of the said acts; which, if not speedily prevented, by some more effectual provisions than have hitherto been made, will be attended with consequences fatal to the British sugar colonies, and greatly detrimental to the trade and manufactures of Great Britain itself. . . .

And that they have carried on the like trade with Holland, and import vast quantities of sugar, rum, and molasses, yearly, from the French, and other foreign sugar colonies, into the British northern colonies, in direct violation of the said act of his present Majesty, without paying the duties imposed thereby. . . .

And that the northern colony traders, to enable them to carry on this trade with, and for the benefit of, France, to the greatest extent possible, often refuse to sell their lumber to the English, without being paid in ready money; which money they carry to foreigners, and lay out in the purchase of their sugar, rum, and molasses, which they refuse to take from the English planters; and likewise purchase a variety of European and East India commodities, which they introduce into all the British northern colonies.

10. Before the War of American Independence the West Indian colonies were dependent on the Americans for estate supplies.

After the war the British Government prohibited the importation of American goods in American ships as they might threaten British shipping.

a. The trade between Great Britain, the West Indies, and America described

Evidence of a British civil servant before the Committee of Trade, 18 March 1784

The course of the trade is as follows: the principal British merchants are concerned with houses in the West Indies to whom they send their ships which carry our goods from hence and who provide cargoes of the West India produce to load them home. These ships are called stationed ships, and seldom if ever vary their course. But there are many others who go to the West Indies to look for freight and are called seekers in contradistinction to the stationed ships. When we exported grain to Portugal and the southern parts of Europe, Madeira and the African islands many of the ships which carried the same when they had left their cargoes of grain, went on to the West Indies to look for freight. The ships also which arrived there from the coast of Africa with negroes wanted freight home. It often happened that freight was not to be had when these ships arrived. The merchants to whom the ships were consigned not being prepared to load them, therefore to save expense and preserve the ships from being eaten by the worm in the West Indian seas, or to avoid the hurricanes in that season of the year, they took on board as much rum, molasses and sugar as would pay for a cargo of lumber in North America, with which they returned in time to receive a cargo for Europe; or if they were not certain of that, and they found a freight in North America for Europe they took it from thence. This trade would be almost entirely prevented by permitting the Americans to bring their lumber and provisions down in their own shipping, and consequently so much injury arise to the West India trade by cutting off this resource from the seekers which might prevent so many of them going out to bring home their own produce.

b. The trade in American ships prohibited

Act of the British Parliament effective 4 April 1788

That no goods or commodities whatever shall be imported or brought from any of the territories belonging to the United States of America, into any of his Majesty's West India islands under the penalty of the forfeiture thereof, and also of the ship or vessel in which the same shall be imported or brought, together with all her guns, furniture, ammunition, tackle, and apparel; except tobacco, pitch, tar, turpentine, hemp, flax, masts, yards, bowsprits, staves, leading, boards, timber, shingles, and lumber of any sort; horses, neet cattle, sheep, hogs, poultry, and live stock of any sort; bread, biscuits, flour, peas, beans, potatoes, wheat, rice, oats, barley, and grain of any sort, such commodities, respectively, being the growth or production of any of the territories of the said United States of America.

And that none of the goods or commodities herein before excepted, enumerated, and described, shall be imported or brought into any of the said islands from the territories of the said United States, under the like penalty of the forfeiture thereof, and also of the ship or vessel in which the same shall be so imported or brought, together with all her guns, furniture, ammunition, tackle, and apparel, except by British subjects and in British-built ships, owned by his Majesty's subjects, and navigating according to law.

c. The prohibition defended in Britain

Report of the Committee for Trade on the Petition of the West India Committee, 31 May 1784

The Committee cannot conclude what they have to report to Your Majesty on this head without observing of how great importance it will be to the security of Your Majesty's islands in the West Indies and the prosperity of those planters, who have offered this representation to Your Majesty; in any future war, that the vessels of Your Majesty's subjects and the sailors that navigate them should be increased in those seas, to the diminution of the naval strength of other countries, so that the planters seem not to be aware that the consequence of success in their present application must eventually be not beneficial, but on the contrary even dangerous to themselves by diminishing those resources of naval strength on which the safety of the British islands particularly depends.

11. In the first half of the eighteenth century the West Indian islands claimed to be Britain's most profitable colonies. By the end of the century the long decline in prosperity had started.

a. Conflicting views on the value of West Indian and American colonies

(i) Leslie, *History of Jamaica*, 1740

What Jamaica is worth to Britain. For this island, of all others, deserves the notice of Great Britain. Barbados is on the decline; we have daily vast numbers of people from that colony, who flock here to better their fortunes; the same may be said of the northern colonies. Indeed Jamaica is a constant mine, whence Britain draws prodigious riches: the five hundred sail of ships, which, as I have showed, it yearly loads, may be computed (at 150 tons each) to amount to 57,000 tons. The export of the island may amount to near 100,000 hogsheads of sugar, reckoning every vessel to carry only 200, by which near 20,000 are maintained at home, and some of them enriched. The next produce of these sugars may be about a million, computing the sugars at only 20s. per hundred weight, and a thousand weight to the hogshead, and the other commodities will bring £100,000 more, all which is returned in manufactures and goods from Great Britain; for, except Madeira wine and rum-punch, they eat, drink, and wear, only the product of Great Britain; and by this means I may venture to affirm, that 40,000 more mouths are fed, besides the numbers that subsist by retailing these commodities, which may be 10,000 in all. In short, by a very modest computation, the Jamaica trade subsists upwards of 100,000 people, and on this island there may be about 40,000 whites; therefore, by this means, Jamaica maintains 140,000 people, all Britons; so you may easily guess, of what importance this place is to Great Britain, and how much it adds to the riches of the British nation, without drawing one half-penny from it.

(ii) *Petition of the Agent for Pennsylvania to the House of Commons,* 16 April 1751

An American agent argues the greater worth of the American colonies to Britain. That the inhabitants of Pennsylvania in particular, and of North America in general, are very numerous; and from their situation, in cold and severe climates, do constantly take off and consume great quantity of woollen and other manufactures of this kingdom, and thereby contribute to the wealth and benefit of Great Britain, in its trade, navigation, and revenues. . . .

And that the British inhabitants in the sugar islands are reduced to a very small number, the ten acre men, who are or should be the numbers and the strength and support of small islands, being in great measure bought out; and the immense produce and wealth of those islands is brought into the hands of a few rich and opulent persons, whose plantations are in general extremely beneficial to them. . . .

And that the said sugar islanders have, on all occasions endeavoured to represent themselves to be as useful as they are wealthy, and as if they were of equal, or even of greater benefit and advantage to their mother country, than the very great numbers of their fellow-subjects in North America, notwithstanding the known nakedness of the slaves in the sugar islands, the small number of white subjects there, and the great heat of their climate; all which render it impossible for them to consume anything like the quantity of woollen, and other British manufactures, taken off by North America; and notwithstanding that the balance of trade between Great Britain and North America is always greatly in favour of the mother country; but between Great Britain and the sugar islands, is apprehended to be as constantly in favour of the sugar islands, and against the mother country.

b. *Profits from slave labour*

Edwards, *History of the West Indies*, 1797

The annual profit arising to the owner, from the labour of each field Negro employed in the cultivation of sugar, may be reckoned at twenty-five pounds sterling money. I reckon thus: a sugar plantation, well conducted, and in a favourable soil, ought to yield as many hogsheads of sugar, of 16 cwt. annually, as there are Negroes belonging to it, the average value of which, for ten years past, may be stated as £15 sterling the hogshead; but, as every plantation is not thus productive and rum, which is generally appropriated to the payment of contingent charges, not being always sufficient for that purpose, I will allow £10 sterling only, as the clear profit per hogshead of the sugar, which therefore is the average value of the labour of each Negro, old and young; and one third only of the Negroes being able people, their labour may be put at £30 a head; out of which however must be deducted, the interest on their first cost, and an allowance for the risk of losing them by death or desertion (their maintenance, etc., being included in the contingent expenses of the estate) for both which I allow fifteen per cent. This leaves about £25 sterling clear, or nearly a fourth part of the actual value of each slave.

c. *British colonies weakened by dispossession of small white settlers*

(i) *Governor of St. Vincent to Secretary of State,* 4 October 1777

Their value. The small and middling white settlers (among which the proportion of those formerly French ones is considerable) may be called the yeomanry of the West Indies, and are by far the most useful and giving the greatest strength to infant colonies. Their ideas are confined to the spot they have fixed themselves on, their wishes circumscribed to attaining only absolute necessaries, with a very few comforts for themselves and family; they never form an idea of quitting the government to live in Europe on the revenue of their American possessions and thus may be deemed permanent inhabitants.

On the contrary the English think only of making a rapid fortune, to enable them to return to Europe to spend it there, leaving only servants on their estates. These are ever attempting to buy out the former class, and very, very often succeed by various acts. The persons thus dispossessed would re-settle on the island with the money for which they sold their old possessions, if they can get grants of small tracts easily and at very little expense. If they cannot, they remove to Martinique, St. Lucia, Trinidad, etc., giving strength to our enemies in proportion as they weaken the British settlement.

(ii) *Petition of Several Planters . . . of Jamaica,* 2 March 1731

Coffee is a crop which small settlers can manage. The chief produce of the island being sugar (the making of which requires large tracts of land, and numbers of negroes, and cattle) the poorer sort of people, whose stocks and plantations are small, cannot carry on the same, and the said island is, for that reason, at present very thinly inhabited with white people; and that the soil, and climate thereof is found by experience to be very proper for coffee, which may be raised by the poorer inhabitants.

d. Competition from the French islands

(i) *Governor of Barbados to Secretary of State,* 31 August 1774

French West India sugar costs less. The French . . . produce the same commodities as we do, in greater abundance and at less expense. They pay lower duties, and they can afford to undersell us, in every foreign market in Europe.

(ii) Edwards, *History of St. Domingo,* 1797

The natural advantages of St. Domingue. It will be found that the planters of Jamaica receive smaller returns from the labours of their negroes, in proportion to their numbers, than the planters of St. Domingo have received from theirs. For this difference various causes have been assigned, and advantages allowed, and qualities ascribed to the French planters, which I venture to pronounce, on full enquiry, had no existence. The true cause arose, undoubtedly, from the superior fertility of the soil; and above all, from the prodigious benefit which resulted to the French planters from the system of watering their sugar-lands in dry weather. This is an advantage which nature has denied to the lands in Jamaica, except in a very few places; but has freely bestowed on many parts of St. Domingo; and the planters there availed themselves of it with the happiest success.

e. English sugar refiners complain of poor supplies and high cost of British West Indian sugar

Petition of Sugar Refiners and Grocers of London, 20 March 1753

The sugar planters have received for their sugars a much higher price than what they did for many years before the commencement of the late war; and notwithstanding these encouragements, instead of increasing their plantations, and sending home a larger produce, they have decreased in their importation ever since the year 1739, upon an average, very considerably.

And that the planters are greater gainers by a small importation than a large one; but the navigation, the revenue, the petitioners, and the consumers of sugar, are great sufferers.

And that the foreign markets are supplied with sugar from the French at less than half the price it is here sold for, exclusive of all duties paid here; and the price of sugars at the British sugar colonies is more than double the price of what it is at the French sugar colonies. . . .

And that the common people of England are deprived of one of the conveniences of life, by the present high price of sugars, and the petitioners of the benefit of supplying them therewith; and that those who can afford it are obliged to pay double the price, which the rest of Europe do for the same commodity; and that there is no possibility of exporting either muscovado sugar or refined, to any port in Europe. . . . And that the inhabitants and proprietors of Jamaica, though they have many hundred thousand acres of land, fit for sugar plantations, which, as they have publicly declared, are sufficient to supply all Europe to cultivate them. . . .

And therefore praying the House to take the premises into their consideration and make it the interest of the British sugar colonies to produce, and send home, a large quantity of sugar to Great Britain, in order to become more useful to their mother country, its trade, navigation, and revenue.

12. The decline of the British West Indian plantation economy was accelerated by the effects of the Napoleonic Wars and by new competition, foreign and British.

a. Ill consequences of the war with France

(i) Marryat, *Concessions to America, The Bane of Britain*, 1807.

The competition of newly captured colonies for British capital and the British market. One grievance, of which the British colonies feel the weight, is the system adopted by the mother country towards the colonies captured from the enemy, which are immediately put on the same favoured footing as her own legitimate possessions, and have her home consumption opened to them. The British market is now clogged with the produce of Demerara, Surinam, Tobago, and St. Lucia; while by the policy of the enemy, the produce of the colonies of Great Britain is excluded from almost every part of the continent of Europe. The cultivation and population of these temporary possessions are augmented by British capital and British speculators; and, as they before were, so they again probably will be, restored to their former owners, with increased means of rivalling the British colonies in the continental markets at a peace, after having done them infinite injury in the British market during war.

(ii) *Petition of the Jamaican Assembly*, 10 December 1811

The decline of coffee. Coffee had been cultivated chiefly for foreign consumption. When the restrictions called by the French the Continental

System were enforced and the markets of Europe shut against the commodity, the numerous proprietors of these valuable estates were at once and without any default of their own reduced to the greatest distress and misery.

b. The competition of other producers

(i) Baring, *An Inquiry into the Causes and Consequences of the Orders in Council*, 1808

An opinion that the West Indies cannot compete with foreign colonies without a monopoly in the market. The destruction of St. Domingo occasioned high prices of sugar and coffee throughout the world: these high prices encouraged an increased cultivation in the islands, which now again produce a general glut of these articles. The present low prices, which are a natural consequence, it is stated, and I believe truly, do not always pay the planter the expense of cultivation. The chasm produced by the sudden loss of St. Domingo, has been now more than filled up by the increased produce of foreign colonies, and especially of Cuba, while the consumption on the continent of Europe has certainly been very much reduced. The British planters, however, were most unfortunately tempted into the competition of raising sugar for those European countries who have no colonies of their own; forgetting that the comparative want of fertility of our islands for ever disables them from supplying any market of which they have not the monopoly; at least, for any longer period than until other colonies are able to overtake them.

(ii) *Sir Stamford Raffles to the Duke of Somerset*, 20 August 1820

East Indian advantages. I find that a sugar-work may be established here at less than one sixth of the expense which must be incurred at Jamaica; that our soil is superior, our climate better, and, as we are neither troubled with hurricanes nor yellow fever, that our advantages are almost beyond comparison greater. For instance, in an estate calculated to afford two hundred or two hundred and fifty tons of sugar annually, the land alone would cost £8,000 or £10,000 in Jamaica, while here it may be had for nothing. The negroes would there cost £10,000 or £12,000 more, while here labourers may be obtained on contract, or by the month, with a very moderate advance, at wages not higher than necessary for their subsistence. . . .

Our advantages over the West Indies are not only in soil, climate, and labour, but also in constant markets. The West Indies always look to the European market, and that alone; here we have the India and China markets, besides an extensive local demand. The only thing against us is the freight, which is of course somewhat higher, on account of the greater distance.

(iii) *Petition of the Committee of Merchants and Planters, Barbados,* 2 October 1812

Petition for protection against East Indian sugar. Your Excellency must be fully aware that should the East India trade be indiscriminately thrown open, without any protecting duties on East India sugar; the West Indies must cease to manufacture sugar, and ruin must inevitably ensue. . . .

(Plea for) such measures as in Your Excellency's great wisdom may seem proper, for obtaining redress of existing evils, and security against the ruinous consequences of a competition in our staple commodity with the East Indies, should the mother country think fit to throw open the East India trade.

13. The effects of the abolition of the British slave trade and the campaign for emancipation.

a. *Increase in the foreign slave trade to rival sugar producers*

Evidence before a Select Committee of the Commons on the Commercial State of the West India Colonies, 6 February 1832

The causes of the severe distress are various. . . . The first is the great extension of the foreign slave trade, that is exceedingly great; in one year, ending 1830, there must have been at least 100,000 slaves introduced into the foreign colonies, about 57,000 of whom were imported into the Brazils alone, according to the returns presented to Parliament last year.

b. Increase in the cost of producing sugar in the British West Indies

Report from a Select Committee on the Commercial State of the West India Colonies, 13 April 1832

Your Committee now advert to the point on which the greatest stress is laid by the West Indians—the abolition of the slave trade, unaccompanied by the abolition on the part of all foreign states.

It is alleged that an increased charge of no less than 15/10d. the cwt. of sugar, is thus occasioned, that is 11/- as the greater cost of rearing slaves in our colonies, than of purchasing them in the foreign colonies, and 4/10d. as the loss sustained by the smaller proportion of slaves effective for work. . . .

Apprehending that this estimate of loss by the abolition laws is somewhat exaggerated, your Committee have no hesitation in submitting to the House their opinion, first, that some loss, and consequently some part of the present distress of the colonies, is occasioned by those laws.

c. Increase in the difficulty of getting capital

Report from a Select Committee on the Commercial State of the West India Colonies, 13 April 1832

This consideration leads your Committee to advert to one cause of the depression of the whole West India interest, which several of the witnesses represent as most important. The agitation of the slave question in Great Britain has tended to diminish the feeling of confidence of the West Indian proprietor in the security of his property, to check the investment of capital, and to increase the difficulty of effecting sales and mortgages.

d. *The financial condition of the estates in the West Indies in 1830*

West India Merchants, *Statements, Calculations and Explanations*, 1830

That many estates have not paid the expenses of their cultivation for the past year, without charging interest on the capital, or even interest on the debts with which the estate may be encumbered, or anything for the support of the families dependent upon them; and that a debt has thus been actually incurred by the proprietors, in consequence of the expenses exceeding the sale of the crop.

That many other estates, more favourably circumstanced than the preceding class, by making better sugar, or by being cultivated at less cost, have not produced enough to pay the interest of the mortgages upon them.

That the remainder of the estates, which are most favourably circumstanced, have yielded so little net income, that, upon the whole, great distress has fallen upon the families of proprietors, and upon all connected with or dependent on the West India Colonies.

14. The gradual repeal of the various laws by which the British market in sugar was reserved on favourable terms to the British West Indies was a blow to the planters in the eighteen-forties.

Schomburgk, *History of Barbados*, 1846

The fiat has been passed, and the monopoly on sugar in favour of the British colonies will be abolished at the commencement of the second half of this century. This sacrifice has been conceded to the free-trade principle. . . .

It became obvious in 1846 that the efforts of a powerful party in England were directed to induce Parliament to resort to the sweeping measure of admitting all sugar and molasses, whether the produce of free or slave labour, at a reduced scale. . . .

Numerous meetings were held, after it was too late to remonstrate; in most cases those who had met came to the resolution that, with their present burdens and restrictions, they were entirely unable to compete with the slave-holding countries in the produce of sugar. . . . They laid claim to the following concessions as an indemnity for the injuries inflicted upon them, and to enable them to compete with Brazil and the Spanish colonies : that the navigation laws be abolished, and the trade in shipping be rendered free; that an unrestricted immigration into the West Indies from all parts of the world be permitted; that the productions of the colonies be admitted into the British markets on the footing of raw materials and be free of import duty; that Great Britain assist the colonies by loans of money secured by Colonial Acts.

15. Sugar producers could calculate the relative costs of producing sugar by slaves or by free workers. Those who remained in production invested in the immigration schemes and new equipment.

a. The cost of free labour to an estate owner

Gurney, *Winter in the West Indies*, 1840

One hundred and seventy slaves, or apprentices, used to be supported on this estate. Now, our friend employs fifty-four free labourers, who work for him four days in the week, taking one day for their provision grounds, and another for market. This is all the labour that he requires, in order to keep up his former extent of cultivation; and willingly did he acknowledge the superior advantage which attends the present system. The saving of expense is obvious. I understand our friend to allow that the average cost of supporting a slave was £5 sterling per annum.

170 slaves at £5 per annum is	£850.
Now he pays 54 free labourers 4/6d. per week one day's labour being set off against rent, for 50 weeks, two weeks being allowed for holidays.	£607. 10. 0
Saving under freedom . . .	£242. 10. 0

b. Capital investment and the cost of labourers on some estates in the eighteen-forties

(i) Mr. Wolley's evidence, *The Sugar Question*, 3 February 1848

In St. Vincent. The average wage per day has been 8d., with house, provision grounds, and medical attendance, which are fully equal to 4d. per day additional. With this rate of wages, and the price of sugar during 1844–45–46, the estate cleared on an average £418 with an average crop of 92 hogsheads; with present prices it would have lost on an average £300 per annum. . . .

Great advantage has been derived in St. Vincent from introducing Portuguese from Madeira; they cost on an average about £125 for twenty-six people introduced; they receive 1/- per day, and a certain amount of rations; they work very well while under contract, and make their children do such work as they are capable of doing, but they demand higher wages when their contract is up. It has been a great evil with the planter that they cannot make long contracts out of the colony, which the home government has always opposed. The St. Vincent planter has the advantage of a custom that if the negro works the day, he must work for a month, or he is liable to a fine for breach of contract, and wages are generally paid only monthly.

(ii) Mr. J. A. Hankey's evidence, *The Sugar Question*, 3 February 1848

In Grenada. Mr. J. A. Hankey stated that he was an extensive West India merchant and a proprietor in Grenada. . . .

The cost on these estates per annum was, during slavery £4. 6s. 3d. per adult labourer. The slave was valued by government at an average £59. 6s. but the government only paid, as compensation, £24. 1s. 4¾d.; the balance remains as a loss to the estates, besides which the estates now have to pay per adult labourer £10. 8s. 4d. per annum, or £6. 2s. 1d. per annum more than was necessary during slavery. . . .

The estates of Mr. Hankey are probably, on the whole, above the average of Grenada estates. They have been fully supplied with capital, carefully managed, and are close to the sea-shore. They are taking off the present crops in Grenada, but are planting no more canes. The ratoons last for about three years. Grenada has not suffered so much from the failure of the West India Bank, as from the disinclination of the merchants to advance money. Mr. Hankey makes no advances to parties having West India property alone, preferring to risk the loss of what is now due, to making further advances. It is one of the worst parts of a West India merchant's business to refuse advances to those who have been well off, but who have only West India property to offer as security. Absentee proprietors have more means and enterprise than residents.

(iii) Dr. Ranken's evidence, *The Sugar Question*, 3 February 1848

In British Guiana. There are 220 sugar estates in the colony, of these 114 have been mortgaged, from 1838 to 1847 inclusive, for £1,006,783. Sixteen estates were mortgaged by non-residents, and ninety-eight by residents. Residents are often in want of money for improvements, non-residents seldom are; having better credit and more capital, they consequently have carried out improvements of agriculture, manufacture, and immigration, on a much larger scale than the resident proprietors. . . .

The quality of sugar has deteriorated in Guiana since freedom, as might be expected from the manufacture requiring great attention. The planters only require sufficient immigration to maintain their cultivation, by supplying the deficiencies now withdrawn. . . . The old colonies . . . have labour infinitely cheaper than it can be hoped for in Guiana. Guiana cannot expect wages to be as low as 4d., as in Antigua, or 8d. as in Barbados. There is no fear of over-production of sugar. There are many staples which could be grown in Demerara, if there were surplus labour. . . .

The colony, therefore, asks, as a remedy for its distresses, protection; for the bill of 1846 has aggravated every grievance created by the Act of Emancipation. They wish for protection against the slave sugar grower; immigration from Africa, with power to form contracts out of the colony.

c. A planter doubts whether the use of immigrant labourers on the estates will enable the planter to compete with slave-produced sugar

Premium, *Eight Years in British Guiana*, September 1846

Coolies might have enabled us to supply the home consumption, and with advantage to ourselves but it is impossible that with them we can make sugar and sell it at as low a rate as the produce of Cuba will be made and sold in England. It is doubtful if the Indian maker of sugar on the European system, will be able to keep his ground against the slave cultivator. In fact, we may say experience is against the probability, for if he could, the sugar of India would long ago have been more abundant in the markets of the continent, which were open to it as well as that of any other country; and if that be the case, if it turns out that the East India planter, with labourers at twopence per day, cannot support the competition, how are we to keep it up at twenty pence to the same people, and thirty guineas of passage-money for five years' service, or six pounds a year in addition to the wages?

d. The use of central factories, new machinery and scientific methods of cultivation recommended for the British West Indies

Schomburgk, *History of Barbados*, 1846

The advantage of a separation of the cultivation of the cane from its manufacture into sugar is now generally acknowledged. The incongruity of the present system must be especially felt in Barbados, where there are estates with ten acres of land under cultivation of the sugar-cane, and to which a windmill and a set of works is attached to produce eighteen or twenty hogsheads of sugar, or, to adduce an extreme case, where only ten hogsheads are made under favourable circumstances. The manufacturing department on a sugar-estate is connected with very heavy expenses, and it would prove more to the advantage of the cultivator if he could sell his canes, and leave the manufacture to those who would devote their whole attention to the means of extracting the largest quantity and the best quality of sugar out of the raw material. The central manufactories in Guadeloupe and Martinique in the West Indies, and in Bourbon in the Indian Ocean, have realized every expectation. . . . Relieved from the manufacturing process, the cultivator of the cane would be able to devote his undivided attention to planting and reaping.

It cannot be denied that the tropical agriculture is at present conducted upon more rational and scientific principles than it was ten years ago, to say nothing of the crude system prevalent in the last century; still there is vast room for improvement. Agricultural chemistry is a science which has only recently attracted attention in the West Indies: nature under the tropics is so prolific, that only in the old and worn-out colonies artificial means were required to refresh the fertility of the soil, and these have not always been employed with judgement and advantage. The husbanding of manual labour is a point of the greatest importance. On many estates the same system is still followed which existed when compulsory labour was in vogue. . . . The use of the plough proves annually of greater advantage to Barbados, but there is still a wide scope for the adoption of other machinery.

The introduction of central manufactories, steam-engines, railways and tramways are points of the greatest importance in the sugar colonies. Cuba is said to possess at present eight hundred miles of railway—the British West Indies only twelve miles.

16. An observer criticises the dependence of the West Indies on cane cultivation for a livelihood.

Davy, *The West Indies before and since Slave Emancipation*, 1854

Is there not a neglect of interest also in the manner in which the agriculture of these colonies is now so restricted—limited in many of them solely to cane-cultivation, and in very few of them comprising any other crop of importance, regardless, as it were, of the varieties of soil, of situation and of peculiarities of climate and equally so of the great capacity of a tropical climate for varied culture? Were the natural advantages made available, how very many valuable productions might be grown, respecting which, trials of them having been already made, there could be no question as to success? It would be tedious to enumerate them, they are so many, whether as manufacturing materials, such as cotton, the coconut palm, the ground nut, etc., or as articles of food, such as besides cocoa and coffee, rice, and various kinds of starch and meal, and many kinds of fruit, especially of the orange kind, fresh and preserved, etc. It is lamentable to reflect that even in these colonies themselves, with few exceptions, fruits which might be had in abundance, of the best kinds, are scarce, and the best of them expensive; and even more lamentable, the fact, that the majority of them, not excluding Trinidad and British Guiana, are dependent, in a great measure, on foreign countries for the greater part of the necessaries of life—for corn, for meat, for fish, salted—to say nothing of the luxuries and comforts.

17. Jamaica in the eighteen-fifties.

a. Lack of labourers for the estates

Sewell, *Ordeal of Free Labour in the West Indies*, 1861

This magnificent country, wanting nothing but capital and labour for its complete restoration to a prosperity far greater than it ever yet attained, is now sparsely settled by small negro cultivators, who have been able to purchase their plots of land for £2 and £3 an acre. With a month's work on their own properties they can earn as much as a year's labour on a sugar-estate would yield them. They are superior, pecuniarily speaking, to servitude; and by a law of nature that cannot be gainsaid, they prefer independence to labour for hire. Why should they be blamed? But the fact remains that the island is nearly destitute of labour; that partly through want of labour sugar cultivation has been abandoned; and by an adequate supply of labour can it only be revived. Covering an area of four millions of acres, Jamaica has a population of 378,000 white, black and mulatto. This makes about eleven acres to each person. In the flourishing island of Barbados, it would contain over five millions of souls, and would export a million hogsheads. Till its present population has been doubled and trebled no material improvement can be looked for. But where is the money—where are the vigour and the energy necessary to obtain this population? Whose fault is it that these are wanting, and that Jamaica, with far greater advantages than Trinidad or Guiana, has failed to follow the footsteps of emancipation?

b. The estates which have survived the disruption

Sewell, *Ordeal of Free Labour in the West Indies*, 1861

He (the planter) was bankrupt before emancipation; but it was emancipation that tore down the veil which concealed his poverty. I speak generally, for I do not doubt that there were many exceptional cases. Many of the three hundred estates in cultivation at the present day are exceptions. There were planters who continued to cultivate sugar after emancipation— who were successful then, and are successful still—and since 1853, when the general abandonment of estates may be said to have ceased in Jamaica, the number of these successful planters has considerably increased. I need not pause to explain that they were all men of capital, and that their properties were economically managed, for both assertions are proved to demonstration by the fact that only first-class estates are in cultivation today.

18. The main features of economic life in the late nineteenth century were the blow of beet-sugar competition, the growth of the banana and cocoa trades and the beginnings of large-scale emigration. The value of small proprietors to the economy was also officially recognised.

a. The competition of beet sugar

Royal Colonial Institute Proceedings, 1876–77

But it is impossible confidently to forecast the future while another element of unfair antagonism remains. There has grown up on the continent of Europe, under the influence of protection and export bounties, an enormous sugar industry, against which our colonies have necessarily to compete. The motive which impelled the first Napoleon to encourage the cultivation of the beet-root for sugar-making may have disappeared, but the injury to English colonial interests has been no less grave than if that motive still existed. We could not complain, of course, of any dimensions the beet industry might assume, if it proved that it could supply the world with sugar at a cheaper rate than we could. But we have every reason to object to a state of things in which excessive production is stimulated by export bounties, and prices in our own market kept down below the natural cost of production, entailing the ruin of our loaf sugar industry. . . . The West India colonies have not remained silent under this state of things. Repeated protests have been made. Conference after conference between England, France, Belgium, and Holland has taken place. . . . In the meantime the English refiners, who would naturally be large purchasers of West Indian sugar, are left in a state of uncertainty, and it may be said that the loaf sugar industry of the United Kingdom has been almost entirely destroyed. . . . It is evident that so long as the inequality is allowed, the West India colonies cannot have that full prosperity to which they are entitled, and which they would certainly possess under a system of international free trade. No one could be expected to invest capital in an industry liable at any moment to be affected by the capricious action of foreign governments.

b. The banana trade

Morris, *Economic Resources of the West Indies*, 1898

At first the fruit was purchased in small quantities from negro peasants in the neighbourhood of Port Antonio. There was practically no capital invested in the cultivation. The settlers were induced to grow bananas in small patches of an acre or two and to deliver the fruit at the port of shipment. In the aggregate these small patches produced bananas sufficient to fill all the first ships engaged in the trade. The fruit trade in Jamaica is now the means of circulating nearly £500,000 annually amongst all classes of the community, and this large sum is immediately available in establishing other and more permanent industries. Bananas come into bearing at the latest in about 15 or 18 months from the time of planting, and as the return is usually from £10 to £20 per acre, the planter is able, with a comparatively small capital, to establish his land in cocoa, coffee, nutmegs, limes, oranges, and coconuts, which, when the bananas are exhausted, will remain a permanent source of revenue. It is on this account that the fruit trade has always been regarded as capable of building up, little by little, an improved condition for the people, not only of Jamaica, but of other West Indian islands suitable for the industry. Latterly, many sugar estates have been converted into banana walks, and all sections of the community have taken part in the enterprise.

c. More sources of employment

Crossman Commission, 1883

It is to the possession of provision grounds that the industrious negro turns with the greatest liking, and there now exists in Jamaica a substantial and happily numerous population of the peasant proprietor class, which easily obtains a livelihood by the growth of the minor tropical products of fruit and spices, cocoa and coffee. This increasing class deducts so much from any available supply of indigenous labour. . . . Again, the negroes have found in other ways means of earning money. Public works in Jamaica, such as the construction of railways, provide them with regular pay at home. Public works in other countries such as the Panama Canal prove a great attraction. The negro who refuses to work on estates in Jamaica will willingly labour for wages on these other undertakings, even when the rate of wages is in reality not higher, but where he imagines himself to be more of a free agent.

d. Emigration

Olivier, *Jamaica, The Blessed Island*, 1936

When I first visited Central America, early in 1911, the United Fruit Company, which had by that time incorporated Mr. Keith's company and the Boston Fruit Company, had 50,000 acres of land in Costa Rica. Most of this was in bananas, some in cocoa, and some parts were used for cattle. . . . There were at least 40,000 Jamaicans working on these plantations, or on other plantations under the Company in the adjacent republics, as labourers, foremen, engineers, schoolmasters, clerks, and managers; a most efficiently organised industrial community under the absolute, though enlightened and benevolent despotism of the United Fruit Company. Jamaicans during this period were emigrating in great numbers not only to Costa Rica, Colombia, Nicaragua and Honduras to plant bananas, but also to Cuba, where the sugar industry was being developed by similar mass production. . . . At the time of which I write labour produced on Costa Rica plantations a far higher return than it could in Jamaica.

e. A royal commission recommends a new agricultural policy

(i) *Norman Commission*, 1897

Encouragement to small farmers. The special remedies or measures of relief which we unanimously recommend are: the settlement of the labouring population on small plots of land as peasant proprietors; the establishment of minor agricultural industries and the improvement of the system of cultivation, especially in the case of the small proprietors. . . . The existence of a class of small proprietors among the population is a source of both economic and political strength.

The settlement of the labourer on the land has not as a rule been viewed with favour in the past, by the persons interested in sugar estates. What suited them best was a large supply of labourers, entirely dependent on being able to find work on the large estates and consequently subject to their control and willing to work at low rates of wages. But it seems to us that no reform offers so good a prospect for permanent welfare in the future of the West Indies as the settlement of the labouring population on the land as small peasant proprietors; and in many places this is the only means by which the population can in future be supported.

(ii) *Norman Commission*, 1897

British Government warned that sugar is not the only interest in the West Indies. It must be recollected that the chief outside influences with which the governments of certain colonies have to reckon are the representatives of the sugar estates, that these persons are not interested in anything but sugar, that the establishment of any other industry is often detrimental to their interests and that under such conditions it is the special duty of Your Majesty's Government to see that the welfare of the general public is not sacrificed to the interests or supposed interests of a small but influential minority which has special means of enforcing its wishes and bringing its claims to notice.

19. The condition of the West Indian sugar industry was improved in the first decades of the twentieth century by the European agreement to remove the bounties to beet sugar, the opening of the Canadian market and the temporary boom in the First World War. Sugar producers spent money on the improvement of sugar production and the Imperial Government set up the Imperial College of Tropical Agriculture.

a. A planter gives reasons for the backwardness of the sugar industry

Lamont, *Empire Review*, August 1902

That the abolition of the sugar bounties, by the spontaneous action of the bounty-giving powers, is eminently desirable, no one but a jam-maker is likely to deny. . . . Behind the great barrier of the bounties other obstacles to prosperity have sprung up unnoticed. . . .

The proprietors of the great estates in Demerara and Trinidad have, as a rule, faced the situation courageously, and spent money freely upon successive improvements in machinery, until at present the best sugar factories of either of these colonies compare not unfavourably, so far as the heavy machinery goes, with those of any country in the world. Unfortunately, however, there has been no corresponding improvement in the management of that machinery or in the manipulation of the juice. In many West Indian sugar houses that important officer, a chemist, is absent. . . .

I turn to the field. Here the case is still more deplorable. The system of agriculture is practically the same that prevailed in the islands in the early days of last century. Except in a few localities, the various operations incident to the preparation and tillage of the soil are all performed by hand at enormous cost, and if a visitor hints that there exist such implements as the plough, the cultivator, the horse-hoe, and the harrow, he is informed that their use is unsuitable to the soil or the climate. . . .

The West Indian backwardness is directly due to two causes; first, the abundance of labourers, working for a low wage; secondly, the extreme rarity of skilled scientific direction. It is the abundance of labour that has stunted the desire for, and the adoption of, labour-saving appliances, both in the field and in the factory.

b. The Imperial College of Tropical Agriculture

Wood Report, 1922

I attach the highest possible importance to the foundation of the new Agricultural College in Trinidad. It is impossible for any industry to compete successfully in the modern world unless it has easy access to the best scientific advice upon practical questions that arise in the course of the daily routine. The College will provide a centre for the prosecution of research and for the gradual propagation of scientific ideas, not only in Trinidad, but throughout the colonies from which its students will undoubtedly be drawn in increasing numbers.

c. The removal of the bounties to beet-sugar producers and the opening of the Canadian market stop the decline in the West Indian sugar industry

Lamont, 'The West Indian Recovery', *The Contemporary Review*, February 1912

If the steady recovery of the last few years continues, a very real prosperity is approaching.

In bringing about this satisfactory change many causes have combined. The removal of the sugar bounties effected by the Brussels Convention of 1903 has undoubtedly been one of them. If it has not done all that was expected of it by its supporters in steadying the price of sugar in the world's markets, even its opponents cannot deny that the Convention has given to planters a new confidence that they cannot be undersold by state-subsidised competitors. With that confidence has come willingness to invest, or ability to borrow, the sums periodically needed for keeping machinery abreast of the times.

Even more than to the Convention, however, credit is due to the preference given by Canada to West Indian sugars at a time when the United States market was suddenly closed to them through the more favourable treatment accorded to the produce of Puerto Rico, Cuba, Hawaii, and of the Philippines. Together, Convention and Preference have arrested the decline of the British West Indian sugar industry.

d. The wartime boom

Colonial Report, Barbados, 1916–17

Thus Barbados enjoyed the combination, unusual in her history, of a large sugar crop and continued high prices. Records were established in revenue and trade, and money was subscribed for local loans. Estates have, for the most part, been cleared of debt, and profits are being largely applied by the estate-owner to the erection of improved machinery and general estate improvement.

20. The success of the late nineteenth-century attempts to cultivate a variety of cash crops became apparent in the early twentieth century. In time these crops were attacked by disease and subject to the competition of large-scale producers in other countries.

a. Coconuts

Wood Report, 1922

The most outstanding feature perhaps of recent development throughout the West Indies is the rise and extension of the cultivation of the coconut palm. This is specially noticeable in Jamaica, Nevis, Dominica, St. Lucia, Tobago, Trinidad and British Guiana. Although some of the plantations are already in full bearing, the greater part are of recent introduction, and the trees are only just beginning to bear fruit. The coconut palm seems to flourish in the West Indies everywhere near the coast, and I should hope that, with the introduction of copra factories, and the better organisation of shipping and marketing the various coconut products are destined to become in the near future an increasingly important factor in the economic life of the colonies.

b. Cocoa

Wood Report, 1922

The cultivation of cocoa forms the main agricultural industry of Grenada and, to a less degree, of Trinidad. It is also grown in small quantities in Dominica, St. Lucia and Jamaica. The high quality of the cocoa produced by Grenada and Trinidad is well known and though affected by the rapid extension of the same industry in the Gold Coast, it would seem that these two West Indian colonies are in a position to hold their own.

c. Cotton

Wood Report, 1922

Sea Island cotton forms the main crop of the islands of Montserrat and St. Vincent; it is also an important crop in the islands of St. Kitts and Nevis. The main obstacles to the prosperity of this industry are the pink boll worm, and the fact that for the present the producer can only find one buyer, namely, the Manchester Fine Spinners Association. There is further difficulty in the cultivation of West Indian cotton, namely, the difficulty of finding suitable rotation crops. The cultivation of cotton, and especially Sea Island cotton, is very exhausting to the soil, and in St. Vincent, which is subject to heavy rains, the cultivation of cotton renders the soil liable to denudation.

d. Limes

Wood Report, 1922

The lime industry is practically confined to Dominica . . . Competition with the Sicilian lemon industry both in the manufacture of citric acid and in the sale of the fresh fruit or its juice, is the most serious factor confronting the industry, the depreciated Italian exchange weighting the scales heavily against the British colonies.

21. The sugar industry and estate labourers in the depression.

a. Imperial preference helps the industry to survive

Olivier, *Speech in the House of Lords*, 23 February 1938

About ten years ago the industry again got into a bad state owing to the over-production of sugar. The price obtainable for sugar was such that the industry could not pay decent wages to these labourers, and employers could not get credit to improve their processes. Mr. David Semple and myself were sent out to inquire into the conditions of the industry. We reported that unless the declared policy of abolishing entirely all Imperial preferences were given up the sugar industry would collapse, and that in the meantime it could not be maintained with any regard to decent conditions for the labouring classes. . . . They not only gave the preference which we recommended, but did rather more than that. Since then His Majesty's Government have carried out another of our recommendations —namely, to endeavour by international means to get some sort of stability in prices.

b. Cane farmers and labourers get no share of the assistance

Olivier, *Speech in the House of Lords*, 23 February 1938

We went all round the West Indies and reported on the conditions in every colony, and we reported universally that the conditions of the working classes were deplorable. . . . I am quite convinced . . . that the conditions of the labouring classes today on all the islands are worse than they were ten years ago.

We said that if the Imperial Government assisted the sugar trade to survive by giving Imperial preference, or if the Imperial Government gave them financial assistance, as they have, by free loans, and enabled the industry to improve their capital equipment, then His Majesty's Government should take care that the farmers and labourers should get some part in the benefit. That, I am afraid, has not been done.

c. The general effects of the depression described by the royal commission

Moyne Report, 1939 (1945)

The prolonged economic depression of recent years found in the West Indies communities ill-equipped to withstand it. Many of the larger producers were severely handicapped as a result of light-hearted over-expansion during the brief period of prosperity which followed the war of 1914–1918, and through this weakness many an otherwise satisfactory concern has been forced out of business, thereby increasing unemployment. The labouring population have never had more than the slightest opportunity to save or establish themselves as economically independent, and for many of them the depression brought complete or partial unemployment, while rates of wages though varying greatly from one colony to another remained at a level meagre enough even were employment continuous. The case of the peasant proprietor is a little better; but he too has generally relied on the cultivation of an export crop and/or on the opportunity to supplement his income by seasonal employment on the estates.

22. The Second World War brought more employment and prosperity. Territories with natural resources have benefited from their exploitation. Since the war West Indian governments have embarked on programmes of varied agriculture and the development of secondary industries in an attempt to employ the growing population and to improve the standard of living.

a. Oil in Trinidad

Blanshard, *Democracy and Empire in the Caribbean*, 1947

Before oil, Trinidad was one more sugar colony, and an entrepôt for South American trade. After oil, Trinidad became the first oil-producing country in the British Empire. The British authorities were slow in making their first oil discoveries, and the first large well was not drilled until 1908. But then the government woke up in time to keep for the people more than half of the island's oil royalties by reserving the oil rights on Crown lands, and today Trinidad could almost support itself from oil and asphalt royalties and taxes. During World War II this one small island, . . . sent 130,000,000 barrels of oil to the united nations.

b. Bauxite in British Guiana and Jamaica

Report of the Mission of United Kingdom Industrialists, 1952

Production of bauxite in British Guiana has been carried on for many years but it was only in 1942 that bauxite was first discovered in Jamaica. Since that time three major companies have taken concessions for mining bauxite on a large scale and one of them is producing alumina from the bauxite before shipment. . . . We were greatly impressed by the scale of operation of the bauxite mining companies and by the immense amount of development work which has been undertaken by them in the last few years. While direct labour employed in the production is relatively small, and probably less than that employed in the construction of the plants and facilities such as ports and loading berths, the start of this industry in Jamaica is bound to have a stimulating effect on the whole economy of the island. This will arise not only from direct wages paid out to those employed, but by the steady growth in the way of ancillary industries providing spare parts and the like, and by the effect of one, at least, of the producers on the traffic carried by the Jamaica Government Railways. It is clear that the further encouragement of bauxite mining and alumina production is likely to be of substantial benefit to the economy of the island. We were also much impressed by the efforts of the bauxite companies to improve agricultural productivity on the relatively low-grade land over which they hold concessions.

c. Tourism in Grenada

Grenada Five-year Development Plan

One of Grenada's most important economic assets is the facilities it offers for the development of the tourist trade. In addition to a beautiful climate which is neither too wet nor too dry the island has a large number of very beautiful beaches which are free from dangerous currents. The southern promontory of the island which, without an extensive irrigation system, is too dry for agricultural pursuits, is suited *par excellence* for tourist development. Indeed all the major tourist development projects undertaken in Grenada in recent years have taken place in this area.

With these natural tourist attractions it is not surprising that the tourist industry occupies a place of prominence in Grenada's economy. In 1961 it was the third largest earner of foreign currency after cocoa and remittances. In that year cocoa exports earned $2·6 million and remittances $2·0 million. Income from tourism amounted to $1·8 million.

In 1957 the industry earned $0·84 million while in 1961 it earned $1·75 million, an increase of 100 per cent in four years. This rate of growth in earnings of the tourist industry has been brought about by a parallel rate of growth in the number of tourists visiting Grenada over the same period 1957–1961. In 1957, 4,300 tourists visited the island. In 1961 a total of 8,000 visited Grenada, 3,700 more than 1957 or an increase of 85 per cent.

d. National development programmes

(i) *Ten-year Plan for Barbados*, 1946–56

In Barbados. The main problem of the colony, however, continues to be that of finding employment. It was therefore urged that the agricultural system should be intensified by means of mixed farming, encouraging the production of nutritionally desirable foods, and that the possibility of developing an export trade in farm produce should be investigated. . . .

Means of developing and promoting secondary industries have not been overlooked. For such a development, Barbados possesses two advantages in a good water-supply and a source of cheap power—natural gas. A beginning has already been made with the establishment of the Government Cassava Factory, the formation of a subsidiary company under the aegis of Barbados Welfare Limited to manufacture salt on a co-operative basis, the selection of Barbados as the site of a plant to test whether cotton spinning can be introduced in the West Indies as a secondary industry, and the proposed appointment of a ceramist to investigate and encourage the development of a pottery industry including the making of tiles and bricks for building.

(ii) *Report of the Economics Committee*, 1949

In Trinidad. We share the doubts expressed by our Agricultural Sub-Committee that our staple agricultural industries . . . could absorb all the manpower which has been released by the cessation of war and the curtailment of labour on the United States Bases. . . . Moreover, further mechanisation of labour in some of the major industries, although contributing to greater output, will probably lead to temporary displacement of fair-sized numbers of land workers previously engaged in those industries. It is expedient, therefore, that any long-term plan of development should include consideration for such persons. In addition to the new opportunities for employment which may be found in the establishment of industries other than agriculture, we are strongly of the opinion that much can also be found in the further development of peasant agriculture. . . .

We have recommended releases of hard currency for the oil and sugar industries, but we consider that the principle should be extended to other approved cases where such releases would materially assist in the development of an industry.

(iii) *A National Plan for Jamaica, 1957–67*

In Jamaica. Planning in Jamaica is a difficult exercise. ... It is difficult first of all, because the relationship between the island's resources and the number of people that those resources have to support, is one of the most difficult in the world to resolve. Secondly, there is the risk of disasters such as a major earthquake or a hurricane, or a substantial change in the price of sugar which can upset any carefully laid plan.

Thirdly, United Kingdom and United States influences have been very strong in influencing the Jamaican pattern and style of life. This has resulted in a diversion of demand in many cases from basic needs to luxuries. This distorts the pattern of demand and also increases the difficulty in any plan to meet the economic, social and political demands which now arise in Jamaica, and which go far beyond the ability of the Jamaican resources to supply. However great the progress involved in any plan it will be impossible to bring Jamaica's standard of living up to that of the United States or the United Kingdom in the next decade.

A fourth factor which makes planning more difficult, and yet has an element of advantage in it too, is the smallness of the Government participation in the economic life of the country. Publicly owned enterprises are few and broadly speaking this is a country where private enterprise is operating most of the economic life. Government planning in many fields is confined, therefore, to the provision of incentives to private investors.

Fifthly, the government is always under severe pressure to provide more jobs, and its planning must on many occasions, and inevitably, leave the long-term and theoretically best economic and social objectives to meet urgent and short-term objectives.

3

Religion and Education before Emancipation

1. One of the many motives which Europeans had in exploring the world outside Europe was the extension of Christendom by settling European Christians abroad.

a. In the newly discovered lands traders and settlers should be good Christians

Letter of Columbus to Ferdinand and Isabella, 1492

So may it please God that Your Highnesses send here ... learned men, who will ascertain the truth of all. .... And I say that Your Highnesses ought not to consent that any foreigner do business or set foot here, except Christian Catholics, since this was the end and the beginning of the enterprise, that it should be for the enhancement and glory of the Christian religion, nor should anyone who is not a good Christian come to these parts.

b. The enslavement of Indians increases the converts among them

Acosta, *History of the Indies*, 1604

Yet I will say one thing which I hold for truth, that although the first entry of the Gospel has not been accompanied (in many places) with such sincerity and Christian means, as they should have used : yet God of his bounty has drawn good from this evil, and has made the subjection of the Indians, a perfect remedy for their salvation. Christianity without doubt augments and increases, and brings forth daily more fruit among the Indian slaves : and contrariwise decreases and threatens ruin in other parts, where have been more happy beginnings. And although the beginnings of the West Indies have been laboursome, yet Our Lord has speedily sent good workmen and His faithful ministers ... with other servants of Our Lord, which have lived holily, and have wrought more than human things. Likewise, prelates and holy priests, worthy of memory, of whom we hear famous miracles.

c. The French Company seeks worthy priests for their colonists in St. Kitts

Du Tertre, *Histoire des Antilles*, 1667–71

The Gentlemen of the Company finding themselves always in difficulties in getting chaplains for the spiritual consolation and the edification of the colonists, were forced to take the first priests who offered themselves for this poor country. They were still so hard to come by, that they did not enquire whether they had the necessary qualities for such a worthy occupation. To get to the root of the evil, and to assure His Majesty that they were following his pious intentions (the King's main intention was that they should strive to spread the Catholic religion, and that the natives should be instructed) and to show the colonists the great concern they had for their spiritual welfare, they decided that no one would be more fitted for these exacting and vital duties than members of the religious orders. For this reason the Company begged the Provincial Father of the Capuchins in Normandy to give them monks to send to St. Kitts.

d. The clergy of the Church of England are criticised in the eighteenth century

Leslie, *History of Jamaica*, 1740

The parish taxes are raised by the Vestry, for the maintenance of the Minister and the poor, and keeping the churches in due repair.

This brings me naturally to consider the church affairs of the island, and I am sorry I am going to give you such a dismal account: you know all the British colonies in America are under the inspection of the Bishop of London; and though His Lordship, no doubt, wishes well to the state of religion in general, and to his own diocese in particular; yet it is surprising that such worthless and abandoned men should be sent to such a place as this. The clergy here are of a character so vile, that I do not care to mention it; for except a few, they are generally the most finished of our debauchers. Messrs. Galpin, Johnson and May are indeed men whose unblemished lives dignify the character they bear. They generally preach either in their own churches, or to a few in some private houses every Sunday; but for others their church doors are seldom opened.

2. Protestantism ended Christian unity in Europe. Religious conflicts in Europe were often reflected in the colonies. Sometimes the colonies were more tolerant in acceptance of religious differences.

a. In English colonies only Governors and Councillors must be members of the Church of England, but all religious opinions are tolerated among the other colonists

Instructions to Governor of Jamaica, 1664

And because we are content, in the infancy of that our plantation, to give all possible encouragements to persons of all opinions and parties to transport themselves thither, with their stocks, for the benefit thereof, that they may not under pretence of scruples in conscience, receive any discouragements there, you shall dispense with the taking the oaths of allegiance and supremacy to those which bear any part in the government, except the members and officers of the council, to whom you are hereby particularly directed to administer the same, finding out some other way of securing yourself of their allegiance to us and our government there; and in no other case suffer any man to be molested or disquieted in the exercise of his religion, so he be content with a quiet and peaceable possession of it, not giving therein offence or scandal to the government; only we oblige you in your own house to the possession of the Protestant religion, according as it is here practised by us in England, and the recommending it to all others under your command, as far as it will consist with the peace and quietness of the island.

b. The French King expels Jews from his colonies and forbids the religious services of non-Catholic Christians

Articles 1 and 3 of the Code Noir, 1685

We instruct all our officials to expel from our islands all the Jews who have settled there; to them, as declared enemies of Christianity, we command to leave within three months from the publication of this edict, on pain of loss of liberty and property.

All public religious observance other than the Catholic, Apostolic and Roman shall be forbidden.

c. Quakers in the Leewards

Governor of the Leewards to Lords of Trade and Plantations, 22 November 1676

In Nevis, are some few Quakers, and in Antigua are sixty; in both islands as many various religions as at home, but most frequent the churches when they like the parson or a fit of devotion comes upon them. . . . The Quakers' singularity and obstinacy have given the Governor more trouble than any others. Not content with the peaceable enjoyment of what they profess in their families, they meet and once disturbed a Minister, for which they were imprisoned and fined, and have since been quiet. They will neither watch nor ward against the Caribbee Indians, whose treacherous and barbarous murders, rapes, and enormities discourage the planters in the Leeward Isles more than anything else. . . . Collections are made for the poor, and by an Act parishioners are also rated, to which all voluntarily submit but the Quakers, whose goods are sold for payment of said rates.

d. Catholic plots are reported in Barbados

Deputy-Governor of Barbados to the Earl of Shrewsbury, 30 May 1689

I, the Council, and Assembly have taken the oath, and all the officers civil and military will I doubt not take it. . . . I shall find means to secure waverers or Roman Catholics. I have already shut up the ringleaders in custody, who when they were at large left the island neither peace nor

safety. These are Mr. Willoughby Chamberlayne and Sir Thomas Montgomerie. . . . Both turned Papists, and behaved so violently and insolently,
corresponding with the Governors, Jesuits and priests of the neighbouring
French islands, from whom they obtained a Jesuit and would shortly have
obtained priests and, if that idolatrous superstition had continued, would
have turned Barbados into a popish if not into a French island. Sir Thomas
Montgomerie went to Martinique, where doubtless great designs were laid
for the conversion of this island and the delivery of it into the hands of the
French by the help of poor Irish servants and freemen, who are the only
papists here; but in six months they gained not a man of note nor, I believe, more than two men or women, high or low. . . . In the infancy of
papistry here they were so bold as to threaten us with fire and faggot, and
told us that we must turn, run or burn.

3. The conversion of Negro slaves to Christianity.

a. The French Government orders that slaves should be bap-
tised

Article 2 of the Code Noir, 1685

All slaves in our islands shall be baptised and instructed in the Catholic
religion, Apostolic and Roman. We instruct the colonists buying newly
arrived slaves that they should inform the Governor and Intendant of it
within one week at the latest, on pain of a summary fine, and they shall
give the necessary orders to have them instructed and baptised in due
course.

b. An objection to religious instruction from a French Governor

Governor of Martinique to the French Government, 11 April 1764

It would offend all the saint-like clergy of France if my views ever got
beyond the sanctuary of your office, but to me religious instruction is an
obligation enjoined upon us by the principles of religion, yet the public
weal and the strongest considerations of social order are opposed to it.

Religious instruction could give to the negroes here new vistas of knowledge, a kind of reason. The safety of the Whites, fewer in number, surrounded by these people on their estates and at their mercy, demands that they be kept in the profoundest ignorance.

c. An objection to the conversion of a slave from an English planter

Ligon, *History of Barbados*, 1657

When I came home, spoke to the master of the plantation, and told him that poor Sambo desired much to be a Christian. But his answer was that the people of that island were governed by the laws of England, and by those laws, we could not make a Christian a slave. I told him, my request was far different from that, for I desired to make a slave a Christian. His answer was, that it was true, there was a great difference in that: but, being once a Christian he could no more account him a slave, and so lose the hold they had of them as slaves, by making them Christians; and by that means should open such a gap, as all the planters in the island would curse him. So I was struck mute, and poor Sambo kept out of the Church.

d. Moravian missionaries work among Antiguan slaves

Coke, *History of the West Indies*, 1808

Many of these Moravian Brethren, melting in pity over the benighted heathens, went forth in the name of their Heavenly Master to instruct them in the things of God. In every quarter of the globe they have extended their labours; and in many places God has blessed and owned their endeavours, by giving them an abundance of souls for their hire. Their missionaries were the first Protestant ministers of the gospel who, with a holy and disinterested zeal, directed their labours to the pious and benevolent purpose of converting the negro slaves in the West Indies. With these views they settled among them in the different islands, and laid the foundation of a Christian Church in Antigua.

e. *Some estates encourage clergy to give religious instruction*

Lewis, *Journal of a West Indian Proprietor*, 25 February 1816

By the overseer of Greenwich's express desire, the Moravian has agreed to give up an hour every day for the religious instruction of the negro children on that property: and I should certainly request him to extend his labours to Cornwall, if I did not think it right to give the Church of England clergymen full room for a trial of their intended periodical visitations; which would not be the case, if the negroes were to be interfered with by the professors of any other communion: otherwise I am myself ready to give free ingress and egress upon my several estates to the teachers of any Christian sect whatever, the Methodists always excepted. . . .

For my own part, I have no hope of any material benefit arising from these religious visitations made at quarterly intervals. It seems to me as nugatory as if a man were to sow a field with horse-hair and expect a crop of colts.

f. *In some territories laws are passed to hinder the missionaries' work with slaves*

An order of the Common Council of Kingston, Jamaica, 1807

WHEREAS it is not only highly incumbent upon, but the first and most serious duty of all magistrates and bodies politic, to uphold and encourage the due, proper, and solemn exercise of religion and worshipping of God:

And whereas nothing can tend more to bring true devotion, and the practice of religion, into disrepute, than the pretended preaching, teaching, and expounding the word of God as contained in the Holy Scriptures, by uneducated, illiterate and ignorant persons, and false enthusiasts:

And whereas the practice of such pretended preaching, teaching, and expounding the Holy Scriptures, by such descriptions of persons, to large numbers of persons of colour, and negroes of free condition, and slaves, assembled together in houses, negro-houses, huts and the yards thereunto appertaining, and also in divers lands and by-places within the city and parish, hath increased to an alarming degree; . . . to the great detriment of slaves who are induced, by divers artifices and pretences of the said pretended preachers, to attend the said irregular assemblies, whereby such slaves are continually kept and detained from their owners' necessary business and employ, and in some cases the minds of slaves have been so operated upon, and affected, by the fanaticism of the aforesaid description of persons, as to become actually deranged:

Be it therefore enacted, and ordained by the Common Council of the city and parish of Kingston . . . that from and after the first day of July next, no person not being duly authorised, qualified, and permitted, as is directed by the laws of this island, and of Great Britain, and in the place mentioned in such licence, shall, under pretence of being a minister of religion of any sect or denomination, or of being a teacher or expounder of the gospel, or other parts of the Holy Scriptures, presume to preach, or teach, or offer up public prayer, or sing psalms, in any meeting or assembly of negroes, or persons of colour, within this city and parish.

And in case any person shall in any ways offend herein, every such person, if a white person, shall suffer such punishment by fine not exceeding one hundred pounds, or by imprisonment in the common gaol for any space, not exceeding three months, or both; or if a free person of colour, or free black, by fine not exceeding one hundred pounds, or imprisonment in the work-house for a space of time not exceeding three months, or both; or if a slave, by imprisonment and hard labour in the work-house, for a space not exceeding six months, or by whipping, not exceeding thirty-nine stripes, or both; as shall be in those cases respectively adjudged.

And be it further enacted and ordained that no person being so licensed or permitted, shall use public worship in any of the places within this city and parish which may be licensed, earlier than the hour of six o'clock in the morning, or later than sunset in the evening, under the penalty of such punishment by fine, not exceeding one hundred pounds, or by imprisonment in the common gaol not exceeding three months, or both, as shall be in that respect adjudged.

g. Missionaries are sometimes successful in persuading the British Government to disallow such laws

Petition to the British Government, 1808

The humble Memorial of the Committee of Deputies of the Three Denominations of Protestant Dissenters

SHEWETH

THAT your Memorialists have learned with deep regret that in an Act lately passed by the Assembly of the Island of Jamaica, entitled, *An Act for the Protection, Subsisting, Clothing, and for the better Order and Government of Slaves, and for other purposes*, certain provisions have been introduced respecting Preachers and Teachers dissenting from the Established Church of England, highly injurious to many peaceable and loyal subjects of His Majesty's crown and government, ...

That if any of those persons, against whom the said provisions appear to have been directed, had been guilty of seditious practices, or other misdemeanours, tending to endanger the safety, or to disturb the peace of the said island, your Memorialists apprehend that the individuals so offending were answerable to justice; and might have been restrained or punished according to the nature and urgency of the occasion, without confounding the innocent with the guilty; whereas, in the present case, your Memorialists believe themselves justified in stating, that, so far from such misconduct having been proved, or the existing laws having been charged with such insufficiency as to demand additional legislative provisions (much less any so vexatious and unjust), it has appeared from most respectable and impartial testimonies ... that great advantage had been derived by the colonists from the labours of that very description of persons who have been silenced and oppressed by the late Act, which, although unsanctioned by the authority of His Majesty, has, nevertheless, been put in full execution.

Your Memorialists therefore, regarding the enactments against which they have taken the liberty to remonstrate, as unconstitutional in their principle, and oppressive in their operation ... humbly pray that your

Lordships will, in your wisdom, be pleased to advise His Majesty to prevent the said Act from passing into law, by refusing thereto his Royal assent.

4. As the humanitarian movement in England against slavery became more effective, the hostility against missionaries in the colonies became more intense.

a. John Smith, missionary in Demerara, writes from prison
John Smith to the London Missionary Society, 12 January 1824

Dear and Honoured Sirs,

You seem to be aware in some measure, of the unceasing animosity which the colonists in general, and the planters in particular, have to the instruction of the slaves, and to faithful missionaries on that account; but you can have no just idea of the rancour and fury they display against a missionary when any report is raised against him, which is not unfrequent, and always has turned out to be false, as far as my knowledge has extended. The following extract from the *Guiana Chronicle* of the 11th of February, 1822, may give an idea of their malicious dispositions towards missionaries :—

'We have had occasion repeatedly to express our opinion of the Sectarian Propagandists, who send forth their missionaries out of a pretended zeal for the salvation of souls. They, the missionaries, to be sure, are too wise and cunning to make direct attacks from the pulpit on public men and measures; but in respect of their wild jargon, their capricious interpretations of the Bible, and the doctrines they inculcate, although in themselves they are to be despised and slighted, yet, in point of the pernicious tendency they may have upon the minds of their hearers, we do think no caution can be too great, no vigilance too strict. The influence they possess on the minds of the negroes is more widely ramified than is imagined, or would be readily believed. It is no longer true to say they are insignificant. . . . From their calling and canting, they have acquired a degree of importance in this Colony not obtainable otherwise.'

Under my persecutions and afflictions, it affords me no small consolation, that the Directors cherish the assurance of my entire innocence. That I am innocent of the crimes which they have laid to my charge, I have not only the testimony of my own conscience in my favour, but the attestation of all my friends, who have made strict inquiries into my conduct relative to this affair. The instructions I received from the Society, I always endeavoured to act upon, and in order to vindicate the Society from the vile aspersions made against it by its enemies, as to its having a concealed object in view; viz. the ultimate liberation of the slaves—I laid over the instructions as a part of the proceedings of the Court Martial on my trial, that publicity might be given to the real object of the Society. . . .

It grieves me, dear Sirs, that I am now a useless burden upon the Society. I have endeavoured from the beginning to discharge my duties faithfully. In doing so, I have met with the most unceasing opposition and reproach, until at length the adversary found occasion to triumph over me. But so far have these things been from shaking my confidence in the goodness of the cause in which I was engaged, that if I were at liberty, and my health restored, I would again proclaim all my days, the glad tidings of salvation amidst similar opposition; but of this I see no prospect. The Lord's hand is heavy upon me; still, I can praise his name, that though outward afflictions abound towards me, yet the consolations of the gospel abound also, and I believe he will do all things well.

I am, dear Sirs, in much affliction,

Your useless, but devoted Servant,

John Smith.

b. James Phillippo, missionary in Jamaica, is refused a licence to preach

Jamaican Newspaper, 10 July 1824

At a court of quarter sessions, held in this town on Tuesday, an application was made by the Rev. James Phillippo, a Baptist missionary, for leave to preach in this parish, but the documents he produced, being without a known seal or signature, were considered unsatisfactory, and leave was refused. He was informed that, in the present perilous state of these colonies, it became the duty of the magistrates to be extremely cautious in granting such permissions; more especially as many of the sectaries in the mother country had declared their avowed intention of effecting our ruin, and had united in becoming publicly and clamorously the justifiers of such a man as Smith, whose seditious practices in Demerara had been proved by the clearest evidence. .... We sincerely hope this example will be followed throughout the island, for there never was a time when more caution was required from the magistrates. The fears we have for some time laboured under, from the efforts of the saints and sectaries in England, seconded by many of our mistaken friends, have induced us to be much too easy in permitting preachers and teachers of all descriptions to be introduced among us, greatly to the injury of the slaves; and it would, perhaps, be a very useful inquiry, in every parish, to ascertain the reduction in comforts they have experienced by the fasts imposed upon them, and the moneys they are obliged to contribute, out of their slender means, towards the support of their teachers. This is a consideration which, in the end, may prove, perhaps, of as much importance to the welfare of the island as the suppression even of seditious practices.

5. Nonconformist pastors were blamed for the slave rebellion in Jamaica at Christmas, 1831. Their chapels were attacked and they themselves were abused or imprisoned.

a. The blame is laid

Report of a Committee of the House of Assembly, 1832

From a mischievous abuse existing in the system adopted by different religious sects in this island, termed Baptists, Wesleyan Methodists and Moravians, by their recognising gradations of rank among such of our slaves as had become converts to their doctrines, whereby the less ambitious and more peaceable among them were made the dupes of the artful and intelligent who had been selected by the preachers of those particular sects to fill the higher offices in their chapels under the denomination of rulers, elders, leaders and helpers.

And lastly, the public discussions of the free inhabitants here, consequent upon the continued suggestions made by the King's ministers regarding further measures of amelioration to be introduced into the slave code of this island, and the preaching and teaching of the religious sects called Baptists, Wesleyan Methodists and Moravians (but more particularly the sect termed Baptists) which had the effect of producing in the minds of the slaves a belief that they could not serve both a spiritual and a temporal master; thereby occasioning them to resist the lawful authority of their temporal, under the delusion of rendering themselves more acceptable to a spiritual, master.

b. A missionary under attack

Knibb to the Secretary of the Baptist Missionary Society, January 1832

I was looking forward with pleasure to the time when I could relieve the Parent Society, but this awful visitation of Providence has for the present destroyed all our prospects. The report being current that I was to be shot, my creditors became clamorous, and I was obliged to do the best my distracted state of mind would allow. I have sold what little things I could to support myself and family, but I assure you that I have not anything to buy the necessaries of life. £84 I had in Stewart Town and the £100 I had in Rio Bueno, are gone in the destruction of the chapels, and my furniture is so injured in hiding it from the rabble, that it will not fetch much. One of Mr. Cantlow's horses has been ruined, and I had to give it away, as I had not money to support it. His other horse and mine are stolen. Every one thinks here that they may abuse missionaries and their property as much as they please. If I can sell my chaise it will pay every debt I now owe; but I must look to you for bread to eat. I deeply feel for your difficulties; I mourn that I cannot relieve them. Had I any money, it should be devoted to the cause which is now suffering, but which will eventually triumph.

c. A missionary imprisoned without charge

Journal of Thomas Burchell, 30 January 1832

In conversation with Capt. Pengelly this evening, I observed that, as I was still kept in ignorance of the cause of my apprehension and imprisonment, both of which I believed to be illegal, without an arrest, a hearing and commitment, or even any reason being assigned for the proceeding, and that too when martial law had ceased, I should apply for permission to return home, to seek there an explanation of such treatment from officers of His Majesty's navy; as also, a redress of my grievances; and that, if I could, I should demand that the whole of my papers, which had been so unceremoniously seized, should be again sealed and forwarded to His Majesty's Government at home for their inspection, that they may be enabled to judge of the legality or otherwise of my confinement.

6. The founding of the nonconformist churches in the West Indies was a hazardous business.

a. A Methodist missionary reports on his difficulties

Missionary in St. Kitts to Methodist Missionary Society, 6 May 1802

You will perceive from the enclosed statement, that the number in our society amounts to two thousand five hundred and eighty-seven; and that the Lord has blessed us greatly in our temporal affairs. Indeed we had more in number than are included in the above statement; but the crop of canes is so great, that many companies of negroes are obliged to work until midnight; and therefore, having no time to attend their classes, I did not take their names into the account.

The Sunday-School I mentioned is nearly established. Our friends are consulting about building a school-house. They urge very much to have a day-school to educate their children in the principles of religion, together with reading, writing and arithmetic. Many white people also press the matter, and say, 'Their children are learning little but vice in common schools.' His Honour the President said, that '*our Sunday-schools deserved* public support', or words to that effect. Many tarry after public service is done, to hear the children sing praises unto God.

Had we four preachers in this island, and two in Nevis, and were the superintendent a man that took delight in training up the rising generation, the above plan might be carried into effect, and the profits resulting from it would be more than sufficient for the maintenance of one preacher. Indeed it would be only another mode, and perhaps a more effectual one, of forwarding the object of our mission. The children at present under our care are about two hundred.

b. A single Methodist missionary for all Jamaica

Coke, *History of the West Indies*, 1808

The removal of Mr. Brazier to the continent, on account of his declining health, and the subsequent death of Mr. Werrill, both of which events happened in the year 1791, placed the societies on the island in a solitary condition. For some time they were left without any missionary, though there was a sufficiency of employment for three or four. . . .

Such was the situation of the societies in the island when Mr. Fish arrived, in 1792. The number in the society amounted to about 170, including those on three or four plantations in the mountains. The violence of persecution had also abated; a few solitary stones were, indeed, thrown occasionally at the chapel, but personal interruption seldom happened.

The care of the whole island now devolved on this single missionary, aided by such internal helps as the societies could produce.

c. Deaths among missionaries

Buchner, *The Moravians in Jamaica*, 1854

There is no mission-field where disease and death have been so active as in the West Indies. A reference to our registries proves this. Since the commencement of the mission in Jamaica in 1754, sixty-four brethren and sisters have been buried here, and how short has been the time of their service!

The following statement will show the length of service of the missionaries who have departed this life in Jamaica :— 6 died within one year; 10 served only one year; 7 served for two years. . . . There was only one who lived to endure the severity of that service for nineteen years!

d. The regular routine of a missionary

Letter from Phillippo to his mother, 1828

Breakfast; conduct family worship, including any persons who may happen to be on the premises. We afterwards go down into the school, which is on the floor beneath us, and which we superintend, and there remain until other engagements require attention. At two o'clock, when at home, I again visit the school, and remain till it is over for the day, concluding as it was begun, with singing and prayer.

About half-past four we dine, then get ready for chapel, class meetings, singing-classes, leaders' meetings, evening adult school, or meetings of some kind or another in town or country every day of the week. They usually commence at six o'clock and continue for an hour and a half. We then take tea, have family prayers, and at nine or half past retire for the night.

This is the regular routine, interrupted, of course, on the week days by services in the country, at Old Harbour, thirteen miles distant, and elsewhere by visits to the sick; by monthly intercourse with members and inquirers, by experience meetings and church meetings, by settlement of disputes and by marriages and burials, etc.

e. For the church to survive slavery must be overthrown

Knibb's Speech to the Baptist Missionary Society, 21 June 1832

For nearly eight years I had trodden the sun-burnt and slave-cursed island of Jamaica, during which time your gratitude has been often called forth by the pleasing intelligence that God was blessing the instrumentality employed. In almost every part of Jamaica Christian churches have been established, which may vie with any in the world for a devout attendance on the means of grace, and for the simple yet fervent zeal of their members.

Hill and dale, street and hamlet, have resounded with the praise and prayer of the African who had been taught that Jesus died to save him, and the sweet and simple strains of the many-coloured slave population have often sounded delightfully on our ears. Success has attended your missionaries in a manner which has appeared to promise the commencement of the millenium.

But I need not say, that all is lost, that our harps are hung upon the willows, and that the voice of praise is no more heard in our streets. A combined Satanic effort has been made to root out all religion; the sanctuaries of God have been broken down with axes and hammers, and the infuriated yell, 'Rase it, rase it, even to the foundations thereof', has resounded through the island. Feeling, therefore, as I do, that the African and the Creole slave will never again enjoy the blessings of religious instruction, or hear of the benefits of that gospel which Christ has commanded to be preached among all nations, and which He has so eminently blessed in Jamaica, unless slavery be overthrown, I now stand forward as the unflinching and undaunted advocate of immediate emancipation.

7. Education for the free population was provided in the West Indies with money given by successful planters. But those who could afford it sent their children to school in England. Religious bodies also provided a few schools for coloured children. The British Government tried to extend religious education to slaves as part of the amelioration policy.

a. Codrington leaves his estates for a college of divinity and medicine in Barbados

Will of Christopher Codrington, 1710

I give and bequeath my two plantations in the island of Barbados, to the Society for the Propagation of the Christian Religion in Foreign Parts, erected and established by my late good master, King William III : and my desire is to have the plantations continued entire, and three hundred negroes at least always kept thereon; and a convenient number of professors and scholars maintained there; all of them to be under vows of poverty, chastity and obedience; who shall be obliged to study and practise physic and chirurgery, as well as divinity; that by the apparent usefulness of the former to all mankind, they may both endear themselves to the people and have the better opportunities of doing good to men's souls, whilst they are taking care of their bodies; but the particulars of the constitution I leave to the Society composed of wise and good men.

b. A writer in Jamaica claims that the free schools are of little use to the public

Long, *History of Jamaica*, 1774

Upon enquiry, in the year 1764, into the state of the several foundations in this island, it appeared that considerable sums had been given and bequeathed for the purpose of erecting free schools; some of which remained unapplied; and others had been so ill-managed, that the public derived but very trivial advantage from them. These foundations are :—

First,   Mannings, in Westmoreland, founded in 1710.

Second,   One in Vere, by charitable donations, 1740.

Third,   In Spanish Town, by devise of Peter Beckford, Esq. 1744.

Fourth,   In Kingston, by devise of John Wolmer, goldsmith, 1736.

Fifth,   At Half-Way-Tree, St. Andrew, by devise of Sir Nicholas Laws, 1695. He gave two acres and a half of land, with a house for a free school; conditioning that any parishioner, paying £5 per annum or £50 down, towards advancement of the school, might send his child thither for instruction. This donation by a law passed in 1738, was established under the control of Governors, to make regulations, appoint teachers, etc., but I do not find that it succeeded.

Sixth,   At Old Woman's Savannah, in Clarendon, by a donation of three acres of land, and sundry subscriptions, 1756.

Seventh,   About 1769 or 1770, Martin Rusea, of the parish of Hanover, devised his estate consisting chiefly of personalty, for erecting and establishing a free school in that parish; but the particular value of this donation, does not yet appear. The assembly, however, have shown a desire to promote it by granting £500 towards its establishment.

All these foundations except that at Old Woman's Savannah were limited to receive boys of the respective parish in which they lay; which, together with their bad regulation has been a principal cause of their failing.

c. Some Jamaicans go to Britain for their education

Long, *History of Jamaica*, 1774

It has long been the custom for every father here, who has acquired a little property, to send his children, of whatever complexion, to Britain, for education. They go like a bale of dry goods, consigned to some factor, who places them at the school where he himself was bred, or any other that his inclination leads him to prefer. The father, in the meanwhile, sends remittance upon remittance, or directs a liberal allowance, that his son may learn the art of squandering from his very infancy; and, not infrequently, to gratify a little pride of heart, that little master may appear the redoubted heir to an affluent fortune.

d. A criticism of the practice of sending children to Britain for education

Long, *History of Jamaica*, 1774

Let me now ask, what are the mighty advantages which Britain, or the colony, has gained by the many hundreds who have received their education in the former? The answer may be, they have spent their fortunes in Britain, and learned to renounce their native place, their parents, and friends. Would it not have been better for both countries, that three-fourths of them had never crossed the Atlantic? Their industry is, in general, forever lost to the place where it might have been usefully exerted; and

107

they waste their patrimony in a manner that redounds not in the least to the national profit, having acquired a taste for pleasure and extravagance of every kind, far superior to the ability of their fortunes. . . . The education they usually receive in Great Britain does not qualify them for useful employment in Jamaica, unless they are bred to some of the learned professions; which nevertheless are not suitable to all, because those professions would soon be overstocked in the island, if every youth consigned from thence was to be trained to physic, divinity or law.

e. Schools in Bridgetown, Barbados

Coleridge, *Six Months in the West Indies*, 1825

There is a large school of coloured children, chiefly free, in the town, which was formerly supported by the Church Missionary Society, but has since been put by the coloured managers of it entirely under the bishop's superintendence. The children are very well behaved, very docile, very sensible of the advantages which they acquire by a system of methodical instruction; and the actual difference between them and their untaught brethren of the same colour and sometimes same condition would convince any unprejudiced witness, that it is not to emancipation but to education that the sincere philanthropist ought to direct his present labours.

Four more schools have been opened by the indefatigable bishop for boys and girls respectively; they are maintained at the expense of government; any colour is admitted upon the simple condition of cleanliness and constant attendance, and instruction is gratuitous. These schools are scattered about in the parts of the town principally inhabited by the coloured people, who are by these means more readily induced to send their children. These children are chiefly of the lowest order of the free coloured and of the domestic and mechanic slaves in Bridge Town and the immediate vicinity. They are not at present taught to write, a point certainly not of any vital importance, and wisely conceded to prejudices which will in due time melt away under a conviction of the propriety of the knowledge and the futility of the prohibition.

f. The British Government supports religious instruction for slaves

Amelioration proposals, 9 July 1823

It would be superfluous to insist upon the indispensable necessity of religious instruction as the foundation of every beneficial change in the character and future condition of the slaves. So deeply indeed is His Majesty's Government impressed with this truth and with the necessity of maintaining an adequate number of clergymen and teachers throughout the West Indies under episcopal control, that if it shall appear that the revenues of the colonies are insufficient for this purpose they will not hesitate to apply to Parliament for such pecuniary grants as may be necessary for supplying the deficiency.

4

Slavery and its Abolition

1. Negro slaves were brought to the West Indies by the earliest colonists and the slave trade soon became an organised traffic in Africa and across the Atlantic.

a. The Spanish King gives a licence for slaves to be imported into the Spanish Empire

Order of the Spanish King, 18 August 1518

Know ye that I have given permission, and by the present (instrument) do give it, to Lorenzo de Gorrevod, governor of Bresa, member of my Council, whereby he, or the person or persons who may have his authority therefor, may proceed to take to the Indies, the islands and the mainland of the ocean sea already discovered or to be discovered, four thousand negro slaves both male and female, provided they be Christians, in whatever proportions he may choose.

b. John Hawkins enters the slave trade with the Spanish Empire

Hakluyt, *Principal Navigations*, 1582

Master John Hawkins . . . being amongst other particulars assured, that Negroes were very good merchandise in Hispaniola, and that store of Negroes might easily be had upon the coast of Guinea, resolved with himself to make trial thereof, and communicated that devise with his worshipful friends of London who became liberal contributors and adventurers in the action. . . . He put off and departed from the coast of England in the month of October 1562, and in his course touched first at Teneriffe, where he received friendly entertainment. From thence he passed to Sierra Leone, upon the coast of Guinea . . . where he stayed some good time, and got into his possession, partly by the sword and partly by other means to the number of 300 Negroes at the least, besides other merchandises which that country yieldeth. With this prey he sailed over the Ocean sea unto the Island of Hispaniola, and arrived first at the port of Isabella: and there he had reasonable utterance of his English commodities, as also of some part of his Negroes, trusting the Spaniards no further than that by his own strength he was able still to master them. From the port of Isabella he went to Puerto de Plata, where he made like sales, standing always upon his guard: from thence also he sailed to Monte Christi another port on the North side of Hispaniola, and the last place of his touching, where he had peaceable traffic, and made vent of the whole number of his Negroes: for which he did not only lade his own three ships with hides, ginger, sugars, and some quantities of pearls, but he freighted also two other hulks with hides and the like commodities, which he sent into Spain.

c. A discussion about the legality of the slave trade reveals how slaves were captured in Africa

Brother Luis Brandaon to Father Sandoval, 12 March 1610

We have been here ourselves for forty years; . . . in the Province of Brazil as well, . . . never did they consider this trade as illicit. Therefore we and the fathers of Brazil buy these slaves for our service without any scruple. Furthermore . . . we here are the ones who could have greater scruple, for we buy these negroes from other negroes and from people who perhaps have stolen them; but the traders who take them away from here do not know of this fact, and so buy those negroes with a clear conscience and sell them out there with a clear conscience. . . . In the fairs where these negroes are bought there are always a few who have been captured illegally because they were stolen or because the rulers of the land order them to be sold for offences so slight that they do not deserve captivity, but these are few in number and to seek among ten or twelve thousand who leave this port every year for a few who have been illegally captured is an impossibility, however careful investigation may be made. And to lose so many souls as sail from here—out of whom many are saved—does not seem to be doing much service to God, for these are few and those who find salvation are many and legally captured.

d. Lengthy trading negotiations on the African coast for slaves and supplies for the voyage

Journal of the Dutch Slaver 'St. Jan', 1659

March 4.	We weighed anchor to proceed on our voyage to Rio del Rey to trade for slaves for the hon'ble company.
March 8.	Saturday. Arrived with our ship before Ardra, to take on board the surgeon's mate and a supply of tamarinds for refreshment for the slaves; sailed again next day on our voyage to Rio del Rey.
March 17.	Arrived at Rio del Rey in front of a village called Bonny, where we found the company's yacht which was sent out to assist us to trade for slaves.
In April.	Nothing was done except to trade for slaves.
May 22.	Again weighed anchor and ran out of Rio del Rey; purchased there two hundred and nineteen head of slaves, men, women, boys and girls and set our course for the high land of Ambosius, for the purpose of procuring food there for the slaves, as nothing was to be had at Rio del Rey.
26 Monday.	Arrived under the high land of Ambosius to look there for victuals for the slaves, and spent seven days there, but barely obtained enough for the daily consumption of the slaves, so that we resolved to run to Rio Cammerones to see if any food could be had there for the slaves.
June 5.	Thursday. Arrived at the Rio Cammerones and went up to look for provisions for the slaves. This day died our cooper.
June 29.	Sunday. Again resolved to proceed on our voyage, as there also but little food was to be had for the slaves in consequence

of the great rains which fell every day, and because many of
the slaves were suffering from the bloody flux in consequence
of the bad provisions we were supplied with at El Mina,
amongst which were many barrels of groats, wholly unfit
for use.

We then turned over to Adriaen Blaes, the skipper, one
hundred and ninety five slaves, consisting of eighty one men,
one hundred and five women, six boys and three girls for
which bills of lading were signed and sent, to El Mina, with
an account of, and receipts for, remaining merchandise.

July 25.   Arrived at Cape Lopez for water and wood.

27.   Our surgeon . . . died of the bloody flux.

Aug. 11.   Again resolved to pursue our voyage towards the island of
Annobon in order to purchase there some refreshments for
the slaves. We have lain sixteen days at Cape Lopez hauling
water and wood. Among the water barrels, more than forty
had fallen to pieces and were unfit to be used, as our cooper
died at Rio Cammerones and we had no other person capable
of repairing them.

Aug. 15.   Arrived at the island of Annobon, where we purchased for
the slaves one hundred half tierces of beans, twelve hogs, five
thousand coconuts, five thousand sweet oranges, besides
some other stores.

Aug. 17.   Again hoisted sail to prosecute our voyage to the island of
Curacao.

e. A transatlantic crossing in a slaver

Voyage of the English slaver 'James', 1675–6

March Wednesday 8th.   Set sail from Dickey's road bound for Barbados.

Thursday 16th. . . . .   A tornado—with much thunder, lightning and
rain. This day I put all my slaves out of irons.

Wednesday 22nd. . . .   I called all my thin slaves aft, which came from

	Wyemba and found 25 of them ... gave my slaves tobacco and pipes.
Tuesday 28th.	Caught fish and agreed to give for every 10 fish a pt. of brandy, gave my slaves 10 fish in their suppers.
Thursday 30th. . . .	Gave the slaves tobacco and pipes and beer in their suppers.
Friday 31st. . . .	Gave the slaves fish in their suppers.
April Monday 17th.	... a stout man slave leaped overboard and drowned himself.
May, Sunday 21st.	Made the island of Barbados at anchor in Kerley Bay.
Monday 22nd.	Mr. Steed went aboard and looked on our slaves.
Tuesday 23rd.	Orders to prepare the slaves for sale on Thursday.
Wednesday 24th.	Our slaves being shaved I gave them fresh water to wash and palm oil and tobacco and pipes.
Thursday 25th.	Mr. Steed came on board to sell our slaves—we sold 163 slaves.
Friday 26th.	We sold 70 slaves.
Saturday 27th.	Sold 110 slaves.
Monday 29th.	Delivered 80 slaves which were part of the 110 which were sold on Saturday.
Thursday 30th. . . .	Went on board with a planter to sell him some of our refuse slaves but he did not like them and I went on shore and gave Mr. Steed an account.
Wednesday 31st. . . .	Mr. Man and myself came on board and sold 5 of our refuse slaves.

2. To regulate slavery in the West Indies the French Government issued an edict for their colonies; in the British colonies the assemblies passed acts to control the conduct of masters and slaves.

a. The French code

Articles from the Code Noir, 1685

4. No overseer shall be put in control of Negroes who does not profess the Catholic religion, on pain of the confiscation of the said Negroes from the masters who have appointed them and summary punishment of the overseers who shall have accepted such appointment.

9. Freemen who shall have had one or more children by cohabitation with slaves, also masters who shall have allowed it, shall each be subject to a fine of 200 lbs. of sugar, and, should they be the masters of the slaves by whom they have had the same children, in addition to the fine they shall be deprived of the slave and the children and she and they be transferred to the hospital, with no possibility of enfranchisement, always on the understanding that this article shall not operate when the free man was not married to any other person at the time of the cohabitation with his slave, shall marry the said slave in the Church, and she shall be freed by this means and the children made free and legitimate.

11. Priests are strictly forbidden to conduct slave marriages if they do not appear to be with the consent of their masters. Masters are also forbidden to use any sanction on their slaves to make them marry against their wish.

12. Children born of slave marriages shall be slaves and shall belong to the masters of the female slaves and not to those of their husbands, if the husband and wife have different masters.

15. Slaves are forbidden to carry any arms or big sticks on pain of whipping and confiscation of the arms by those who have caught them . . .

16. Slaves belonging to different masters are also forbidden to collect together by day or by night under pretext of marriages or other occasions, either on their masters' estates or otherwise, and even less in the open

road or distant spots, on pain of corporal punishment which cannot be less than the whip and branding, and, in repeated cases or other aggravating circumstances can be punished by death . . .

22. Masters shall be obliged to provide each week to their slaves of eighteen years old and more, for food, 2½ measures of cassava flour, or three cassavas weighing 2½ lbs. each at least, or some equivalent provision, with 2 lbs. of salt beef or 3 lbs. of fish, or some equal value; and to children weaning until ten years old, half the above subsistence.

26. Slaves who are not fed, clothed and maintained by their masters, as we have here ordained, may report the fact to our Procurator General and put their complaints in his hands, in each case, or if the information comes from others, the masters shall be summoned at their request but without cost; which will be the same process as we would wish pursued for crimes and barbarous and inhumane treatment by masters against their slaves.

27. We declare that slaves may own nothing which does not belong to their masters; and everything which they receive for their work, or through the gift of other people, or otherwise, whatever the claims may be, shall be regarded fully as the property of their masters, even children of slaves. . . .

33. Any slave who has struck his master, his mistress or the husband of his mistress, or their children to cause a bruising or bleeding, or on the face, shall be punished by death.

38. Runaway slaves who have been missing for a month from the day when their master reported it to the Justice, shall have their ears cut and shall be branded with the *fleur-de-lys* on one shoulder; if they run away for another month, also from the day of the report, they shall have their tongue slit, and be branded with the *fleur-de-lys* on the other shoulder and the third time, they shall be punished by death.

43. We instruct our officials to take criminal proceedings against masters or overseers who have killed the slave belonging to them or under their command, and shall punish the murderer according to the brutality of the circumstances; and should they have received absolution, our officials are allowed to set the masters or overseers free but they require to obtain an official pardon from us.

59. We grant to those who have been enfranchised the same rights, privileges and immunities enjoyed by people born free: wishing that the benefit of acquired liberty may produce in them, as much for their persons as for their goods, the same effects that the good fortune of natural liberty offers to our other subjects.

b. Jamaican slave law

Clauses from *Laws for the Government of Negro Slaves*, 1787

II. Every master, owner, or possessor of any plantation or plantations, pens, or other lands whatsoever, shall allot and appoint a sufficient quantity of land for every slave he shall have in possession upon or belonging to such plantation or plantations, pens, or other lands, as and for the proper ground of every slave, and allow such slave sufficient time to work the same, in order to provide him or her, or themselves with sufficient provisions for his, her or their maintenance: and also all such masters, owners, or possessors of plantations, pens or other lands, in ground provisions at least one acre of land for every ten negroes that he shall be possessed of on such plantation, pen or other lands, over and above the negro grounds aforesaid, which lands shall be kept up in a planter-like condition, under the penalty of fifty pounds.

III. That no master, owner or possessor of any slave or slaves, whether in his or her own right, or as attorney, guardian, trustee, executor, or otherwise, shall discard or turn away any such slave or slaves on account or by reason of such slave or slaves being rendered incapable of labour or service to such master, owner, or possessor, by means of sickness, age or infirmity, but every such master, owner, or possessor as aforesaid shall be, and he is hereby obliged to keep all such slave or slaves upon his, her or their properties, and to find and provide them with wholesome necessities of life, and not suffer such slave or slaves as aforesaid to be in want thereof, or to wander about, or become burthensome to others for sustenance.

IV. That every master, owner, or possessor of slaves shall, once in every year, provide and give to each slave they shall be possessed of, proper and sufficient clothing, to be approved of by the justices and vestry of the parish where such master, owner, or possessor of such slaves resides.

V. That all masters and mistresses, owners, or in their absence, overseers of slaves, shall, as much as in them lies, endeavour the instruction of their slaves in the principles of the Christian religion, whereby to facilitate their conversion, and shall do their utmost endeavours to fit them for baptism, and, as soon as conveniently they can, shall cause to be baptised all such as they can make sensible of a Deity and the Christian faith.

XI. That if any person hereafter shall wantonly, willingly, or bloody-mindedly kill any negro or other slave, such person so offending shall, on conviction, be adjudged guilty of felony without benefit of clergy, and shall suffer death accordingly for the said offence.

XII. Any person or persons, that shall wantonly or cruelly whip, beat, bruise, wound or shall imprison or keep in confinement without sufficient support, any slave or slaves, shall be subject to be indicted for the same in the supreme court of judicature, or in either of the courts of assize, or courts of quarter sessions in this island.

XVIII. That every field slave on such plantation or settlement shall on work-days be allowed, according to custom, half an hour for breakfast, and two hours for dinner; and that no slave shall be compelled to any manner of field-work upon the plantations before the hour of five in the morning, or after the hour of seven at night, except during the time of crop.

XXI. And whereas it has been found by experience that rebellions have been often concerted at negro dances and nightly meetings of the slaves of different plantations, when such slaves are generally intoxicated; and it has been found also that those meetings tend much to injure the healths of negroes; Be it therefore enacted, by the authority aforesaid, that if any overseer, or in his absence any book-keeper, or other white person having the care and management of any plantation or settlement, shall knowingly suffer any slaves to assemble together and beat their military drums, or blow horns or shells, every such overseer, book-keeper, or other white person so offending, shall for every such offence, upon conviction thereof, upon an indictment in the supreme court of judicature, or before the justices of assize, suffer six months' imprisonment.

XXIII. That if any slave shall offer any violence, by striking or otherwise, to any white person, such slave, upon due and proper proof, shall, upon conviction, be punished with death, or confinement to hard labour for life, or otherwise, as the court shall in their discretion think proper to inflict; provided such striking or conflict be not by command of his or their owners, overseers, or persons instructed over them, or in the lawful defence of their owners' persons or goods.

XL. Any slave who shall pretend to any supernatural power, in order to affect the health or lives of others, or promote the purposes of rebellion shall upon conviction thereof suffer death, or such other punishment as the court shall think proper to direct.

3. Slave life on the plantations.

a. Seasoning new slaves

Young, *A Tour through the Windward Islands*, 1791–2

From the late Guinea sales, I have purchased altogether twenty boys and girls, from ten to thirteen years old. It is the practice, on bringing them to the estate, to distribute them in the huts of Creole negroes, under their direction and care, who are to feed them, train them to work, and teach them their new language. For this care of feeding and bringing up the young African, the Creole negro receives no allowance of provisions whatever. He receives only a knife, a calabash to eat from, and an iron boiling pot for each. On first view of this it looks like oppression, and putting the burden of supporting another on the negro who receives him; but the reverse is the fact.

When the new negroes arrived on the estate, I thought the manager would have been torn to pieces by the number and earnestness of the applicants to have an inmate from among them. The competition was violent, and troublesome in the extreme. The fact is, that every negro in his garden, and at his leisure hours, earning much more than what is necessary to feed him, these young inmates are the wealth of the negro who entertains them, and for whom they work; their work finding plenty for the little household, and a surplus for sales at market, and for feeding his stock. This fact was in proof to me from the solicitations of the Creole negroes in general (and who had large families of their own) to take another inmate, on conditions of feeding him, and with a right to the benefit of his work. As soon as the young negro has passed his apprenticeship, and is fit for work in the field, he has a hut of his own, and works a garden on his own account.

b. Organisation of plantation work

Renny, *History of Jamaica*, 1807

On plantations, the Negroes are generally divided into three classes, called gangs; the first of which consists of the most healthy and robust, both of the males and females, whose chief business it is, before crop-time, to clear, hole, and plant the ground; and during crop-time to cut the canes, feed the mills, and attend to the manufacture of the sugar. It is computed, that of the whole body of the Negroes, on a well-conditioned plantation, there is commonly one-third of this description, exclusive of domestics and tradesmen, such as carpenters, coopers, and masons. The second gang is composed of young boys and girls, pregnant females, and convalescents, who are chiefly employed in weeding the canes, and other light work, adapted to their strength and condition; and the third gang consists of young children, attended by a careful old woman, who are employed in collecting green-meat for the pigs and sheep, or in weeding the garden, and gentle exercise of that nature, merely to preserve them from the habits of idleness.

The first gang is summoned to the labours of the field a little before sunrise, by the blowing of a conch shell. They bring with them, besides their hoes and bills, provisions for their breakfast, and are attended by a white person, and a black superintendent who is called the driver. The list is then called over, and the names of all the absentees noted; after which they commence their labour, and continue at work till eight or nine o'clock, when they sit down in the shade to breakfast, which has been in the meantime prepared by a certain number of women, whose sole employment is to cook. This meal consists of boiled yams, eddoes, ocra, calalue, and plantains, or as many of these vegetables as can be easily procured; and the whole when seasoned with salt, and cayenne pepper, is a very agreeable and wholesome breakfast. In the meantime, the absentees generally arrive, when they are punished by a certain number of lashes from the driver's whip, in proportion to the aggravated circumstances of the crime. After half an hour's intermission from labour, their work is again resumed. They toil till noon, and are again allowed an intermission. Two hours are now allotted for rest and refreshment, one of which is commonly spent in sleep. Their dinner is now provided, composed of the same materials with their breakfast, with the addition of salted meat or pickled fish, of which each Negro receives a weekly allowance. At two o'clock, they are again summoned to the field, where, having been refreshed, both by rest and food, they now manifest some signs of vigorous and animated application: although it is an undoubted fact, that one British labourer will perform three or four times more work, than a Negro in the same period. At sunset, or very soon after, they are released from their toil, and allowed to return to their huts; and when the day has been wet, or their toil unusually severe, they are sometimes indulged with an allowance of rum. They do not, in general, labour longer than ten hours every day, Sunday excepted. In the crop season, however, the arrangement is different; for at that time such of the Negroes as are employed in the mill, and boiling-houses, often work late, frequently all night; but, in this case, they are commonly divided into watches which relieve each other.

c. A visitor observes the life of the slaves

Sloane, *History of Jamaica*, 1707

They have Saturdays in the afternoon and Sundays, with Christmas holidays, Easter, called little, or *Pickaninny*, Christmas, and some other great feasts allowed them for the culture of their own plantations to feed themselves from potatoes, yams and plantains, etc., which they plant in ground allowed them by their masters. . . .

They formerly in their festivals were allowed the use of trumpets after their fashion and drums made of a piece of a hollow tree. . . . But making use of these in their wars at home in Africa, it was thought too much inciting them to rebellion, and so they were prohibited by the customs of the island. . . .

The Negroes have no manner of religion by what I could observe of them. It is true they have several ceremonies, as dances, playing, etc., but these for the most part are so far from being acts of adoration of a God, that they are for the most part mixed with a great deal of bawdry and lewdness. . . .

The parents here, although their children are slaves for ever, yet have so great a love for them, that no master dare sell or give away one of their little ones, unless they care not whether their parents hang themselves or no. . . .

The punishments for crimes of slaves are usually, for rebellions, burning them by nailing them down on the ground with crooked sticks on every limb, and then apply the fire by degrees from the feet and hands, burning them gradually up to the head, whereby their pains are extravagant. For crimes of a lesser nature gelding or chopping off half of the foot with an axe. These punishments are suffered by them with great constancy.

For running away, they put iron rings of great weight on their ankles, or pothooks about their necks, which are iron rings with two long necks riveted to them, or a spur in the mouth.

For negligence they are usually whipped by the overseers with laicewood switches till they be bloody and several of the switches broken, being first tied up by their hands in the mill-houses.

d. Food and provision grounds

Young, *A Tour through the Windward Islands*, 1791-2

In the case of the negro feeding himself with his own provisions, assisted only with salt provisions from his master (three pounds of salt fish, or an adequate quantity of herrings, per week, as in St. Vincent), the situation of the negro is in proportion to his industry; but generally speaking it affords him a plenty that amounts to comparative wealth, viewing any peasantry in Europe.

On my estate at Calliaqua, forty-six acres of the richest ground are set apart for the negro gardens, where they work voluntarily in the two hours they have every noon to themselves, on the half holiday in the week, and Sundays; and their returns are such that in my negro village, containing eighty-five huts, there is scarcely one but has a goat and kids, two or three pigs, and some poultry running about it. All this flock is plentifully fed from the negro's garden. . . .

Of the salt provisions given out to the negroes, the finest sort are the mackerel salted from America, and the negroes are remarkably fond of them. My brother H. (who is a manager at once properly strict, and most kind, and who is both feared and beloved by all the negroes) indulges them by studying to give a variety in their provisions; pork, beef, and fish of different sorts. A negro prefers pork to beef; one pound of pork will go as far as two pounds of beef in his messpot. This little attention of Mr. H. to the negroes' wishes, shows how much of their comfort must ever depend on the master's regard to them.

e. Measures are taken to discourage rebellion among the slaves

Leslie, *History of Jamaica*, 1740

They are so far superior in number to the Whites, that one should think it would be unsafe, considering all circumstances, to live amongst them. The reasons of the planters' security are these: the slaves are brought from several places in Guinea which are different from one another in language, and consequently they can't converse freely; or, if they could, they hate one another so mortally, that some of them would rather die by the hands of the English, than join with other Africans in an attempt to shake off their yoke. None of them are allowed to touch any arms, unless by their Master's command, or go out of the bounds of the plantation to which they belong, without a special permit signed by their owner or overseer. They are kept in such awe, that they are afraid even to make the least thought of liberty appear. And when they see the Whites muster and exercise, there can be no terror in the world greater than what they lie under at that time. 'Tis true, the *Creolian* Negroes are not of this number; they all speak English, and are so far from fearing a muster that they are very familiar with it, and can exercise extremely well.

f. A slave revolt

Governor of Jamaica to Lords of Trade and Plantations, 31 August 1690

On the 29th July last all the negroes on Mr. Salter's estate in the mountains in the middle of the island broke out into rebellion, to the number of more than five hundred, forced the dwelling house, killed the caretaker and seized fifty fuses and other arms with quantities of ammunition.

They marched to the next plantation, killed the overseer and fired the house, but the slaves therein would not join them. They then returned to the great house, loading their great gun with nails, and ambushing the skirt of wood next the house.

The alarm being given, about fifty horse and foot marched against them and there was a slight skirmish. Next day more foot came up and the negroes left the house for the canes, where the foot came in on their rear, killed some, wounded others and captured their field guns and provisions and put them to rout. Thirty choice men then pursued them through the woods, killed twelve and took all their provisions. Sixty women and children have since come in, who report that many have died of wounds and that they have few good arms. Fresh parties are after them, but I am afraid that so many will be left as to be a great danger to the mountain plantations.

This rebellion might have been very bloody, considering the number of negroes and the scarcity of white men. There were but six or seven whites in that plantation to five hundred negroes, and that is the usual proportion in the island, which cannot but be a great danger.

g. *Runaway slaves*

Advertisements in Jamaica Royal Gazette, 1782

MARIA, a Washer, bought from James Elford, Esq., the initials of whose name she bears on one of her shoulders:— She eloped early in October last and has been frequently seen at Port-Royal, where it is imagined she is harboured among the shipping: . . .

WILLIAM, a slim made Waiting-Boy, and a Postillion; 18 months ago purchased from Mrs. Susannah Gale:— He eloped at Christmas, and has been a cruise to sea on board the *Hercules* Privateer; was apprehended on board about ten days ago, but made his escape on landing: he passed on the late Capt. Graham of the *Hercules* as a free man, and assumed the name of GEORGE. . . . As he may, in all probability, attempt the like imposition on others, and may endeavour to get off the island, all captains of men of war, masters and commanders of merchant-men, and other vessels, are hereby cautioned against admitting the said Slave WILLIAM on board, otherwise they shall, on conviction, be prosecuted in the rigorous manner the law has directed.

MARY, a stout, young House Wench, about 16 years old, eloped eight weeks ago, was seen twice since in Liguanea. It is supposed she is harboured by the Watchmen, as she has been seen in Kingston selling plantain. Whoever will secure the above runaways in gaol, or deliver them to the Subscriber, at his pen in Liguanea, or to Mr. J. Davidson, Wharfinger in Kingston, shall receive FIVE POUNDS Reward.

N.B. As the Subscriber intends leaving the island by an early opportunity, he will dispose of his pleasant and agreeable Penn in Liguanea, generally known by the name of GREIG'S PENN, together with all his Household Furniture, Negroes, Horses, Carriages, etc., either by public or private sale.

h. Discussion by a governor of "An act for the better regulating slaves and rendering free negroes and mulattoes more useful and preventing hawking and peddling"

Governor of Jamaica to the Council of Trade and Plantations, 1730

It having been alleged, and I believe very justly, that the number of free mulattoes and free negroes daily increase, and that their houses and habitations are often times receptacles of rebellious and runaway slaves; either their idle and indolent life, or their supplying the runaways with powder, arms and ammunition, may prove of pernicious consequence to the island if not prevented; . . . and by free negroes hawking and peddling about the street with several goods and merchandise and provisions, by whom the runaway negroes (as is alleged) are likewise supplied. The Legislature hath thought proper in this bill to restrain them, under severe penalties from such practices for the future; and to oblige them to go upon all emergencies in pursuit after rebellious negroes, at the command of any magistrate, or military officer. This will render them more useful to the country, and though this law is thought by some to be severe, yet for my own part I think it a good one, and could have wished that a clause had been inserted in it, that no mulatto, Indian, or Negro should hereafter be made free, unless the owner allotted them a sufficient maintenance during life.

4. The abolition of the British slave trade was finally enacted in 1808 after several unsuccessful attempts. In Crown colonies the British Government tried to prevent any illegal importation of slaves by requiring a slave register to be kept.

a. An opportune time

Castlereagh to Governor of Jamaica, 14 January 1808

At a time like the present, when it is found that by the too great increase of colonial produce, the markets of the world are over-stocked, and the price proportionally reduced, an experiment for putting an end to a traffic, attended always with inhumanity and injustice might be tried with the least possible damage to the interest of the colonies; it becomes in this case the interest of the West India planter to prevent the increase of cultivation and the breaking up of new lands. The existing stock of negro labourers being sufficient for a cultivation, found already too extensive, it naturally occurred that by due attention to management and morals the present number of slaves might be kept up without further importation: and as it is known that on several estates the negro population increases, it is believed that by due management that increase may be made general. His Majesty therefore feels a just confidence that when the first moments of apprehension and alarm shall have subsided the subject will be considered in its true light, and as the planter must see that a more extensive cultivation will merely tend still more to clog the markets and reduce the price of commodities they will be reconciled to a measure which excited them to a generous attention to their labourers as the surest means to maintain and increase their number.

b. The argument of the opposition

Parliamentary speaker at a debate, 1808

Will any man tell me, notwithstanding the bold unsupported assertions of the noble Lord, respecting the rigour in the treatment of the slaves—which he cannot prove, and therefore will not permit me to disprove—that the traffic as carried on by us, is not conducted with more humanity than it is by any other country in it?

Now that trade which you throw away as inhuman, France and other nations will be anxious to acquire, and this you must prevent; you must prevent the Slave Trade from being carried on by other countries, or your attempt at abolition is worse than vain. . . .

Let us for an instant take a view of the amount of the property which would be swallowed up or thrown into the hands of the enemy. The value of these colonies, in their present state, is no less a sum than £90,000,000, and the debts due are as high as £3,000,000, while the annual profit derived to this kingdom from the imports from the West India islands is at least

£10,000,000; and the loss of this immense property is the prospect we have in view while arguing this measure.

c. Slave registration in Trinidad

Order-in-Council, 26 March 1812

To provide more effectually for the prevention of the illegal and clandestine importation of slaves into the Island of Trinidad . . . establishment of a public registry for the registration and enrolment of the names and descriptions of all negroes, mulattoes, and mustees, who are now, or at any time hereafter shall be held in a state of slavery within the said island, and of the births and deaths of all such slaves. . . .

From and after the said final closing and authentication of the said original registry of slaves in the said island, it shall not be lawful to hold or detain in slavery, nor to use or treat as a slave, in the said island, any negro, or mulatto, or other person, who shall not have been first duly registered as a slave, according to the directions hereinbefore contained, but that every negro, mulatto or other person within the said island, not so registered as a slave, shall be deemed and taken to be free, except only fugitive slaves from any other island or place in the West Indies.

5. In 1823 the British embarked on a strong policy for the amelioration of the conditions of slavery. This amelioration policy was introduced in Crown colonies by Order-in-Council and was also strongly urged on the colonies with assemblies. The planters resisted and by their resentful attitudes made the slaves suspicious that they were being denied the freedom which they thought the British Government intended to give them.

a. The amelioration policy introduced

Resolutions of the House of Commons, 15 May 1823

That it is expedient to adopt effectual and decisive measures for ameliorating the condition of the slave population in His Majesty's colonies.

That through a determined and persevering, but at the same time judicious and temperate enforcement of such measures, this House looks forward to a progressive improvement in the character of the slave population, such as may prepare them for a participation in those civil rights and privileges which are enjoyed by other classes of His Majesty's subjects.

That this House is anxious for the accomplishment of this purpose at the earliest period that shall be compatible with the well-being of the slaves themselves, with the safety of the colonies, and with a fair and equitable consideration of the interests of private property.

b. *Reforms proposed by the British Government*

Secretary of State to Governors of islands with assemblies, 9 July 1823

It is my purpose rather to point out such changes in the law as may be conveniently adopted at present and which will (it is hoped) lay the foundation for a further and more effectual reformation. I am therefore to direct you to lay before the Colonial Legislature of — the following remarks and propositions; and you will not fail to press upon that body the importance of directing their immediate and most serious attention to them.

.   .   .

The next subject to which I must draw your attention is the manumission of slaves, every unnecessary obstacle to which must be removed. Although it appears from the recent returns that taxes have in almost every colony been imposed on manumissions, I am gratified to learn that they have in practice been generally discontinued.

I have next to advert to the subject of the sale of slaves in satisfaction of the debts of their owners. Among the whole range of projected improvements in the colonial system there is perhaps none which on an attentive consideration will be found to present more difficulties than this. . . .

I have now in addition to those instructions, to direct, that you will cause some effectual law to be submitted to the legislature for preventing any domestic punishment whatever until the day following that on which the offence may have been committed, and even then not except in the presence of one free person besides the person under whose authority the punishment may be inflicted.

The last subject to which I propose at present to advert is the necessity of insuring to the slave the enjoyment of whatever property he may be able to acquire.

In conclusion I have most earnestly to impress upon you the necessity of proceeding to carry these improvements into effect not only with all possible dispatch but in the spirit of perfect and cordial cooperation with the efforts of His Majesty's Government.

c. The amelioration proposals meet with strong resistance

Two Resolutions of Jamaican Assembly, 11 December 1823

Resolved, nem. con.—That this House cannot contemplate without sensations of astonishment and the most serious apprehension, the measures which have been adopted by the Commons House of Parliament in their unanimous vote of the 15th May last; as if the machinations of a powerful and interested party were not sufficiently active for the work of destruction, the sanction of ministerial authority has been made subservient to their views, and a decree has gone forth whereby the inhabitants of this once valuable colony (hitherto esteemed the brightest jewel in the British Crown) are destined to be offered a propitiatory sacrifice at the altar of fanaticism ...
Resolved, nem. con.—That this House, impressed with a due sense of their own dignity, and the integrity of the colonial character, set at nought the malicious and unfounded aspersions which have been cast upon the inhabitants of Jamaica. Proud of their attachment to His Majesty, His family and Government, devoted to the interest of those they represent, and alive to the impulse of humanity, the House need no Pharisaical dictator to prompt them to the discharge of their duty, but will, if left to their own guidance, steadily pursue the line of conduct which comports with the loyalty of their feelings, their regard to the safety, honour, and welfare of the island, and the peace and happiness of their fellow-subjects and dependants.

d. The Jamaican Assembly's attitude defended

Speech of Barrett to meeting of West India planters, 1 May 1833

And what was the Assembly of Jamaica commanded at once to accomplish?

1. To abolish Sunday markets.
2. To admit slave evidence.
3. To sanction marriage.
4. To abolish taxes on manumission.
5. To prevent the separation of families.
6. To regulate punishments.
7. To establish savings banks.

It is not surprising that they hesitated to obey, without reflection, these imperative commands of the Colonial Office. The order was sudden and unexpected; it was conveyed in an unusual mandatory tone. Time was required for consideration, and to prepare their constituents for this novel mode of government. . . . And it must not be forgotten that the Colonial Legislatures are freely chosen by the people; that purity of election has always existed in the West-India islands; and, consequently, that the representatives of the people dare not outrun or disregard the opinions of their electors.

e. Some slaves in British Guiana demand immediate freedom

Governor of British Guiana to Secretary of State, 24 August 1823

Their views . . . they stated to be unconditional emancipation. I expostulated with this body for at least half an hour, and explained how much such conduct put it out of my power to carry into effect His Majesty's beneficent views for bettering their condition: explained the abolition of the flogging of females and of the carrying whips to the field as but first steps in the intended measures. These things they said were no comfort to them. God had made them of the same flesh and blood as the whites, that they were tired of being slaves to them, that they should be free and they would not work any more. I assured them that if by peaceful conduct they deserved

His Majesty's favour they would find their lot substantially though gradually improved, but they declared they would be free.

f. Christmas rebellion in Jamaica, 1831

Bleby, *Death Struggles of Slavery*, 1853

During the day we learnt that there was reason to apprehend unpleasant occurrences at the close of the holidays; for some of our own members had heard people belonging to the Baptist Society declare their intention to 'sit down, and not return to work, after the holidays.' . . . This information awakened some alarm in our minds; and led us to express the hope that no slave-members of the different missionary churches would take part in the proposed attempt to resist the existing laws of the land, and the legal authority of their masters, as it would not fail to bring a reproach on our common Christianity, and be made the pretext for persecution and oppression. A series of religious services were held, which occupied from ten o'clock to six, with scarcely any intermission; during which we alluded more than once to the information we had received in the morning, and earnestly cautioned all the people not to give heed to the unfounded and mischievous reports that were in circulation, as to their freedom having been given by the King, and to have nothing to do with those persons who were disposed to create mischief, and lead them astray. We pointed out to them the hopelessness of any attempt, on their part, to resist the authorities and the law; and advised them, whatever others might do, to go quietly and peaceably to their work when the holidays ceased, and await patiently the time when the Lord, in His good providence, should bring about a change in their condition.

g. A Protector of Slaves declares the need for emancipation to avert further rebellion

Private Letter from Protector of Slaves, British Guiana, 1832

As to my office, it is a delusion. There is no protection for the slave population; and they will very shortly take the matter into their own hands, and destroy the property. The only way of saving these countries is to give the slaves a reasonable share in the produce of their labour.

I am desperately unpopular, although I am sure I have not intended to do my duty captiously. But the fact is that this colony is in a state of rebellion; the administration of justice obstructed or totally defeated—no taxes paid—the most vehement clamour, not only against the laws themselves, but against the lawmaking power. . . . You have brought forward the slave to a certain point of civilisation and intelligence, and he perceives the utter insufficiency of your system either for his further advancement or for his control. What should be given to the slaves is *such a state of FREEDOM as they are now fit for*.

6. Dissatisfied with the limited effects of the abolition of the slave trade and the amelioration policy, the humanitarians in England campaigned for the emancipation of slaves. They were bitterly fought both in and out of Parliament by a determined opposition of planters and merchants. The Act of Emancipation was finally passed and those who had foretold immediate disorder in the West Indies were proved wrong.

a. Two views on the morality of slavery

(i) Speaker at an Abolition Meeting, 1832

Slavery defined. What then is slavery? Slavery in the West Indies is the forced servitude of every black man found on those islands, who cannot by legal documents prove his liberty; this violent constraint is exercised during his life without wages, while the master only is the judge of the kind, degree and time of labour, and of the subsistence which the slave shall receive. The master may, moreover, imprison, beat, scourge, wound, and otherwise injure the body of the slave at his own discretion, and may depute the same power to whom he pleases, even to a fellow slave. Slaves possess no legal right in any kind of property; for however obtained, whatever they have belongs in point of law to their master, who may dispose of that which they have acquired, as well as of themselves or of their children, in the same manner as cattle or land may be sold; while the creditor or tax-gatherer may seize the slave and sell him to a distant proprietor, and so tear him from his parents, his wife, his children, and his home, for the debts of his master; or he may be devised by will to a cruel tyrant or severe task-master without the power of remonstrance, or even the right of redemption on any terms.

(ii) Barrett, *Speeches on the West Indies,* 1833

The guilt for slavery must be shared. If slavery is an offence which ought to be discontinued, it is an offence common to the nation. The army which conquered Jamaica, which first garrisoned and then settled that island, carried with them no slaves; they were planters before they became slave-owners. Slaves were sent to them in English ships; torn from Africa by English dealers and spoilers. English laws promoted the traffic, and English capital maintained it. So greedy, in those days, was this country for the trade in Man, that shortly after the Restoration, a grant of land in the colony (of Jamaica) could only be obtained on condition of cultivating it by Negro Slaves. The soldier carried to Jamaica nothing but his arms; when he became a planter, he had no resource but his own strength and industry. He did not go in search of the Negro in Africa; the Negro was brought to him; and the King of England, by and with the advice of his Council, compelled him to purchase, if he desired to escape from the condition of a daily labourer, and aspired to be an owner of land and a free-holder. Thus the planter became a slave-proprietor not by the choice of his will, but by the force of law. It is not fair—it is not honest—it is unjust and cruel for the people of England to reproach the planter with the unavoidable consequences of their own act, and to load him with obloquy at the moment that they are about to make him the victim of their guilt.

The Colonial Secretary admitted the vastness of the interests which are involved in this question; he admits, that on its successful settlement depend the lives and fortunes of a large proportion of our fellow-subjects, and the welfare, both spiritual and temporal, of 800,000 slaves. By a hasty, an imperfect, or ill-considered measure, the numerous body of persons dependent on the colonies, who reside in England, may be ruined; the free inhabitants of the colonies may be massacred, or be engaged in civil war with the newly-emancipated slaves; and those slaves themselves, that we design to civilise, and to make happy, may be driven back to the barbarism, the vices, and the sufferings of savage life. None of these events can happen without inflicting on England a heavy loss in wealth, in commerce, in reputation, and a substantial power.

b. Negro slaves and English workers compared and contrasted

(i) Barrett, *Speeches on the West Indies*, 1833

Conditions of Negro slaves and English workers compared. If time allowed, I might moot the question, whether despair is known in the dwelling of the Negro. The Militia ballot, the tax-gatherer, the heartless bailiff, and the brutal press-gang, are strangers to him. He is equally unaccustomed to repine over a sick wife without medicine and medical attendance, and famishing children; to see his hearth cold, and his hut roofless, and his aged parents dragging out a miserable existence in the parish poor-house. He has a master; and that master supplies all his wants; repairs all his misfortunes; protects him from his own improvidence, and from every injury and enemy, and, I may add, he protects him too often even from the laws he has transgressed. There is not a peasant in the world that walks abroad with a more contented countenance and a more confident bearing than the Colonial Slave. . . .

It must be confessed that the requisition of the Colonial Minister to discontinue the flogging of women has not been obeyed. . . . I own that for a moment I felt ashamed that I was a Colonist. I was restored to my self-esteem by recalling to my recollection that . . . within a very few years whipping was the punishment of women confined for their offences in the houses of correction and prisons of England. I, for my part, have not the slightest doubt that these female offenders owe their late and tardy exemption from the cat-o'-nine tails to the outcry that was raised in this country against the whipping of black women in the colonies. The Negro Philanthropists forgot for a long time, in their abhorrence of whipping Negro women in Jamaica, that white women were hourly flogged in Great Britain. They have been compelled, from very shame, to correct the anomaly; and the females of England have to thank their sisters of the West Indies that they have exchanged the scourge for the tread-mill.

It is long since we limited the hours of slave labour, or able-bodied slaves, to ten hours the day, while the factory children of this humane and pious kingdom have been toiling fourteen and sixteen hours—their labour being in unwholesome and confined manufactories, and the slaves' in the pure and open air. Our black slave children do not betray the sickly countenances, the stunted figures, the incipient deformity and squalid appearance, the ragged and dirty persons of the labouring infants of England.

(ii) Wilberforce, *An Appeal on Behalf of the Negro Slaves of the West Indies*, 1823

Conditions of Negro slaves and English workers contrasted. Indeed, the West Indians . . . have even distinctly told us,—that these poor degraded beings, the Negro slaves, are as well or even better off than our British peasantry; a proposition so monstrous, that nothing can possibly exhibit in a stronger light the extreme force of the prejudices which must exist in the minds of its assertors. A Briton to compare the state of a West Indian slave with that of an English free man, and to give the former the preference! . . . I will not condescend to argue this question, as I might, on the ground of comparative feeding and clothing, and lodging, and medical attendance. Are these the only claims; are these the chief privileges of a rational and immortal being? Is the consciousness of personal independence nothing? Are self-possession and self-government nothing? Is it of no account that our persons are inviolate by any private authority, and that the whip is placed only in the hands of the public executioner? Is it of no value that we have the power of pursuing the occupation and the habits of life we prefer; that we have the prospect, or at least the hope, of improving our condition, and of rising, as we have seen others rise, from poverty and obscurity to comfort, and opulence, and distinction? Again; are all the charities of the heart, which arise out of the domestic relations, to be considered as nothing; and, I may add, all their security too among men who are free agents, and not vendible chattels, liable continually to be torn from their dearest connections and sent into a perpetual exile? . . . But, above all, is Christianity so little esteemed among us that we are to account as of no value . . . all the consolations and supports by which religion cheers the hearts, and elevates the principles, and dignifies the conduct of multitudes of our labouring classes in this free and enlightened country? Is it nothing to be taught that all human distinctions will soon be at an end; that all the labours and sorrows of poverty and hardship will soon exist no more; and to know, on the express authority of Scripture, that the lower classes, instead of being an inferior order in the creation, are even the preferable objects of the love of the Almighty?

Let me ask, is there, in the whole of the three kingdoms, a parent or a husband so sordid and insensible that any sum, which the richest West-Indian proprietor could offer him, would be deemed a compensation for his suffering his wife or his daughter to be subjected to the brutal outrage of the cart-whip—to the savage lust of the driver—to the indecent, and degrading, and merciless punishment of a West-Indian whipping?

But I will push no farther a comparison which it is painful and humiliating to contemplate: let it however be remembered, that it is to those who have professed insensibility to this odious contrast that the destiny of the poor slaves would be committed, were we to leave them to the disposal of the colonial legislatures.

c. There is no compromise with slavery

Speaker at an Abolition Meeting, 1832

What are our demands? Some careful people, who have an extreme tenderness for the lives of the slaves, but a much greater anxiety for the lives of the oppressors and masters, will say, 'We are friends of the slave, we abominate slavery—it is a system of iniquity, the offspring of injustice, and the parent of misery, and oppression, and cruelty. But then the planters have all their property involved in the business, their subsistence depends upon it; and they cannot remedy it without impoverishing themselves, their families, the slaves, and the revenues of the country: besides, to emancipate the slaves suddenly, would endanger their own welfare and future prosperity. Let the slaves learn to enjoy liberty—prepare them for it by the knowledge of the Scriptures and of religious duties. . . .'

To prepare the Negroes for liberty before they enjoy its blessings, is like the policy of the over-fond mother, who would have her child taught to swim before he enters the water, and while his limbs are bound. . . .

We would say, then, let the oppressed go free, break every yoke, undo the heavy burdens, proclaim liberty to the captives. . . . Grant to the Africans so long enchained, . . . perfect, immediate, generous liberty, with all the privileges, security, and good government of British subjects. Let them enjoy the privileges of religion, . . . and be rendered eligible to every elevation and honour of civilised society. Let no longer fleecy hair and dark complexion be barriers to personal advancement and honourable occupation. Let all enjoy a community of privileges of service and advantages, and then justice and truth shall be the shield and buckler and the golden rule shall prevail. . . .

Who does not know, that knowledge and slavery are incompatible? The one cannot flourish, without destroying the other. But progress in knowledge is inseparable from every species of amelioration. Tell of a plan of gradual emancipation, without improving the negroes in knowledge, and you tell of your own folly. Speak of preparing the negroes for liberty, without cultivating their minds, and you render your proposition unworthy of all regard. . . .

Whatever might be the result of immediate emancipation, by the wise and parental authority of government, the result of emancipation wrought out by the negroes for themselves, would unquestionably reek with blood.

Immediate emancipation is a certain remedy, and it is the only remedy at once righteous in principle, and safe in fact. Delays are dangerous. Delay in duty, that is, in what is morally right, is criminal as well as dangerous.

d. The abolition of slavery accepted in Parliament

Resolutions passed, 12 June 1833

1. That it is the opinion of this Committee that immediate and effectual measures be taken for the entire abolition of slavery throughout the colonies under such provisions for regulating the condition of the negroes as may combine their welfare with the interests of the proprietors.

2. That it is expedient that all children born after the passing of any Act or who shall be under the age of six years at the time of passing any Act of Parliament for this purpose, be declared free; subject nevertheless to such temporary restrictions as may be deemed necessary for their support and maintenance.

3. That all persons now slaves be entitled to be registered as apprenticed labourers and to acquire thereby all rights and privileges of free men; subject to the restriction of labouring, under conditions and for a time to be fixed by Parliament, for their present owners.

4. That towards the compensation of the proprietors, His Majesty be enabled to grant to them a sum not exceeding £20,000,000 sterling, to be appropriated as Parliament shall direct.

5. That His Majesty be enabled to defray any such expense as he may incur in establishing an efficient stipendiary magistracy in the colonies, and in aiding the local legislatures in providing, upon liberal and comprehensive principles, for the religious and moral education of the negro population to be emancipated.

e. The day of emancipation

Madden, *Twelve Months' residence in the British West Indies*, 1835

From the day the Abolition Bill was passed the 1st August was looked forward to with intense interest; with extravagant hopes by one party, and groundless apprehension by the other. The Ides of August, however, are come—and, what is more, they are passed and not a single riot occurred throughout the island, and not a single man, woman or child, was butchered to make a negro holiday. This conduct of the great unchained was very provoking, to be sure; for a great many prophecies were to be fulfilled on the 1st of August, 'or thereabouts', as Mr. Moore would say! but somehow or another, the predictions have not been accomplished; and, unfortunately for the prophetic character of the Cobbetts of Jamaica, they are never likely to be accomplished. The House of Assembly judiciously decided that the 1st of August should be a holiday, and the negroes were recommended to observe it as a day of prayer and thanksgiving. All the sectarian places of worship were accordingly thrown open, and they were thronged with the negroes to an unprecedented extent.

5

Emancipation and Apprenticeship

1. By Act of Parliament slaves were declared apprentices, slave owners were compensated and provision was made to transform a slave society as smoothly as possible into a free community.

An Act for the Abolition of Slavery throughout the British Colonies; for promoting the industry of the manumitted slaves; and for compensating the persons hitherto entitled to the services of such slaves

Preamble to the Act of Emancipation, 1833

Whereas divers persons are holden in slavery within divers of His Majesty's colonies, and it is just and expedient that all such persons should be manumitted and set free, and that a reasonable compensation should be made to the persons hitherto entitled to the services of such slaves for the loss which they will incur by being deprived of their right to such services: And whereas it is also expedient that provision should be made for promoting the industry and securing the good conduct of the persons so to be manumitted, for a limited period after such manumission: And whereas it is necessary that the laws now in force in the said several colonies should forthwith be adapted to the new state and relations of society therein which will follow upon such general manumission as aforesaid of the said slaves; and that, in order to afford the necessary time for such adaptation of the said laws, a short interval should elapse before such manumission should take effect, be it therefore enacted. . . .

That from and after the First Day of August One thousand eight hundred and thirty-four all persons who in conformity with the laws now in force in the said colonies respectively shall on or before (Aug. 1, 1834) have been duly registered as slaves in any such colony and who on (Aug. 1, 1834) shall be actually within any such colony and who shall by such registries appear to be on (Aug. 1, 1834) of the full age of six years or upwards, shall by force and virtue of this Act, and without the person's execution of any indenture of apprenticeship, or other deed or instrument for that purpose, become and be apprenticed labourers.

2. Could the Act of Emancipation transform the slaves and masters into a free community smoothly?

a. The dangers attending emancipation are vividly stated by an opponent

Speech of Barrett, 1833

By a hasty, an imperfect, or ill-considered measure, the numerous body of persons dependent on the colonies, who reside in England, may be ruined: the free inhabitants of the colonies may be massacred, or be engaged in civil war with the newly emancipated slaves; and those slaves themselves, that we design to civilise and to make happy, may be driven back to the barbarism, the vices and the sufferings of savage life. None of these events can happen without inflicting on England a heavy loss in wealth, in commerce, in reputation, and in substantial power. . . .

Most cautious and guarded, and almost unimpeachable, should be the plan, which is to pass through so many perils; a plan which is meant to confer a great boon, but may inflict boundless and intolerable wrong.

b. The success of the Act depends on the attitudes taken towards it by both Whites and Negroes

Madden, *Twelve Months in the West Indies*, 30 May 1834

Whether the recent measure that is to come into operation on the 1st of August will prove successful or otherwise must mainly depend on the temper of the colonists, and the co-operation of the colonial legislature. As for the negroes, nothing short of infatuation can cause them to oppose it.

They have much to lose, they have little to gain by opposition to a measure which confers on them present advantages and prospective liberty. If they have any ground for discontent, it is the length of the probationary term of apprenticeship; the necessity for which they may not understand, and the probability of seeing its termination they may be unable to comprehend. On the other hand, the white people have many things opposed to their interests or their prejudices to irritate their feelings: they have injury to property, deprivation of power, and interference with colonial legislation to resist and even to avenge. The magistrates of the country have what they deem the insult to brook, of transferring their authority to a stipendiary magistracy—strangers in the land, and appointed by an obnoxious government.

c. A governor explains the Act

Proclamation of Governor of Barbados, 22 January 1834

On the 1st of August next you become free from absolute slavery, and at the same time you become apprentices, under regular laws, to your present owners. Any offences you may then commit against your masters will be punished by magistrates sent from England for the purpose of administering the law between you and them.

All slaves who have been regularly engaged in cultivation, or in the manufacture of sugar, including all tradesmen, remain apprentices to their masters for six years from the 1st August next, ending in 1840; and all domestic slaves remain apprentices for four years from the 1st August next, ending in 1838.

The reason why labourers and tradesmen have a longer period of apprenticeship than domestic servants is, that the former class are not required by law to work more than 45 hours in the week; by which you gain extra time equal to one day in every week, except on emergencies such as tending cattle and the preservation of your masters' properties.

The domestic class is not to enjoy this exemption from labour, and therefore their apprenticeship is shorter than that of labourers.

If you at any time absent yourselves from your work, or neglect it, you will have to make good the time lost, or neglect so occasioned, to your master.

After the 1st August next no female apprentice can be punished by the whip or cat, or be imprisoned by their employer's authority; but they will be liable to imprisonment or hard labour by the magistrates.

All slave children under six years of age on the 1st August next, or who may be born after that day, become free.

The law requires you to support your children so made free; for if you neglect to do so, they will have to go through a servitude to their mothers' owners until they attain 21 years of age.

By the Act of Parliament it will be rendered more easy for you to purchase your discharge from apprenticeship, than it was your freedom when slaves.

You cannot fail now to understand the advantages secured to you by the King and Parliament; but you must be orderly and industrious, and do your duty honestly and faithfully to your present owners.

The law is strong, and the law will punish you if you do not work.

In England, idle people and those who will not work, are taken up as vagabonds and vagrants; and the same laws will be in force here.

England is to pay twenty millions of pounds sterling for your gradual freedom. You can only deserve or understand this blessing by a course of good conduct, by obeying the laws, and being dutiful to all those entitled to your services, and to whom you will have to look for the rewards of your labour when you become perfectly free.

d. The first reactions

Governor of Windwards to Secretary of State, 26 August 1834

I have the honour and satisfaction to state to you that perfect tranquillity, by my latest accounts, exists in all the islands of the Windward Government.

Grenada, on the commencement of the apprenticeship system, was partially disturbed by refractory negroes on two estates. The prompt action of the civil and military authorities immediately restored order.

In *St. Vincent* one estate only struck work, and order was soon restored.

In *Tobago* and this island the negroes have been perfectly orderly and steady at their duties.

You will of course receive despatches from the respective chief authorities of *Demerara, Trinidad, St. Christopher's* and *'Dominica*, all of which have in the new state of things been considerably agitated.

In my capacity as Commander of the Troops, I received an application from the Lieutenant-Governor of Trinidad for a reinforcement, which I saw strong objections to complying with; and the enclosed letter, subsequently received from Sir George Hill, will satisfy you it was unnecessary, and that the unfortunate feeling of the negroes there was fast subsiding.

In *St. Christopher's*, where martial law had been proclaimed and some severe examples made you will be glad to find the military means, aided by the militia, were found ample; and by my last despatches . . . the disturbance in that island was fast settling down.

The Windward squadron, under Captain Strong, of the *Belvidera*, afforded as usual the most cheerful and important services in aid of the troops; and *Grenada* and *Trinidad* will each receive a ship to aid in maintaining the public tranquillity.

3. The period of apprenticeship was intended to let both masters and ex-slaves get accustomed to living and working in a free community.

a. The Secretary of State explains the intention of the British Government

Circular Despatch, 19 October 1833

In effecting, throughout extensive dominions of the Crown, so vast a change as that from slavery to freedom, His Majesty's Government and Parliament agreeing in their views, deemed it indispensable to provide for a transition state, of longer or shorter duration, but of which they fixed the maximum, during which the present master and slave should continue bound to each other by mutual obligations, securing the one a limited portion of labour, and to the other a certain maintenance and protection, and the principal object of these enactments was to make temporary provision for the continued cultivation of the soil and good order of society, until all classes should gradually fall into the relations of a state of freedom. . . . But as these legislatures were expressly authorised to fix the term of this apprenticeship, provided it did not exceed a certain duration, so it is clearly within their province, should they deem it safe and prudent so to do, to dispense with it altogether, and to pass at once to a state of unrestricted freedom. I do not anticipate the probability, and I should be disposed to doubt the prudence of such a course. . . . But you will distinctly understand, that you will not be authorised to give your assent to any Act creating an intermediate state of a different description or subjected to restrictions of a different nature from those contemplated by Parliament. The term of apprenticeship may be shortened, the hours of compulsory labour may be fewer, the burthens imposed may be made lighter; but no distinctions must be allowed to be drawn between those at present free and those at present slaves, of a different character from, or to a greater extent than those which have been sanctioned by Parliament.

b. *Antigua bypasses apprenticeship*

(i) *Legislature to Governor of Antigua*, 2 November 1833

Reasons given. We do not, we confess, discover any sufficient reason referable to this island, why an unrestricted emancipation should not answer as well in 1834 as in 1838 or '40; and we are perfectly satisfied, that no possible future efforts during so short a term of years can bring the slaves of most of the other colonies to the same state of religious and social improvement as that to which those of Antigua have already reached.

It cannot have escaped the observation of your Excellency, even during your short residence among us, that there are circumstances in the condition of this colony which invite more to such a favourable change than perhaps in any other; among these may be suggested the all-important and paramount one of an utter dependence, from peculiarity of climate and the absence of unoccupied lands, except those of absolute sterility, of the labourer on the proprietor and capitalist for the means of procuring food; and that a large portion of the population, whether bond or free, could not hope for the means of subsistence except by some laborious occupation in one of those frequent periods of long drought especially to which we are almost annually subject.

(ii) *Proclamation of the Governor*, June 1834

Conditions of full freedom in Antigua. First—that their condition will be no longer that of reliance on their masters for food, house-room and clothing; their new position will remove them from this close connection with their former owners, and they will henceforth have to depend for the necessities of life on the honest and industrious labour of their own hands.

Secondly—that whilst the utmost benefit of the laws, and encouragement from the owners of plantations will be given to those who labour industriously and live soberly and honestly where they are permitted to reside, the magistrates will be by law empowered to order to be taken up and brought to deserved punishment, all such as shall wander about in idleness, or attempt to make a living by robbery, theft or any dishonest means: and the masters, who are required by the Act just passed not only to establish unrestricted freedom, but to let their steady, orderly and reputable dependants remain in undisturbed possession of their present habitations or houses, for twelve months to come, may, nevertheless, avail themselves of the right which the same Act gives them, namely, to expel from their estates such as shall be guilty of 'insubordinate, quarrelsome, disorderly or riotous behaviour, or drunkenness, theft, trespass, or other gross delinquency'.

c. A Special Justice in Jamaica cites his district as an example of apprenticeship working well

Report of Special Justice in St. Mary, 17 March 1835

I have 16 sugar estates to visit; the mills are kept about for different periods, 12, 16 and 18 hours, as it suits the convenience of the estate. I am not aware of any difficulty whatever in taking off the crops. Some managers pay wages for spell-work, some give time in return, and some give rum, sugar and salt provisions; some managers employ the apprentices 45 hours in crop time and out of crop time; the labourers giving up 4½ hours weekly for an allowance of salt fish.

There is the best disposition on the part of the apprentices to work for wages, throughout this district; they not only take them when offered, but prefer them to any other arrangement. There is an opposition in some cases to give wages; where they have been tendered, the apprentices readily sell their own time. I have the assurance of many managers for this good disposition in the apprentices. Where the new system is fairly tried, and faith kept with the apprentices, the manager has no trouble beyond those delinquencies which occur in all countries.

The apprentices appear to consider the new system as a great blessing, and are eager to have every advantage the law has given them. There is one great difficulty in carrying the new system into effect, as regards the hours of labour; there is no uniform hour of rest appointed for the field people. Many of them conceive they are cheated out of their time; the want of clocks and watches is much felt: in a few instances watches have been given to the constables attending in the field. I do not consider that the irritation against the 'invasion of their rights', as the proprietors and managers term the new system, has yet subsided; they find great difficulty in looking upon their late slaves as their equals in the court of law and justice.

With respect to the frequency of complaints, I consider they will not be disposed to commit offences when they are more acquainted with the laws. Such has been my experience on those estates where I have taken the most trouble to explain to the apprentices the obligations of the law on both parties, master and servant. Complaints are no longer made from those properties.

In conclusion, I do consider, as far as my district is concerned, that it is a fair example of the good working of the new system under the Abolition Law; and that it requires nothing more than fair play on the part of the managers to bring the apprentices to a state fitted for perfect and absolute freedom when the term of service expires. I am not aware that any steps have been taken by proprietors or managers in my district to establish schools or instruct in any way their apprentices, or to encourage marriage among their servants.

4. Generally apprenticeship did not work well.

a. Obstacles to the fair working of apprenticeship appear promptly

(i) *Report of Committee to enquire into the working of the new system of labour*, Jamaica, 13 November 1834

As the planters saw them. The failure of the system is attributed principally to the following causes:—

1st. To the domestic authority of the master (which formerly constituted the main controlling power) having been so entirely destroyed, that he cannot now exercise over the negro apprentices even the reasonable extent of authority which a master may in England over his apprentices.

2nd. To the local magistrates having been, at the same time with the masters, deprived of all power and authority to aid in maintaining the peace of society, and in enforcing the law.

And lastly; to the altogether inadequate number of stipendiary magistrates, and the unfitness of many of them to discharge properly the difficult and important duties entrusted to them, from their entire ignorance of the peculiar habits and dispositions of the negroes, or of the fair and reasonable quantity of labour which they are competent and ought to perform.

(ii) Madden, *Twelve Months in the West Indies*, 24 November 1834

As the apprentices saw them. The dislike to the apprenticeship, on the part of the negroes may be referred to three heads.

1st. Incapacity, or at least unwillingness, to comprehend prospective advantages.

2nd. Reluctance to labour without wages.

3rd. Disposition, in some instances, to withhold their own time, and that of their children under six years of age, as a retaliation for past grievances, real or imaginary; or the recent deprivation of their old allowances.

b. *Shortage of magistrates from England*

Address of Governor of Jamaica to Assembly, 26 November 1834

That the number of special magistrates originally sent out from home was insufficient for the duties they had to perform, was my impression from the commencement; and in consequence of my representations on that subject, an additional number have been granted. Several of these have been already appointed by me from amongst the residents of this island, and the rest, I am assured, will be sent out by the first opportunity. All the vacancies which have occurred since my arrival have been filled up by persons already established here, and I have strongly recommended to the government their confirmation. Some of your local magistrates have been appointed by me to the special commission, and I have procured the unsalaried services of other persons eminently qualified for the duty. Between those now employed, and those whom I have the certainty of having . . . at my disposal, there will be fifty persons qualified to act as special magistrates in this island, and I anxiously hope that His Majesty's Government will, in consequence of my more recent representations, feel themselves justified in making a further increase in the number already appointed.

c. *Apprentices not to be subject to the jurisdiction of local justices*

Lieutenant-Governor of St. Lucia to Secretary of State, 20 January 1836

In my despatch of the 12th instant I made your Lordship acquainted with the unwarrantable conduct of a Mr. Goodman, who, in his capacity of justice of the peace, ordered an apprenticed labourer to be publicly whipped in the market-place in the town of Soufrière, although two special magistrates were then residing on the spot.

Having minutely inquired into the circumstances connected with this case, I can come to no other conclusion than that this illegal punishment was committed in direct opposition to my authority, and with a view to impress on the minds of the negroes that the power of punishing them was still vested in the local magistracy.

Your Lordship will observe, by Mr. Goodman's letter, that he states he punished the apprentice in question on his own voluntary confession of his guilt, but by the report of the special magistrate the theft was positively denied by the prisoner.

5. Conditions of life under apprenticeship.

a. *Vexations of the ex-slaves*

(i) Sturge and Harvey, *West Indies in 1837*

We had a long talk today with a negro, introduced to us by a friend as one on whose veracity we might depend. He appeared to be a serious, respectable man. The substance of his statement was, that their wages of one shilling currency, a day, (about five-pence halfpenny sterling), were not sufficient to maintain them. He had a wife and six children, and an old mother to support; of whom, two of the children only were able to earn anything. They could not manage without 'minding' their little stock. He said that if a labourer was five minutes after time in the morning, the manager stopped his pay for the day. He complained also that he had just received thirty days notice to quit, because he refused to allow one of his children, whom he wished to put into a trade, to go to the field, although he promised that all his other children should be brought up to estate labour. . . . In conclusion, however, as the labourers could not now be locked up in the dungeon and flogged, the change in their circumstances was yet as he emphatically expressed it, 'Thank God, a great deliverance from bondage'.

(ii) Madden, *Twelve months in the West Indies*, 24 November 1834

The vexations of the negroes may be thought trivial, but in reality they are not so. . . . In all that respects the mode of administering their supplies, of apportioning their times of labour, of defining the nature and extent of the jurisdiction of the special justices, the matter is so vaguely expressed in the Act as amended here, that loopholes are left for innumerable vexations, which it is not in the power of the special magistrates to prevent or punish. These vexations consist in withholding the customary allowance of salted provisions, rum, and sugar, or, where they are continued, of exacting from the negro such extra labour as the law has allotted for the necessary cultivation of the negro grounds.

(iii) Sturge and Harvey, *West Indies in 1837*

A great grievance to which negroes are subjected, is the practice of fining gangs in *time* for bad work. If an overseer is, or pretends to be, dissatisfied, he calls in one or two people before the magistrate; who mulcts the whole gang, idle and industrious together, in two, four, or even eight, of their Saturdays.

(iv) Sturge and Harvey, *West Indies in 1837*

The children however had not proper attendance when sick, as their parents were usually compelled to repay the time they devoted to them. The planters expected the parents would apprentice their children, and resorted to severe measures to compel them to do so; but the mothers resisted to extremity. It was at length found that it would not do to be so hard upon mothers.

(v) Sturge and Harvey, *West Indies in 1837*

We learn that considerable distress prevails among the aged and infirm part of the population. When the Abolition Bill was passed, a number of these were superannuated and pensioned on the different estates; but the provision made for them is too often totally inadequate to their maintenance. We heard today, of a poor woman who was allowed only a *dog*, which is about three farthings sterling, per day, from the estate on which she had spent her youth and strength as a slave.

(vi) Hinton, *Memoir of William Knibb*, 1849

The law made here, and now in operation, is a most abominable infringement upon the abolition act. That was bad, this is worse. I pray to God that it may be disallowed. Apprentices are now valued higher than when slaves. One named Bailey, from Georgia estate, who was nearly flogged to death during martial law, paid £75 currency for his term of apprenticeship last week. Charles Campbell's son, a boy of eight years of age, was valued at £21. 6. 8d. I wished to assist my servant George (he is a house servant); for his three years and a half they valued him at £60. The fact is, that, under the abolition act, they were purchasing themselves so fast that this law was made to stop them. This is the third time the law has been altered unfavourably to the apprentice. How can the poor things be expected to understand or to relish such continued changes, and all for the worse?

b. *Different views of planters*

(i) Sturge and Harvey, *West Indies in 1837*

Sometimes planters and ex-slaves are both satisfied. One who had introduced on his estate a system of remuneration and task-work observed, that the negroes now did more work in six days than formerly in eighteen. Another, the owner and attorney of several estates, observed that his people did more work in the last two days in the week for which they received wages, than in the other four; and a third, who had conferred complete freedom on his apprentices, said that they were more industrious than before, and that his property suffered less from pilfering.

(ii) *Memorial of Planters of Trelawney, Jamaica*, May 1835

Wages do not always produce the desired results. That the apprenticeship system in this island, established under the Abolition Act, has, after nine months' trial, confirmed the anticipations of all practical men of its ruinous consequences; and your memorialists have now the miserable prospect before them that, in a short period, the cultivation of the staple productions of this island must cease. . . .

Your memorialists beg leave to state, that all the work which can now be got from apprentices, even with a liberal price paid to them for their own time, is confined exclusively to the manufacturing of sugar; and from the consequent neglect of the cane field, the usual plant canes have not been established, nor the ratoon canes or grass fields duly attended to. The falling off in the next year's crop must necessarily be serious; and the same evil will annually increase until it terminates by the gradual throwing up of sugar estates, notwithstanding the assertions to the contrary of inexperienced persons, who flatter themselves with false hopes.

6. Under slavery the discipline of slaves was the concern of the master; the control of the ex-slaves became a public concern and a matter for public comment.

a. The controls loosened

Evidence before Committee of House of Assembly, Jamaica, to enquire into the working of the new system of labour, 31 October 1834

The want of active controlling power; uniformity in the hours of labour: accustomed formerly to work by the rising and setting of the sun as their guide, the labourer required no other direction; but they are now referred to specified hours for labour, which they cannot yet comprehend; the power of the master is now superseded by the authority of the magistrate. In one case under my charge, in a very populous district in St. Ann's, the magistrate has not visited an estate with 190 people but once since the 1st of August, although frequently required to do so; the consequence of which is, a gradual disorganisation of order among the people. Shortly after the 1st of August they were civil, well behaved and obedient, but from want of necessary control they turn out to work when they like, do what they choose, take what days they like—in fact, do as they think proper.

b. More cases for the courts

Sturge and Harvey, *West Indies in 1837*

One of us went this morning to attend the sitting of the House of Assembly. In the lobby he was introduced to the Chief Justice of the island, who said, in the course of a few minutes' conversation, that it was not to be supposed that crime had really increased because there were now heavy calendars. Cases came before the magistrate, which were formerly decided by the masters. The peaceable and orderly conduct of the people had exceeded his anticipations; and there was no one he believed, who would deny, that the general result of emancipation had more than equalled his expectation.

c. A Stipendiary Magistrate reports on his estate cases

Report of a Stipendiary Magistrate in St. Vincent, 15 June 1836

I am sorry that I am unable, in my return for the month of May, to report to your Excellency on the decrease of crime amongst the apprenticed labourers; though so far as regards complaints in the relative character of master and apprentice, there is a continued diminution.

The slight protection afforded to the safety of the provision grounds holds out a great temptation to idle and ill-disposed apprentices to neglect the cultivation of their own grounds, and to live by plundering from the industrious; but the motive for which I am in hopes will shortly be decreased, by compelling those whose grounds are not cultivated to work them in a gang on their own days.

In the number of punishments inflicted, I beg to inform your Excellency that the gang on one estate, consisting of 46 apprentices, viz. 18 males and

28 females, were sentenced to one day's extra labour for not working properly; this being deducted from the 115 punishments there will remain only 65.

d. A missionary comments on the penal system

Hinton, *Memoir of William Knibb*, 1849

Some of the special magistrates flog most cruelly, and I fear will create much discontent. If the Anti-Slavery Society were to send out one or more staunch men, who would be present at the trials of apprentices, and faithfully report them, they would do great good. It would be a check upon the magistrates which they would much feel.

Through great mercy we are all well, and matters are quiet, which would not be the case were not the negroes the most patient people upon earth. Oh! this thrice-cursed apprenticeship!—nothing but blood, murderous cells, and chains! I think nearly forty young and old females pass my door in chains every morning. Not one school is yet established, whilst most abominable cells and treadmills are being erected all over the island! This is to prepare the poor things for freedom! You tell me to be quiet, and I am; but if I were at home, I would publish what I know as far as I could travel.

7. The end of apprenticeship came earlier than was planned because the system lost support generally.

a. A governor wishes apprenticeship to continue

Governor of British Guiana to Secretary of State, 19 March 1836

I assure your Lordship that I should much regret and lament the doing away of the apprenticeship. I deprecate any sudden change or the abandonment of a system which, in British Guiana at any rate, so completely answers. Neither the planters nor the labourers are prepared for any immediate alteration. . . .

In thus advocating the continuance, for the present, of a system which, to a hasty observer, may appear to be too favourable to the interests of the planter, as put in opposition to those of the labourer, I beg to explain to your Lordship, that I am influenced solely by what I conceive to be the general good, and that the apprentice system (if carefully superintended in its details) appears to me to be equally necessary and advantageous to both parties. If I was susceptible of being influenced by unworthy motives, the continued opposition and ill-will I have experienced on the part of the most influential of the planters would rather have induced me to have arrived at the conclusion, that the apprenticed system ought to be abolished. I am, however, of a decidedly contrary opinion; the managers and the labourers are daily approximating; not only wages for additional labour are becoming more common, but large fields of sugar canes are weeded or cut down by agreement. Labour is, in fact, finding its level and its value; nothing can be going on better, and I do not think that the permanent well-being of the labourer would be accelerated by any immediate change of system.

b. A missionary wishes to end apprenticeship

Knibb to a friend, 7 January 1836

I am in a land of half freedom, where there is much that is pleasing, and much more to annoy. Every effort has been made in certain quarters to prevent the system from working, but hitherto in vain. The general conduct of the emancipated Africans is above all praise; nor do I believe that there is a population on the earth among whom less crime is committed. We only need perfect freedom to make the colony prosperous. This must come, and the sooner the better. I bless God for what has been done, but I do not like the apprenticeship system, because it is unjust; yet it is not slavery, and it must issue in freedom. I do all I can to prevent oppression, nor do I stand by any means alone; but do it I will, if I should stand alone. I have told the magistrates respectfully, but firmly, that let the consequence be what it may, no one shall oppress my people with impunity.

8. At the end of apprenticeship ex-slaves were no longer bound to the estates and many found other occupations.

a. Where will ex-slaves work after apprenticeship?

Sturge and Harvey, *West Indies in 1837*

No planter who has treated his apprentices kindly and has habitually employed them for wages in their own time, entertains a doubt, that he will be able to carry on the cultivation of his estate by free labour. Such, it may be confidently anticipated, will be benefited, rather than injured by emancipation. Those, however, who have pursued a contrary course, will suffer a deserved retribution. It cannot be anticipated, that every individual labourer should continue in his present employment; and it needs no extraordinary foresight to point out the parties who will sustain the loss, resulting from the diminution of labourers. . . .

To such views as these, is opposed the fear that the negroes will be tempted, by the abundance and fertility of the waste lands, to become small settlers, and independent cultivators. We do not think such an alarm reasonable, and we deprecate any attempt to evade the difficulty, by lessening the free agency of the labouring population. It would be possible to deprive freedom of its substance and value, by restrictive laws, devised with subtlety, and executed with violence. It would be possible to reduce the negroes to a hybrid condition in the social scale, which should possess neither the efficiency of slavery, nor the energy of freedom. . . . But the die is cast upon freedom: nothing less than unfettered freedom can save the colonies: freedom, protected, not circumscribed by new laws. In a country of mountain fastnesses, the negroes can only be prevented from squatting on the crown lands, by being suffered to acquire them honestly by purchase. They will not occupy them to a greater extent than the demand for agricultural produce for the island markets will enable them to do with pecuniary profit. Mutual competition will speedily abate the desire for independent cultivation.

b. Barbadians who stay at home have little alternative to working on the estates

Sewell, *Ordeal of Free Labour*, 1861

The population here, as I have said, is extremely dense, averaging 800 persons to the square mile. . . . In Barbados, therefore, labour has always been abundant, and the island, which out of 106,000 acres has 100,000 under cultivation, presents the appearance of a perfect garden. All this, practically considered, is owing in a greater degree to an adequate labouring population than to the special benefits of abolition. But no credit is due to the Barbadian plantocracy for retaining that adequate labouring population in their employ. To the latter it was the option of work at low wages, and on most illiberal terms, or starvation.

c. Grenadians pursue various occupations

Sewell, *Ordeal of Free Labour*, 1861

In this island the majority of emancipated field labourers continued to pursue their agricultural calling, and if some have engaged in trade, or have emigrated to other islands, the only wonder is that more have not done so, when wages are as low as from five shillings to two and sixpence sterling per week. But it must not be supposed that of the 14,000 Grenadian Creoles at present engaged in agriculture, all are in a subservient position. Only 6,000 are actually on the estates, and the remainder, preferring a greater independence than would be there allowed them, have rented cottages, or are living in their own houses, and may be seen travelling along the roads every morning to their daily work.

d. Planters in Trinidad fail to hold workers

Sewell, *Ordeal of Free Labour*, 1861

The labourers, as soon as they were free, asked, and for a time received, higher wages than the planters, encumbered as their property was with debt, could afford to pay; and when this rate of wages was subsequently reduced, the majority of the emancipated deserted the estates to better their condition and to seek a more independent livelihood. A very large number purchased small tracts of land and began to plant for themselves; a few squatted on crown lands, of which the government holds an enormous proportion; while many took to trade, and setting up as petty shopkeepers in the towns, pursued a calling more congenial with their tastes and inclinations. The planters vainly endeavoured to remedy the evil; in vain they adopted most stringent measures to prevent the increase of small proprietors, and keep up, by such unnatural means, a sufficient labouring force for the estates. They imposed heavy taxes on all lands and buildings except those devoted to sugar manufacture. But their measures were futile.

e. Many squatters find cheap or free land in the interior of British Guiana

Commission Report in British Guiana, 1848

The system of freeholds (as it is called here) appears one of the crying evils of the day, and is indeed little better than a licensed system of squatting. Where whole districts present but a scene of abandoned estates it is very easy to purchase land for a trifling consideration; and thus members combining, deserted plantations are bought up and villages quickly formed on their sites. There are great numbers too, who strictly speaking *squat* up the rivers and creeks, that is, settle themselves on Crown land without any title whatever. The forest teeming with game and the rivers with fish, afford them plentiful subsistence; and the ground with very little tillage yields them an abundant supply of provisions. They carry on a small trade in firewood, charcoal, etc., but by day the greatest part of their lives is spent in absolute idleness.

9. Flight from the estates in Jamaica.

a. *Missionaries encourage free villages immediately after emancipation*

Account of Visit with Phillippo, 1861

A visit to this township was most interesting, it being the first of those numerous settlements of the enfranchised slaves which sprang into existence immediately after emancipation. . . . It comprises about fifty acres of land: twenty-five acres were purchased in the commencement of 1835 by Mr. Phillippo as peculiarly eligible for village settlement on account of the good roads about it and its proximity to Kingston and Spanish Town. . . . In June 1838 two months before entire freedom was proclaimed the first lot of land was purchased by Henry Lunan formerly a slave and headman on an adjoining plantation. I record his name to mark with especial emphasis this commencement of a new era not only of liberty but of an independent peasantry in the island of Jamaica.

b. *Free villages to make ex-slaves independent of estate rents*

Hinton, *Memoir of William Knibb*, 1849

I do hope that, if you can, you will assist me in forming a free village at this place, so that should any of our members, as I know they will, be the victims of treachery, scorn or trickery, they may have a home. The inveterate enemies of the blacks will find that a few such purchases will afford them an asylum, so that a peasant, with a little freehold, may defy their scorn, and go to any estate he pleases to work, and return to his home and family when he has fulfilled as an hireling his day's employ. While the landowners have all the land, they can, and they will, and they do, daily oppress the people, by demanding abominable high rents for their houses. In many cases, though the house is no better than a hog-sty, I have seen demands of eight shillings and fourpence per week rent, and at the same time only one shilling and eightpence per day for wages, so that a man must work five days to pay for his house and grounds. Even this does not satisfy some of them, but they try to make the man pay rent, the wife pay rent, and each of the children pay rent; and I have seen, and if I come home I will produce, the papers where a Baptist has been charged at the rate of £150 per annum for his house and grounds, the outside value of which, if sold, was not £40.

c. The ex-slaves purchase land

Report on Jamaica by James Anderson, Civil Engineer, 1841–2

It has of late become very general, indeed ever since the measure of emancipation was complete, among those Negroes who have saved a little money to purchase one, two and three acres of ground, occasionally ten acres, and some have even acquired upwards of twenty acres for which they have to pay from three to £10 sterling, per acre, and in some instances a higher price, but £6 sterling per acre may be considered as the average price for good ground; upon which the Negro erects his cottage, and occasionally with a good deal of taste.

d. Number of smallholders multiplies

Governor of Jamaica to Secretary of State, 14 December 1840

The accompanying statement shows that a large increase has taken place from 1838 to 1840 in the number of proprietors of small freeholds in the several rural parishes of this island; the increase consisting almost entirely of emancipated negroes.

It appears that the number of such freeholders assessed in 1838 was 2,014; and in 1840, 7,848.

10. A judgement on the effects of emancipation.

Sewell, *Ordeal of Free Labour,* 1861

The act of British emancipation has been widely abused; but its detractors must live among the people it disenthralled if they would learn the value at which it can be estimated. . . . I have not assumed, in aught I have written, that the West Indian Creole is yet capable of self-government. I have simply endeavoured to show that, under freedom, sources of industry and prosperity have been opened that, under slavery, would have remained closed for ever. I have endeavoured to show that for the West Indies, freedom has been the best policy. . . . If emancipation did no more than relieve the West Indian slave from the supervision of a task-master, I should have nothing left to say. . . . But freedom, when allowed fair play, injured the prosperity of none of these West Indian colonies. It saved them from a far deeper and more lasting depression than any they have yet known. It was a boon conferred upon all classes of society: upon planter and upon labourer; upon all interests: upon commerce and agriculture—upon industry and education—upon morality and religion. And if a perfect measure of success remains to be achieved, let not freedom be condemned; for the obstacles to overcome were great, and the workers were few and unwilling. Let it be remembered that a generation, born in the night of slavery, has not yet passed away, and that men who were taught to believe in that idol and its creations still control the destinies of these distant colonies. Reluctantly they learnt the lesson forced upon them; slowly their opposition yielded to the dawning of conviction; but, now that the meridian of truth has been reached, we may hope, that light will dispel all the shadows of slavery, and confound the logic of its champions when they falsely assert that emancipation has ruined the British islands.

6

Social Conditions since Emancipation

1. In the Act of Emancipation the British Government under-took to make a grant for the education of newly emancipated Negroes. The money was paid to religious bodies to enable them to run schools. Here are some of the aims which govern-ments and philanthropists hoped to achieve through education.

a. An Anglican clergyman advocates the importance of having an educated labouring class after apprenticeship

Report by Rev. J. Stirling to British Government, 11 May 1835

A system of control now secures their conduct. Five years hence their performance of the functions of a labouring class in a civilised community will depend entirely on the power over their minds of the same prudential and moral motives which govern more or less the mass of the people here (in England). If they are not so disposed as to fulfil these functions, pro-perty will perish in the colonies for lack of human impulsion; the Whites will no longer reside there, and the liberated Negroes will probably cease to be progressive, the law having already determined and enforced their civic rights. The task of bettering their condition could be further advanced only by *Education.*

b. The Imperial Government uses the religious bodies to promote education

Latrobe Reports on the use of the Negro Education Grant, 1837–8

The great object contemplated by the outlay of the money voted by Par-liament for these schools is the moral and religious education and im-provement of the Negro population.

Keeping, however, in view the liberal and comprehensive principles upon which Her Majesty's Government ... have availed themselves of the agency and co-operation of the different religious bodies previously engaged in promoting education in the colonies, it will be the duty of the inspector to maintain a strictly impartial bearing towards the various institutions in the West Indies, whose schools it will be his duty to visit, and carefully to avoid any proceeding which may be calculated to excite a feeling of jealousy, or the apprehension of undue interference in their respective systems.

c. A missionary sees his pupils as the pastors and lawyers of the future

Methodist missionary to a new colleague, 2 January 1835

I trust he will remain long enough in the missionary field, to see some of the sable emancipated infants we are now receiving into our schools, respectably and successfully occupying their stations in the pulpit, on the bench and at the bar. Let the 'liberal and comprehensive principles' of H.M. Government be brought to bear on them and there is little doubt that such will be the result. Your missionaries can furnish from their schools some fine specimens of superior intellect and consequent aptitude in learning.

d. Governor MacLeod proposes that his government should establish government schools in Trinidad

Governor of Trinidad to Secretary of State, 13 October 1841

There is perhaps no British colony, where, from the mixed nature of its inhabitants, which I have before stated, the necessity of some general plan of education is more required than in Trinidad.

The number of immigrants we are receiving renders the demand of an extension of the means of education of greater consequence every day, and while there appears a willingness and readiness on all sides to aid in this desirable object, yet the difference of languages and religion make it more imperative that the system to be adopted, should be one, under the control of the government, not only with a view to make it accessible to all parties and creeds, but to cause the language spoken to be that of the country to which this colony belongs.

Your Lordship will not fail to think this most essential when I tell you that two-thirds of the natives still speak exclusively either Spanish or French, and I conceive it absolutely necessary that people living under British rule and claiming the benefit of British subjects, should be able to read the laws by which they are governed.

e. The Imperial Government calls on West Indian governments and West Indian labourers to pay for their own education after 1845

Circular Letter to Governors from Secretary of State, 10 October 1845

I have to request that, whilst intimating to the legislature of the colony under your government, the cessation of the assistance which was so liberally afforded by Parliament during the earlier years of freedom, to secure a favourable commencement of the work of education, you will state that the successful prosecution of it must necessarily depend upon the colonists themselves, that H.M. Government commit it to their hands, and to those of their representatives, in the confidence that it will engage their anxious attention.

At the same time that you make this communication to the legislature, you will, if you shall deem it likely to be productive of good effects, convey to the labouring population of the several districts, through the stipendiary magistrates, the clergy, the missionaries, or any other channel which you may prefer, an exhortation in Her Majesty's name expressing Her Majesty's earnest desire, that they should make every exertion in their power to obtain instruction for themselves and their children; and that they should evince their gratitude for the blessings of freedom, by such present sacrifices for this object as shall make freedom most conducive in the end to their happiness and moral and spiritual well-being. . . .

Her Majesty cannot doubt, that if the labouring classes at large should be animated by the same spirit of steady and patient industry, which ought always to accompany good instruction, the boon of freedom will not have been bestowed on them in vain, but will give birth to all the fruits which Her Majesty and other well-wishers have expected from it.

f. The Principal of Codrington College proposes a new effort to revive education

Rawle to an English friend, 8 April 1847

My chief vocation will be to get all the educational system of the island remodelled; for it is now deplorable. Almost all the Sunday schools have expired by inches, and the day schools fail to draw children and are under untrained and apathetic masters. . . . We must make a stir for the education of the people, or the grant will not be continued by the legislature; for everybody must see that it is a wretched failure and waste of money under the present system.

The little observation which I have made of the Negro character is favourable. . . . They have not yet got clear of the habits of slavery, and are under none of the influences which are found most civilising in England. Their superiors do not mix with them; the ladies cannot on account of the climate; and the clergy, except in few instances, have not got into the way of close pastoral superintendence. What they want is personal contact with us; and I have no doubt that, if they had it, they would improve rapidly. I shall probably stock my big house with curate, master and mistress, etc., being most anxious to put an end to this state of things.

2. After 1838 many of the laws, which had been based on a division between slaves and free men, had to be repealed. The British Government used its powers to prevent the freedom of ex-slaves being limited by new laws. It also influenced West Indian governments to make laws needed in a fully free community.

a. The British Government instructs governors of Crown colonies to amend old laws and to make new ones

Circular despatch to governors of Crown colonies, 15 September 1838

The new legislation required in the West Indies will have for its first object the repeal of obsolete or inapplicable laws, or parts of laws, affecting persons of free condition. . . .

The second general object of the new legislation will be the introduction of laws calculated to meet the new exigencies of society. Her Majesty's Government are very unwilling to multiply such enactments beyond the necessity of the case; but there are some main topics, respecting which new laws are evidently indispensable. Without attempting to make a complete enumeration of these, I may mention the law which regulates the mutual rights and duties of masters and servants, the law for the prevention and punishment of vagrancy, the law of marriage, the militia law, the law for the maintenance of the poor, the law respecting police, and the law for preventing the unauthorised occupation of land.

b. The British Government withholds approval of two Antiguan laws

Secretary of State to Lieutenant-Governor of Antigua, 27 January 1842

In the Report of the Attorney-General on an *Act for the summary punishment of riotous conduct*, that gentleman states that this Act is taken almost verbatim from the British Act of Parliament, and does not appear to him to be open to any objection. If I rightly understand what is the Act of Parliament to which reference is thus made, this statement is not accurate, because the penalties are more than double in pecuniary amount, and because in certain cases they are still more severely enhanced in kind. . . .

The 5th clause of the *Act for authorising the finding of apprentices* . . . enacts that 'all indentures and deeds and agreements in writing entered into for such purpose (that is to serve in Antigua) which would be valid and effectual in the place where made, shall be to all intents and purposes valid and effectual in this island'.

... To ratify in a colony, contracts for the performance of services there, which contracts have been made beyond its limits, and elsewhere than in the United Kingdom, is directly opposed to the principle of all the Emigration Acts, and Orders in Council, which expressly declare invalid every such contract. To give validity in Antigua to any contract which would have been valid at the place where it was made, is to the extent, to incorporate into the local law, the laws of all countries, civilised or barbarous, from which labourers may be drawn.

I think it probable that these consequences were neither designed nor foreseen, still as they would apparently follow in point of law, and as attempts might occasionally be made to enforce them, you will recommend the Legislature of Antigua to repeal the clause in question, and in the meantime Her Majesty's decision on this act will be suspended.

c. The British Government presses the immediate reform of prisons on West Indian assemblies

Circular despatch to governors, 13 August 1838

I have the honour to transmit to you a copy of an Act of Parliament which has been passed entitled *An Act for the better government of prisons in the West Indies*. . . . I am aware that the necessity for such an Act may be much greater in some colonies than in others, and I have no reason to doubt that, in some at least, every disposition will be evinced by the Legislature to correct evils and abuses in their prison discipline and arrangements. . . . Her Majesty's Government, however, felt it necessary that an immediate remedy should be applied to such evils as may be removed by the adoption of an uniform system of superintendence and inspection throughout the West Indies. . . .

It will be your duty, in conjunction with the council, to examine and revise the regulations at present in force respecting the government of prisons, and to make such alterations and additions as appear to be requisite, in order to insure the maintenance of good order and discipline, and the proper care and treatment of the prisoners. In doing this you will especially keep in view the importance of due classification of the prisoners, so far as this may be compatible with the present buildings.

You are further authorised by Her Majesty to appoint one or more persons, on whose qualification for the office you can rely, to inspect the prisons within your government, for the effectual discharge of which duty ample powers have been given by this Act. In the first instance, you will appoint one or more of the special justices to this office, as it will form an appropriate part of their duty, and one which they may easily and beneficially discharge, now that they have been relieved from the onerous functions imposed on them by the late apprenticeship code. . . .

The power with which you are entrusted of removing any improper officers, will be exercised with firmness and decision, whenever such a measure is required, by circumstances coming to your knowledge.

The extreme power of declaring a prison unfit to be used as such, is intended to apply to cases in which such a measure is the only method of preventing those evils which would otherwise result from the confinement of prisoners in a place obviously defective in those arrangements which are essential to the health and proper treatment of the prisoners. I would instance, as an example, any prison in which, owing to the insecurity of the building, the prisoners, in order to prevent escape, are subjected to modes of restraint which would only aggravate their punishment, and which in a suitable building would not be necessary; or any prison in which the cells are so constructed as to be injurious to health, or to inflict needless pain.

3. After emancipation the planters no longer provided medical care for estate workers. They, and the people who had taken up other occupations, were without medical attendance for a long time. In the eighteen-fifties there were several severe epidemics.

a. Medical attention is no longer provided for estate workers

Premium, *Eight Years in British Guiana*, 1 January 1843

On many estates the planters have discontinued the practice of paying the doctor to attend their labourers, and the latter, instead of making arrangements with the medical man to secure his attendance, with that reliance on the Whites which has hitherto been part of their nature, for habit is hardly a strong enough word to express some of their peculiarities, throw the blame on their masters, when a coroner's inquest finds that the person has died without medical attendance—an old law wisely and humanely requiring that an inquest (or similar investigation) shall be held on every one who dies without being seen while ill by a practitioner.

b. Doctors advocate sanitation laws for new villages

Premium, *Eight Years in British Guiana*, 1 January 1843

Some medical practitioners in the neighbourhood of the larger villages which have lately sprung up from the sale of land, have represented strongly to the governor the mortality which has occurred from want of attendance, during the prevalence of epidemic diseases. I heard of one village which had lost eighteen children from whooping-cough, not one of whom was visited by a doctor. Those gentlemen urged on his Excellency the necessity for some sanitary enactment, to make it imperative on people to employ the usual means for the preservation of life; and quoted instances to show that the governments of all nations recognised the necessity for arbitrary laws when public health was endangered, believing that in such cases people could not be safely left to themselves. Our own quarantine laws and local regulations during the existence of cholera will occur to anyone as parallel instances.

c. Towns are badly sited and badly drained

Davy, *The West Indies before and since Slave Emancipation*, 1854

Most of the towns . . . are situated on the leeward coast, close to the sea, and mostly in low situations equally unfavourable for ventilation and drainage, for coolness consequently, and the absence of malaria or noxious effluvia. Not one of them that I am acquainted with, is provided with sewers, or is efficiently drained, or is well supplied with water—great and fatal omissions in regard to the health, comfort, and welfare of their inhabitants.

d. A missionary during the cholera epidemic

Diary of Phillippo, 28 October 1850

Sunday: went to prayer-meeting as usual. A large congregation. . . . Went to Passage Fort. Called at several houses. Saw several persons dead and dying. Called at the hospital and found more dead there, and the hospital in a filthy state. Preached to a thin congregation, owing to the great mortality in the neighbourhood. Called again at the hospital, and ordered a nurse to be procured. From thence went to Cumberland Pen; several cases of the disease existing, and several deaths. The Kraal Pen had been in a dreadful state, but was somewhat improving. The Farm Pen, the property of Lord Carrington, was rapidly decimating; several had been interred without coffins, and numbers were being taken with the epidemic every hour. I prayed with all the patients, and returned to town at dark. Preached in the evening to a large congregation.

e. The epidemics lead governments to take measures against contagious diseases

British Guiana Royal Gazette, 14 August 1851

It must be generally admitted, we think, that there is every desire on the part of the people of this colony, to improve its sanitary condition. The misfortune, perhaps, may be that there has been more of zeal than discretion in the matter, and that we have been more ready to do something, than to know exactly what is best to be done. This, however, is a deficiency under which we shall, probably, not labour long. Thanks to the prevalence of cholera in Jamaica, and the visit to the colony of a Medical Inspector appointed by the Home Government, we have at last reached that stage in sanitary knowledge, which has resulted in two bills being laid before the Court of Policy, one, the *Public Health*, and the other, the *Nuisances Removal and Contagious Diseases Prevention Bill.* . . .

That sanitary legislation of a sound nature is urgently called for in this colony, we hold to be as indubitable, as that prevention is better than cure, and that it is the duty of government to protect the public to the utmost of its power, from impending calamities. When, therefore, we find that, cholera has reappeared in Jamaica, and that yellow fever is hastening its victims to the grave in Surinam, it is high time that the Legislature of British Guiana should begin 'to set its house in order'.

f. A new mental hospital in Kingston

Harvey and Brewin, *Jamaica in 1866*

In 1837 no spectacle was more harrowing than that of the lunatic ward of this hospital, where, in small square cells, round a court-yard, the patients were singly confined, some of the raging maniacs being chained like wild beasts.

The new lunatic asylum is built on the harbour beyond the penitentiary: it contains two hundred patients, in nearly equal proportion of the sexes. It is not too much to say that the cleanliness and ventilation are perfect. The medical director, Dr. Allen, relies much on employment, imitation and moral influence: there is no mechanical restraint. We thought the institution would compare with the best in the mother country. Dr. A. is full of resource in improving the structural arrangements and devising occupation: he showed a pardonable pride in explaining how much work had been done on the land and in the house, to the great benefit of the patients and the reduction of expense.

4. The high death rate in the eighteen-fifties left many children orphans. Orphanages started by private persons were sometimes assisted by the governments.

a. In British Guiana

Dalton, *History of British Guiana*, 1855

The Georgetown Orphan Asylum has lately been instituted, and promises to become one of the most creditable establishments of the colony. Its principal advocate and supporter has been the Chief Justice, Mr. Arrindell, who, with his excellent lady, are unremitting in their attention to the numerous inmates who have already crowded into its handsome and hospitable walls. It has hitherto received the cordial support of the charitable of nearly all the religious denominations of the community, and has likewise obtained a liberal grant from the local legislature.

b. In Trinidad

Ordinance for Promoting the Education and Industrial Training of the Children of Indian Immigrants, 1 October 1856

Whereas a school for the education and industrial training of the children of Indian immigrants has been established in the ward of Tacarigua, by and at the expense of Frederick William Burnley Esquire, other like schools may be established by voluntary contributions in other parts of the colony and it is expedient that use should be made of such institutions: Be it enacted . . .

1. It shall and may be lawful for the Governor upon application made to him by the person establishing, or the Directors or Managers of any such school to direct the Agent General of Immigrants and the Inspector of Schools, or either of them, to examine and report to him on its condition and regulations; and any such school as shall appear to the satisfaction of the Governor and shall be certified under his hand to be efficient for its purpose shall be held to be 'An Indian Training School' under the provision of this Ordinance.

3. It shall be lawful for the Agent General of Immigrants to direct any child or other descendant of any Indian Immigrant introduced into this colony at the public expense with the consent of the father if living and resident of this island, or any such child being an orphan or abandoned by his parents to be sent to any such Indian Training School provided that no such child shall be so sent who shall be above the age of ten years.

4. That no child who shall be so sent to any such Indian Training School

shall be liable to be retained at such school after he shall have reached the age of fifteen years, except with his consent.

7. It shall be lawful for the Governor to defray out of the public moneys appropriated to Immigration for the cost of the maintenance and clothing of any child who may be sent to any such Training School by the order of the Agent General of Immigrants during the time that he may remain at such school, such sum not exceeding ten pounds per annum for every such child as the Governor shall deem fit.

5. The middle decades of the nineteenth century were bad years ; the rural populations isolated by the reduction in the number of estates, uneducated, unassisted by governments, suffered greatly.

a. A plea to the Government of Jamaica to give help to the small settlers in time for them to become the backbone of the country

Report of Stipendiary Magistrate for St. Thomas in the Vale, 1854

A general decadence prevails over the large properties and old establishments. On the other hand, the thousands of well-cultivated settlements, with their tastefully arranged cottages and gardens, which have given quite a different appearance to the country since August 1838, bespeak the prosperity and comfort of the occupants, and present a cheering prospect and an encouraging hope for the future.

At first, these settlements were sufficiently near the estates to enable the cottagers to labour on them, returning to their own homes every evening ; a very important consideration in several points of view ; but the abandonment of the estates has operated in two ways to prevent this ; the labour is no longer required, and the settlements have become too isolated and far removed from cultivated estates. When we consider that the comparatively few large properties which are still upheld, must, in the course of events, follow the fate of others which have been either abandoned or cut up into small settlements, . . . we cannot but foresee the rapidly approaching importance which must very soon attach to these small settlements and their yeomanry of possessors. . . .

If ever there was a time when it was necessary that something should be done by a government for a people, this is the people, and now is the time. The country has hitherto done little or nothing or worse than nothing for them.

b. *The Government of Jamaica charged with keeping the mass of the people ignorant*

Sewell, *Ordeal of Free Labour*, 1861

It would be false to deny that the most deplorable ignorance prevails throughout the lower orders of society, and especially among the field labourers. How could it be otherwise when the planter's policy has been to keep the people uninstructed, and the government has never even encouraged education, much less insisted upon it as one of the most important of reciprocal duties between a free state and its citizens. No general system of public instruction has been introduced in Jamaica, and it is surely unreasonable to expect that this people, or any other people, could acquire a knowledge that has never been placed within their reach. It is estimated that there are 65,000 children in Jamaica between the ages of five and fifteen, and for their education the Legislature voted last year the sum of £2,950—less than a shilling for the instruction of each child during a space of twelve months.

c. *Underhill, a visiting Baptist minister, describes and accounts for social evils in the eighteen-sixties*

Underhill Letter, 5 January 1865

All accounts, both public and private, concur in affirming the alarming increase of crime, chiefly of larceny and petty theft. This arises from the extreme poverty of the people. That this is its true origin is made evident by the ragged and even naked condition of vast numbers of them, so contrary to the taste for dress they usually exhibit. They cannot purchase clothing, partly from its greatly increased cost, which is unduly enhanced by the duty which it now pays, and partly from the want of employment and the consequent absence of wages.

The people, then, are starving, and the causes of this are not far to seek. . . . The simple fact is, there is not sufficient employment for the people; there is neither work for them, nor the capital to employ them.

d. Remedies suggested by Underhill

Underhill Letter, 5 January 1865

1. A searching inquiry into the legislation of the island since emancipation—its taxation, its economical and material condition—would go far to bring to light the causes of the existing evils, and, by convincing the ruling class of the mistakes of the past, lead to their removal. Such an inquiry seems also due to this country, that it may be seen whether the emancipated peasantry have gained those advantages which were sought to be secured to them by their enfranchisement.

2. The Governor might be instructed to encourage by his personal approval and urgent recommendation the growth of exportable produce by the people on the very numerous freeholds they possess. . . .

3. With just laws and light taxation, capitalists would be encouraged to settle in Jamaica, and employ themselves in the production of the more important staples, such as sugar, coffee, and cotton. Thus the people would be employed, and the present starvation rate of wages be improved.

. . . It is more than time that the unwisdom—to use the gentlest term—that has governed Jamaica since emancipation should be brought to an end; a course of action which, while it incalculably aggravates the misery arising from natural, and, therefore, unavoidable, causes, renders certain the ultimate ruin of every class—planter and peasant, European and Creole.

e. Imperial Government replies to a petition for more land from 'the poor people of St. Ann's parish' that they should work steadily and save their earnings

'*The Queen's Advice*', 14 June 1865

I have received Her Majesty's command to inform them (the petitioners), that the prosperity of the labouring classes, as well as of all other classes, depends, in Jamaica, and in other countries, upon their working for wages, not uncertainly, or capriciously, but steadily and continuously, at the times when their labour is wanted, and for so long as it is wanted; and that if they would use this industry, and thereby render the plantations productive, they would enable the planters to pay them higher wages for the same hours of work than are received by the best field labourers in this country; and as the cost of the necessities of life is much less in Jamaica than it is here, they would be enabled, by adding prudence to industry, to lay by an ample provision for seasons of drought and dearth; and they may be assured, that it is from their own industry and prudence, in availing themselves of the means of prospering that are before them, and not from any such schemes as have been suggested to them, that they must look for an improvement in their condition; and that Her Majesty will regard with interest and satisfaction their advancement through their own merits and efforts.

f. Protest against police action in St. Thomas before the Morant Bay riots

Petition to the Governor from Paul Bogle and others, October 1865

We, the petitioners of St. Thomas-in-the-East, send to inform your Excellency of the mean advantages that have been taken of us from time to time, and more especially this present time, when on Saturday, 7th of this month, an outrageous assault was committed upon us by the policemen of this parish, by order of the Justices, which occasioned an outbreaking for which warrants have been issued against innocent persons which we were compelled to resist. We therefore, call upon your Excellency for protection, seeing we are Her Majesty's loyal subjects, which protection if refused we will be compelled to put our shoulders to the wheel, as we have been imposed upon for a period of 27 years with due obeisance to the laws of our Queen and country, and we can no longer endure the same, therefore is our object of calling upon your Excellency as Governor-in-Chief and Captain of our island.

6. Under Crown colony government some able and determined governors worked hard to improve the economic and social conditions of the islands.

a. Lord Harris in Trinidad

Davy, *The West Indies before and since Slave Emancipation*, 1854

Fortunately for the island, the nobleman presiding over its government is fully sensible of the real wants of the community, and is exerting himself to supply them—creating hope where there was almost despair, confidence where there was mistrust, and, it is believed, a more healthy tone and feeling generally. He has instituted model and training schools, which it is said are doing well and to be of great promise, as to an improved and efficient system of education. Under his directing influence, the roads are undergoing substantial repair, and new ways of communication are being made; bridges are being constructed; pipes laid for supplying water to the principal town; and other public works of a useful kind are in progress.

b. Sir John Peter Grant in Jamaica

Gardner, *History of Jamaica*, 1873

In reviewing the events of the past six years, it is evident that a marked improvement in the existing condition and future prospects of the island has been effected. The discontent which once characterised so many of the people is now rarely witnessed. Taxes are more cheerfully paid, because it is known that they will be carefully expended for legitimate purposes. Education is extending, and Christian churches are flourishing. Crime is under control. Industrious habits are stimulated by the prospects of success, while the commercial and agricultural condition of the island alike indicate steady but real progress. To Sir John Peter Grant no small share of the credit of this state of things is due, nor has he lacked the assistance of able and zealous co-workers.

7. The payment of the Anglican clergy from public funds was criticised by members of other churches. In Trinidad and St. Lucia Catholic clergy were also paid from public funds.

a. Baptist objections in Jamaica

Speech by Knibb in England, 7 June 1845

I believe in free trade, not merely in sugar, but in religion too. I would never cast such a slur upon the episcopalians who tell us . . . that they number all the talent, that they possess all the energy, and have engrossed all the wealth of the church, as to suppose that they loved their religion so little that they did not like to pay for it. Others may say so if they please, and may assert that unless Christianity is supported by the state it will fall. I believe no such thing. . . . I do not say that feeling will not sometimes rise that these striplings should step in when we have been twenty years toiling for the poor slaves, and were binding up their broken hearts when they were scarcely born, or if they were born, were playing at marbles at Oxford or Cambridge. . . . But do not suppose, Christian friends, that our people are caught; not at all, our congregations still stand, fair, clear, and numerous.

b. A Governor points out that the Established Church is maintained at the expense of members of other denominations

Governor of the Windwards to Secretary of State, 13 January 1857

They can scarcely be satisfied with a system under which their food and other necessities are taxed for the support of the clergy of the Church of England, while they have to pay their own clergy either by voluntary effort as in the case of the Wesleyans and Moravians, or by fees as in the case of the Roman Catholics. . . .

There can I think be no doubt that the influence of the Church of England in the several West India legislatures is greater than among the people at large, and in view of all the circumstances, my own conviction is that the wisest policy which the authorities of that church can pursue is to submit cheerfully to the decisions of the respective legislatures regarding ecclesiastical grants and especially to avoid any controversy, which will bring prominently forward for discussion the merits of the existing system.

c. The contribution from public funds made to Anglicans and Catholics in Trinidad contrasted

De Verteuil, *Trinidad*, 1858

The majority of the population are Catholics in several of the British West India islands, viz. in Dominica, Saint Lucia, Grenada, and Trinidad; but, in every one of them, the Church of England has the lion's share. In Trinidad, where the catholic religion is now, and has, since the capitulation in the year 1797, always been supported from the general funds of the colony, the church of 45,000 catholics cost the colony £4,500, and that of 17,000 episcopalians, £5,500, besides extra allowances. For the last thirty-four years the catholic bishop had been in the receipt of £1,000 per annum as his stipend : our present governor, . . . has, by the advice of a protestant committee, and with the aid of an irresponsible council, reduced that sum to £500 sterling.

d. The Governor of Trinidad deprives a Catholic bishop of the stipend and official recognition because he is not a British subject

De Verteuil, *Trinidad*, 1858

The present administrator of the diocese being an alien, the governor has withheld the entire stipend; and even refuses to recognise the bishop's authority *in matters of church hierarchy*. The withholding of the administrator's stipend, because he was an alien, was a questionable right, . . . because the catholics of Trinidad, and not the administrator, have to bear the consequences: but, to refuse to recognise the authority of the latter in the appointment of parish ministers, is an undue interference, and an assumption of prerogative, of which every liberal and impartial man cannot but disapprove.

8. In the second half of the nineteenth century all governments maintained primary schools to a varying extent. Schools and colleges for secondary and further education were also started; there were frequent arguments about the nature of these schools and who should attend them.

a. The British Government continue to give urgent advice on education even after the Negro Education Grant is withdrawn

Circular Despatch, 26 January 1847

Nor will a wise colonial government neglect any means which affords even a remote prospect of gradually creating a native middle class among the negro population, and thus, ultimately, of completing the institutions of freedom, by creating a body of men interested in the protection of property, and with intelligence enough to take part in that humbler machinery of local affairs which ministers to social order. . . . To inculcate the principles and promote the influences of Christianity. . . . To diffuse a grammatical knowledge of the English language, as the most important agent of civilisation, for the coloured population of the colonies. . . . To communicate such a knowledge of writing and arithmetic, and of their application to his wants and duties, as may enable a peasant to economise his means, and give the small farmer the power to enter into calculations and agreements.

An improved agriculture is required in certain of the colonies to replace the system of exhausting the virgin soils, and then leaving to natural influences alone, the work of reparation. The education of the coloured races would not, therefore, be complete, for the children of small farmers, unless it included this object.

The lesson books of colonial schools should also teach the mutual interests of the mother country and her dependencies; the rational basis of their connection, and the domestic and social duties of the coloured races. These lesson books should also simply set forth the relation of wages, capital, labour and the influence of local and general government on personal security, independence, and order.

b. A missionary describes his schools

Buchner, *The Moravians in Jamaica*, 1854

Several of the larger schools, numbering from fifty to one hundred scholars, are kept by teachers educated in our Normal School; those numbering below forty children are mostly kept by young women, who possess sufficient knowledge to conduct an infant school, and whose moral and religious character qualify them for the office. . . . Reading, writing, arithmetic, Bible-history, religious instruction, and in some cases grammar and geography, are taught in these schools.

c. The Baptists establish a college to train West Indian ministers

Phillippo, *Jamaica*, 1843

The people are literally hungering and thirsting after righteousness; they have been endeavouring to carry on the service of God among themselves because they were unable to obtain other instruction, but they have at length made an effort which will prove to their advantage.

From this wonderful concurrence of animating circumstances, and the co-operation of other favourable events, how bright and glorious becomes the prospect of the future! But the most interesting feature by which that prospect is distinguished, so far at least as human instrumentality is concerned, is that which regards the employment of native labourers, many of whom, possessing zeal, talent, and piety, are now rising up in our churches. Irrespective of other advantages, it is almost impossible to conceive how much such an agency will contribute to the general diffusion of knowledge and religion, especially with that training which they are about to receive in the theological institution now founded by the Baptist missionaries, in connection with the parent society.

d. A legislator gives an opinion on how public money should be spent on middle class education

Member of Court of Policy, British Guiana, 1 March 1853

Then, there was another question—how far were they justified as a legislative body in taking the money paid by all classes of the community to provide for a school for the higher classes? He thought it was their duty to provide instruction for the lower classes; and it might even be proper to support a grammar school; but to go as far as was now proposed, to give high salaries for professors and masters, and to make a sort of college of the institution, was what he could not consent to do. . . .

The object was not to provide education for the highest officials and the richest merchants; but to assist the middle classes in having their children taught reading and writing and grammar, to speak and write their own language properly, history and geography, the knowledge of other countries, the French, Spanish, and other languages, and book-keeping. That was the knowledge that was wanted for storekeepers and officials in the buildings; not Latin and Greek—the Classics as they were called. . . . Those who wish to make their children doctors and lawyers and officers in the army, could keep them in the school till they were thirteen or fourteen years of age, and then send them to Oxford or Cambridge; but he did not think that the people's money should be spent for the purpose now intended. He did not insist that Latin and Greek should be left out of the list of instruction; but they should be paid for by the parents who wished to have them. He did not think it would be justice to the community to support this proposition.

e. A visiting inspector contrasts the social background of those who attend the secondary schools in Trinidad

Keenan Report, 1869

Upon the subject of secondary education, feeling runs high in the colony. There are some who would rank it next to sacrilege to touch a penny, or disturb even a form, of the Queen's Collegiate School. There are others who, if they could, would with a single stroke annihilate it. Similarly, the Catholic College has its champions and its foes. . . .

The first thing likely to strike a person . . . is the strangeness of the fact that whilst the white population, which is only between 5,000 and 6,000 furnishes 142 pupils to the collegiate establishments, the coloured population, which, exclusive of the coolies, numbers from 60,000 to 70,000, furnishes only 37 pupils. Twenty-four of the coloured pupils are in the Catholic College, and 13 in the Queen's Collegiate School.

Lord Harris provided that every encouragement should be given to all, however humble their birth. No such encouragement, however, is afforded to the poor in the Queen's Collegiate School, for the high rate of fees effectually bars the door against them; and at the Catholic College the authorities plead that they derive no aid from the state to enable them to give places on moderate terms to the poor.

The next conclusion . . . is, that the Queen's Collegiate School has not obtained the confidence of the people generally. Of the 68 pupils on its rolls, 28 are the sons of members of the Civil Service. This is a large proportion of the whole attendance. The children of the public officers receive a most excellent education, which, however, is mainly paid for by the taxes of the people. The Queen's Collegiate School is therefore a great boon to the public servants of the colony. But is the interest of the public servants to be primary and paramount in the consideration of this question? In measuring the relative acceptability of the two colleges to the people of the colony, I have to turn to the other classes—the merchants, the planters, and the professional men. And how does the case appear from this point of view?

In the Queen's Collegiate School there are 14 sons of merchants; at the Catholic College there are 41. At the Queen's Collegiate School there are 13 sons of planters or of proprietors; at the Catholic College there are 41. At the Queen's Collegiate School there are 10 who are the sons of professional men or of others; at the Catholic College the number is 22. The Queen's Collegiate School has 28 sons of members of the public service, exclusive of 3 who are the sons of rectors; whilst the Catholic College has only 6.

These facts are conclusive. They require no comment. The people flock to the non-endowed college; not because its education is better than that which the Queen's Collegiate School affords, but because the principle of its foundation—the introduction of the religious element—is more acceptable to them.

f. High schools encouraged in Jamaica in the hope that a government college will follow

Methodist missionary to Methodist Missionary Society, 7 December 1875

Quite an agreeable excitement has been created among us by the appointments made on behalf of our High School. . . . Hope is expressed that our society will not allow this to be an ephemeral undertaking. I, for one, do not expect that it will be. Nevertheless it will not be a success and permanent blessing without constant pushing. Government seems to hesitate with regard to any further effort to establish a college for the colony. I don't think the idea is abandoned, but there seems to have come over the entire country a sense of its deficiency and unpreparedness for a college, and along with it the feeling that a few good high schools established in different parts of the country by religious societies or private individuals will do the needful, and prepare a sufficient number of youths from time to time, to render a college worth maintaining. Providence directs!

g. *Disproportionate spending on primary and secondary education justified by the claim that pupils can pass from one to the other*

House of Assembly in reply to Governor of Barbados, 2 February 1891

The House in admitting that one-third of the vote for educational purposes is spent annually in making provision for the intellectual wants of 500 or 600 students who attend the higher grade schools, while the remaining two-thirds are spent on the schools in which instruction is afforded to upwards of 23,000 of the children of the people, desire respectfully to draw attention to the Education Act, under which it is possible, as has been already proved, for children of the people to pass by progressive stages not only from the elementary to the highest grade schools but also to one of the English universities, at the expense of the colony.

9. In the last quarter of the nineteenth century governments were worried about neglected and vagrant young people, whom they regarded as potential criminals.

a. *Child labour is condemned in Barbados*

Report of Kendal District Inspector of Schools, 1891

I protest that child labour is an abomination and a disgrace, and that we must reach out towards a day when there shall be no half-timers, no exemption from schooling until all that we can teach has been learned, or the age of 14 at least has been attained. How can we speak of enlightenment when we use saplings for fuel and cut the green corn for fodder. How dare we boast of freedom when thousands of children are doomed to premature toil. . . . What pride can we take in reckoning our industries, if when able-bodied men are indolently roaming the country, rusting in workhouses, or rotting in taverns, children of tender age are toiling in factory, work-shop, and field, at the expense of their physical growth, their intellectual development, and their moral welfare. I hope and believe that ere long some Wilberforce will arise to open the eyes of the nation to this abuse, to avenge the children of the poor, and to claim in the name of humanity, childhood for children.

b. *Young criminals have not received education*

Governor of Barbados to House of Assembly, 3 March 1876

Apart from motives of philanthropy is it not the duty of the state, especially with our teeming population, amongst whom there must necessarily be a huge amount of poverty, which never fails to beget crime, for its own safety to make provision, that the rising generation may be trained to habits of industry—for a living they must have—and if they are not taught to seek it by habits of industry and self-reliance, they will obtain it by fraud.

We may shun the duty of training them in their youth, but if we do, we cannot escape the task of providing for them as criminals in after years.

... The Chaplain says that out of 256 boys in the Juvenile Prison during the year 1875, only 28 had been under any instruction whatever, previous to their committal to prison. He says that the Juvenile Prison 'is at present nothing but a nursery for Glendairy Convict Prison' and he asks—not for the first time—for some institution 'to which our half-starved, neglected and ignorant children can be sent'.

c. *The juvenile population of Jamaica*

Report of the Commission on the Juvenile Population of Jamaica, 1879

(i) *In towns*. We find that there is a tendency amongst portions of the rural population to gravitate towards the towns and Kingston especially. The class to which we refer are moved by a desire to obtain their livelihood by other means than agricultural labour, and by the hope of that casual employment at high rates which is often to be obtained in towns. As a rule such persons are not qualified for skilled labour, and as there is no constant demand for such services as they can render, they pass a considerable part of their time in idleness, and so fail to make adequate provision for the care of their families. ...

The dwelling places of a considerable proportion of the poor classes in towns are of a most miserable description, many of them being unfit for human habitation. They consist of single rooms opening into a common yard. In these rooms families are herded together under conditions that defy the simplest observances of decency. . . .

Of other sources contributing to juvenile vagrancy, one is to be found in the large number of young women of no settled occupation, who proceed to the towns hoping to obtain domestic situations. They furnish a supply much in excess of the natural demand, and failing to find employment often fall victims to the temptations to immoral life that surround them. . . .

The parents of such children do not send them to school. They will not, and in some instances of exceptional poverty they perhaps cannot, pay school fees. But even where a free school is available they do not trouble themselves to see that their children attend. Moreover parents of this class too often do not provide their children with food, so that the latter are obliged to seek it for themselves during the hours when they should be at school.

Nor do such parents apprentice their children to trades.

(ii) *In the country.* There has been a tendency for many years on the part of the class from which estates' labour is drawn to retire from such labour, and to settle themselves upon their own holdings in the mountain districts. The movement has been observable for a long period, but has become much more marked in certain parts of the island during the last eight or nine years. Of such persons there are many who endeavour to settle themselves within reach of a chapel and a school, and who are prosperous and respectable in themselves and in their families. But there is a class who appear to prefer to place themselves at a distance from civilising influences and to live in idleness. This class is largely recruited by the youth of both sexes arriving at the age of puberty, who, being able to take care of themselves, throw off all parental control, form illicit connections, build themselves a hovel, plant a provision ground that enables them to live in almost perfect idleness, produce children, remain with one another just as long as it suits them, and then part to form fresh connections of an equally transient character. The same practice is also stated to exist on estates.

Estates' labour is now to some extent supplied in parts of the island by what are known as roving gangs. Young men and women, drawn mainly from the worst class of the mountain population that we have mentioned, varying in age from sixteen and fourteen upwards, band themselves in gangs, and move about from estate to estate, labouring for rarely more than a fortnight in one place and returning to their own habitations in the intervals.

10. In the last decades of the nineteenth century the educational provision was frequently criticised. The critics complained about the cost, the poor results, the quality of teachers and the curricula.

a. Results in Jamaica disappoint Royal Commissioners

Crossman Report, 1883

The average expenditure for five years' periods has been as follows:

1862 to 1866	.	.	£3,700
1867 to 1871	.	.	7,200
1872 to 1876	.	.	19,300
1877 to 1881	.	.	23.400

Census of Year	Able to read and write	Able to read only	Total	Centisimal Proportion of persons above 5 years old	Number of children attending school
1861	50,726	68,333	119,059	31·3	33,521
1871	71,076	81,398	152,474	35·0	40,610
1881	115,418	115,750	231,168	45·7	67,402

These results show decided progress, but progress by no means in proportion to the increase in expenditure. In 1881 the expenditure was six times as great as in 1861, but the number of children attending school and the number of these able to read and write was only twice as great. This is the more serious when we remember that, after deducting the adult whites (8,000) and 80 per cent of the adult coloured population (60,000), it would appear that out of 250,000 adult Negroes only 22,000 are yet able to write.

This is a most unsatisfactory and discreditable state of affairs.

b. *Attack on undue economy in education*

Report of Inspector of Schools, Trinidad, 1886

In the Jamaica Education Report, 1883, the following are given as the cost of Education per head in the countries named: Jamaica, 10d; Trinidad, 1/8d; Barbados, 1/8d; British Guiana, 2/6d; Great Britain, 3/5d; United States, 6/8d.

Considering that the educational system of Jamaica is reported as far from perfect, and that expenses and wages in Barbados are much lower than here, . . . Trinidad comes well out of the comparison if cheapness is considered as a test. The comparison shows at all events that the working of our educational system has been conducted with much economy . . . but there is no more reason (if anything rather less) why cheapness should be sought for in educational than in any other services. In no other department is cheapness considered the chief aim. In education, as in other branches, the utmost economy consistent with efficiency ought certainly to be practised, but the crying for a reduction of an educational expenditure is merely a form of asking that the schools should be crippled.

c. *Need for scientific education in British Guiana*

Daily Chronicle, 7 March 1890

What we want in this colony are men who have received a scientific education:—engineers, chemists, mineralogists, electricians: men who will be able to bring every resource of science to bear in developing the country.

At present the majority of these have to be imported at high salaries. The young Creole is no worse for being able to construe a little Livy or Horace; but if the time in teaching him the resources of his own colony has been occupied in cramming his unwilling mind with Latin grammar, then it is not much to say that his education has been on wrong lines. . . . The alumni of Queen's College will make very nice gentlemanly clerks in Government offices; but they are not turned out to the battle of life equipped with weapons of modern precision.

d. Attack on curricula for neglecting the need for agricultural development

Report of Inspector of Schools, Trinidad, 1889

The present system of high class education is producing a superabundance of doctors and lawyers, some of whom follow their profession here, some elsewhere, while the system of primary education produces many clerks and would-be schoolmasters, but comparatively few practical agriculturists or first class mechanics.

It is no doubt desirable that the inhabitants of the colony should be afforded facilities for educating their sons to follow these professions, but surely in an essentially agricultural community such as this, in an island with thousands of fertile acres waiting to be opened up and cultivated, it is not too much to expect that at least equal facilities will be given for the education of the youth of the colony in those pursuits which tend to develop the resources of the island.

11. Occupation, class and colour at the beginning of the twentieth century.

Olivier, *White Capital and Coloured Labour,* 1906

Practically all these small holdings are owned by the black peasantry and coloured people, the acreage varying from less than an acre to 50 or 100 acres. Next in number to the nearly pure negro peasant class comes the considerable coloured class of mixed African and European descent, which largely supplies the artisans and tradesmen of the community. Very many of this class are landowners and planters, many are overseers and book-keepers on estates, many commercial clerks, and some are engaged in the professions of law and medicine. Many clergy of all the Protestant denominations are black or coloured; so are all the elementary schoolmasters and schoolmistresses and some of the teachers in the few second grade schools. . . . The whites predominate in the governing and employing class, and as merchants or planters direct and lead the industrial life of the island.

12. A comprehensive scheme for agricultural education was proposed by the Imperial Government in 1899. Some parts of it worked better than others. Outside the schools Agricultural Societies tried to influence farmers through instructors.

a. The scheme proposed by the Imperial Government

Circular Despatch from the Secretary of State, 4 October 1899

The scheme comprises three distinct systems of agricultural instruction adapted to the needs of different classes of the community, viz:—

(i) Higher agricultural education imparted at existing high schools and colleges and by the medium of public lectures.

(ii) The maintenance of Agricultural Schools for selected pupils who will be treated as apprentices.

(iii) The teaching of the principles of agriculture in elementary schools. I propose to deal with these three systems *seriatim*.

(iv) It is intended to appoint lecturers in agriculture at the principal high schools and colleges in the West Indies under whom boys of fourteen years and upwards attending the school will have the opportunity of specialising in the subject. A Cambridge graduate of distinction has already been appointed in this capacity at Harrison College, Barbados. Another will be probably appointed at the High School at Jamaica and it may possibly be found desirable later on to appoint similar lecturers at colleges in Trinidad and British Guiana. It is hoped that the opportunities thus afforded of obtaining a thorough knowledge of scientific agriculture will be readily embraced especially by the sons of owners and managers of estates in the West Indies.

Agricultural schools on apprenticeship lines are being established in St. Vincent, St. Kitts, St. Lucia and Dominica, each affording accommodation for 25 boys. The boys will be fed, clothed, and trained free; and admission to the schools is to be regarded as a sort of prize, to be awarded on the recommendation of Inspectors of Schools or other responsible persons to boys in elementary schools about fourteen years of age who have passed the IVth Standard, and who show moral and intellectual aptitude for instruction. . . . Preference will be given to promising boys trained at these schools in making appointments to junior posts under the Department of Agriculture.

In dealing with the question of teaching the principles of agriculture in elementary schools it seems desirable to reiterate, that the object of the scheme is not to teach farming in schools, but, to quote from an able memorandum by the Archbishop of the West Indies, 'to have the entire youth of an agricultural country intellectually trained in an atmosphere favourable to agriculture, so that they should grow up interested in it, and that they should learn . . . that agricultural work is not only fit for slaves'. The chief immediate difficulty in instituting such instruction is the ignorance of agriculture which is displayed by the majority of elementary teachers, and in some cases also by Inspectors of Schools. In the future all knowledge of this subject will have to be made compulsory on all who wish to become teachers; but the existing teachers must be afforded opportunities of becoming acquainted with it. . . .

I need hardly remind you that a change in education, amounting almost to a revolution, cannot be effected by mere machinery, but requires the local co-operation of all concerned: and I am confident that you will do all in your power to secure such co-operation on the part alike of your subordinate officers, and of the people of the colony under your government.

b. *Opposition in British Guiana to the idea of higher education in agriculture*

Daily Chronicle, 22 August 1899

At any rate, it is certain that for some time to come such things as agricultural science would mean little more than a frivolous waste of public money. Suggestions of this sort presuppose a taste for agriculture amongst the pupils and their parents, whereas generally speaking no such sentiment exists in Demerara. The process of alienating the people from the soil has proceeded in this colony to an extreme unknown in most of the other West Indian possessions. There is not the slightest evidence that the class of youth who would be able to win agricultural exhibitions and benefit by the services of a science professor has any desire to take up agriculture for the making of his daily bread. On the contrary, it is by these people that the strongest aversion is entertained against the tilling of the soil. To their mind it is an ignoble calling, to be adopted only as a last resort, when all other means for gaining a livelihood fail. . . . Nor has the colony at the present time any opening for the class of person that a scholarship in agriculture would tend to produce. If we had a dozen or so of such young men, equipped with a high technical knowledge of agriculture and allied subjects, it would be puzzling to know what to do with them. They would hardly be prepared to accept positions as overseers, and they would not have the practical training to qualify them for anything higher on a sugar estate. . . .

In Jamaica, Trinidad, and other islands in the West Indies, young men, the sons of colonists in comfortable circumstances and with the prospect of having a little capital when they reach their majority, become overseers on coffee, cocoa, or sugar estates with the object of ultimately becoming agriculturists on their own account. But we find no such tendency in British Guiana. The same class of Creole youth in this colony supposes that the acceptance of the position of overseer would mean a fall in his social status, and his one aspiration is to get a footing somewhere in the government service.

c. An Agricultural School eventually wins support

De Lisser, *Twentieth Century Jamaica*, 1913

A few miles to the north of Kingston is an institution which has been established but for a few years now—the Hope Farm. It is an agricultural college, and when reporting on it about five years ago, its Director bemoaned the circumstance that while so many of the Jamaica youths of the better working class and peasant-proprietor class were very fond of sitting at a desk with pens stuck prominently behind their ears, they showed no inclination whatever to profit by the opportunities afforded by the government to acquire a good education in scientific agriculture and stock-rearing. Only three years later he was writing in quite a different strain. He then had as many pupils as he could accommodate, and others were applying for admission to the College Farm. The youths were apt learners, good workers—altogether he was pleased with them. He had a little misjudged the class he had written about, though by no means wittingly.

d. The value set on agricultural education in elementary schools

Report of Inspector of Schools in British Guiana, 1903

Agriculture has now been one of the extra subjects since March 1901, and although the text books in use (*Blackie's Tropical Readers*, Books I and II) are used in a large number of schools as reading books for the three highest standards, yet it is disappointing to find so few children presented for examination. If the grant for reading in the upper standards were reduced from $1.38 to $1, and the grant for agriculture increased from $1 to $1.38, schoolmasters might be induced to pay more attention to this subject, but under a reapplication of grants it would be well to make provision for more thorough instruction by making a condition for earning the maximum grant that schools should be furnished with pots and boxes, or where possible a small garden for the purpose of demonstrating and giving object lessons on the growth of plants and the nature of soils.

e. Agricultural societies extend their work

Olivier, *Jamaica the Blessed Island*, 1936

The establishment of local branch societies had been intended, but did not at first make much progress. One travelling instructor was employed, ... and an instructor in bee-keeping. The Society took steps to promote and extend the manufacture of Jippa-Jappa (Jamaica Panama) hats, a strictly local industry, by distributing the fibre plant in suitable districts and by holding classes.

The branch societies slowly grew; they began to invite the presence of the travelling instructor at their meetings and for visits to members' holdings. Two, and then three, part-time instructors were added. More and more instructors, to be assigned to particular districts, had to be found and worked on full time. ...

The journal became popular, articles in it were read and discussed at meetings. Reports of branch meetings began to appear in the newspapers. Correspondence with the Central office increased steadily.

	Direct Members	Branches	Branch Members	Agricultural Instructors
In 1897 there were	364	6 with	300	1
In 1910 there were	500	63 with	3500	11

The work of the instructors is the Society's most influential function. They attend all meetings of branches, report to the office the attendance and the subjects discussed, give addresses on technical topics of current importance, and generally deal with local agricultural interests. They assist in the work of Agricultural Loan Banks, and help to establish them.

13. Improvement of public sanitation which took place in the later years of the nineteenth century, and the application of new knowledge about tropical diseases made the West Indies healthier to live in. The population increased at a rapid rate.

a. The death rate reduced

Lamont, 'The West Indian Recovery', *The Contemporary Review*, February 1912

Another factor in the new prosperity of the British West Indies is undoubtedly the surprisingly rapid improvement in the sanitation of the towns, and in the healthiness of the islands generally. . . . Vigorous and sustained campaigns against the mosquito have succeeded in practically eliminating yellow fever, and in greatly diminishing the prevalence of malaria, the twin scourges of the tropics in olden days. The death-rate of West Indian towns can now stand comparison with that of almost any European cities.

b. Jamaica's population increases

De Lisser, *Twentieth Century Jamaica*, 1913

The population is increasing at the rate of more than thirteen thousand a year, we may safely conclude that by the close of the second decade of this century—that by the year 1920—the people of Jamaica will number nearly if not quite a million. And they will continue to increase long after that date, for the colony's birth-rate is one of the highest in the world, while its death-rate is under twenty-two per thousand of the inhabitants. Its health conditions are steadily improving, year by year some further step is taken in the way of sanitation, and the gospel of personal cleanliness is more persistently preached. . . . Every step towards such improvement will directly benefit the working classes, who more than any other are affected by what is bad or backward in the conditions of the present.

c. Some diseases persist

Wood Report, 1922

The general conditions of health and sanitation in the West Indies are not yet satisfactory. The vital statistics taken over a period of years reveal a rate of mortality, more especially among infants, that is far too high.

Thanks to strict quarantine regulations, yellow fever is now unknown in the islands, where fifty years ago or even less its annual toll was heavy. There remain, however, malaria, dysentery, hookworm, yaws, typhoid, tuberculosis and venereal diseases. . . .

The problem of infantile mortality, largely the result of ignorance and apathy on the part of parents, is being tackled in several colonies by energetic committees of ladies who are interesting themselves in the matter. . . . Baby Saving Leagues have been organised, and I hope before long they will be established in every colony. Where established they are already showing appreciable results; for instance, the medical report for St. Kitts for this year shows a reduction of infantile mortality of 25 per cent., although here, as elsewhere, the task is rendered difficult by the high percentage of illegitimate births, the primitive character of social standards, and unhealthy housing conditions.

14. West Indians first emigrated in large numbers to Panama to work on the cutting of the canal. Then they went to Central America and to the United States, until they were stopped in the nineteen-twenties.

a. Migration to Panama for higher wages

Olivier, *Jamaica, the Blessed Island*, 1936

When the United States Government resumed the construction of th. canal [in 1904], emigration thither revived, and when I was in Jamaica there were between forty and fifty thousand Jamaicans in the Canal Zone. These men were earning 3/4d. to 4/- a day, whereas in Jamaica they would have been earning 1/6d. or perhaps 2/-. The wages on the canal were not limited by considerations of profit. The builders were determined to get the work done; they had the United States Treasury to finance them and they were prepared to pay whatever was necessary to obtain the labour they needed. A Jamaican planter could not pay more than he would recover in the sale of his produce.

b. Migration to Central America

Annual Report of the Isthmian Canal Commission, 1913–14.

Apparently these West Indians who have been accustomed to the high wages and higher standards of living prevalent on the Canal Zone, have not chosen to return to their homes in the islands, but have chosen to seek employment on construction work in other fields. Over 2,000 were sent to Honduras and thousands of others have gone to Costa Rica and Bocas del Toro.

c. The end of migration creates grave problems

British Guiana Daily Chronicle, 4 September 1924

We have seen it stated that upwards of 1,000 persons emigrated annually from Barbados to the United States; we have also noted that Trinidad claimed an exodus in one year of 3,000 while Jamaica complains that there is an annual drain of 1,500 souls from that island, not to reckon the thousands who flock to Cuba annually to reap the harvests, and some of whom return. The drain from the lesser islands of Grenada, St Lucia and the Leeward Islands is quite as appreciable; and with the sudden damming up of this flow a serious outlook has to be contemplated. The West Indian islands may be regarded as developed to their full, under the present fiscal system of the United Kingdom. We do not by this mean to convey that every square rod of land is cultivated in any of them, save only perhaps Barbados; but that they have reached the normal extent of their development must be conceded by all as is evidenced by their emigration statistics.

d. Development works might save the situation

Grenada 'West Indian', 30 August 1924

A serious problem will soon force itself on the governments of the West Indies with regard to conditions of work for the people of the West Indies. The door of the United States is barred; emigration to Cuba is threatened with prohibition; Maracaibo offers no good opportunity; there might be no quarter to turn for help in the future. Unless well-considered development works are started, there is likely to be great social ferment in these islands.

15. After the First World War West Indians were critical of the social and economic policies of the colonial administration. Criticism became more intense with the depression in trade which severely affected the living standards of town and estate workers.

a. **Two views on the achievements of the colonial administration**

(i) *Speech of A. R. C. Lockhart in Roseau,* 2 October 1921

In Dominica, Crown colony government is charged with causing all activities to stagnate. Ladies and Gentlemen: I congratulate you on being here tonight in such large numbers. . . . The time has come when we can no longer submit to the manifest disadvantages, and humiliations of Crown colony rule, (loud cheers) and are resolved to have a voice in the making of the laws we have to obey, and the imposition of the taxes we have to pay. (cheers) . . . We see the evils of the present system everywhere in the colony, and they can be summed up in the word 'stagnation'. (Hear, hear.) Stagnation in trade and industry from the want of adequate communications either by land or sea, stagnation in the provision of educational facilities, stagnation in every public social service—in sanitation, in medical care of the labouring class in the country districts, and in organised charity for the disabled and sick poor. As in the case of every man, so is every institution approved or condemned by its works.

(ii) St. Johnston, *A Colonial Governor's Note Book,* 1936

An ex-governor lists the work he did in Antigua at the beginning of the thirties. My address was well received, and I may say, now, six years afterwards, that no less than seven out of the eleven projects I had touched upon were brought about, chiefly through the help of the Colonial Development Fund. These were Housing, Land Settlement, Water Supplies, partial assistance to Agriculture in a Gyrotiller, a Bacterial Laboratory, a Health Campaign under a specialist, and a new Hospital for Lepers. The Colonial Development authorities rejected my schemes for roads and for railway extensions (I think the idea that these would be merely bolstering up an inevitably moribund sugar industry seized their minds, which I considered rather a short-sighted policy, but I may have been wrong); while my scheme for improved schools was ruled to be outside their jurisdiction. I should add that if my roads scheme had been accepted it would have found ordinary employment for a great number of people who desperately needed it in the following two years, instead of special grants for 'relief' having to be made by the Imperial Exchequer, and it would also have ended the continual complaints that were levelled—(by people who did not realise that road-construction needs special funds)—against the government for 'neglect of the public roads'.

b. An official suggests primary school education has stood still for thirty years

Report of the Commissioner of Education, British Guiana, 1925

The first impression which the primary schools make on the mind of the visitor is that they have not been altered in any important respect for at least thirty years. The buildings, the furniture, the books, and the slates all suggest the eighties or nineties of last century. The curriculum has, no doubt, been modified in certain directions, but the modifications are too few and feeble to dissipate the general atmosphere of late Victorianism.

The sanitary conditions of the majority of schools are rightly condemned by medical and enlightened lay opinion. There is no systematic physical training, and a large number of schools have not sufficient space, either indoors or outdoors, to carry out this branch of education. No serious attempt is made to provide any manual instruction at any stage of the child's school life. Very few schools have furniture suitable for infant hand-work; and at the other end of the scale there is neither accommodation.

staff nor apparatus provided for the purpose of introducing the elder boys to wood-work or any other craft, or the elder girls to cookery, mothercraft, or any of the necessary duties of women in the home.

The evil results of these material defects are intensified by another factor which is even more important—the employment of unqualified and under-paid teachers, who are a danger to the schools and the community. . . . If an assistant teacher is now, with the cost of living at its present high level, worth only from $8 to $15 a month to the community, he or she is unfit to mould the minds and characters of the next generation of citizens.

c. Responsibility of Church and State in providing school facilities is not clearly defined in British Guiana

Report of the Commissioner of Education, British Guiana, 1925

My objections to the present methods of administration do not prevent me from appreciating to the full the great services which the churches have rendered to education in the past. I appreciate, also, the fact that it will be a long time before the Commissioner of Education can hope to find else-where than in the churches any organised body of public opinion which will take more than a languid interest in educational progress. But the present insanitary condition of many schools, and the general lack of furniture and equipment, are due to the fact that each party—the churches and the state —has been able to prove to its own entire satisfaction that the responsibility rested upon the other. In the meantime the physical welfare of the children has been lost sight of. It is essential, therefore, that in the future the rela-tions of the two parties should be clearly defined, and that each should accept full responsibility within its own sphere.

d. Reforms will cost money

Report of the Commissioner of Education, British Guiana, 1925

Like the law, education seeks to provide for each wrong an appropriate remedy, but the costs must be paid in both instances. The introduction of practical work into the infant school system, the establishment of central schools for the elder children (where education can be conducted on practical and modern lines), of a technical school for 'vocational training', and of a training institute for teachers, the provision of domestic and other forms of science teaching for girls, the improvement of the physical conditions of the schools, and the guarantee of an adequate pay to a properly trained and qualified teacher, will all cost money.

e. *Cipriani accuses the administration of building a golf course in Trinidad before a T.B. sanatorium*

Cipriani in the Legislative Council, 1929

The government know—it is no secret—the terrible toll taken of the labouring classes by tuberculosis and ankylostomiasis (hookworm) in this colony. The government also know what are the remedial and preventive measures, but what have they done besides making their usual empty promises in the past, as they are willing to make in the future, and will make again this morning? . . . I happened to discuss with him (the governor) the necessity of erecting a sanatorium, and reminded him of the promise . . . that there would be no golf course on the St. James' pasture until the sanatorium was erected. There has been no meeting of the Tuberculosis Association called since. The golf course exists, but the sanatorium has not yet been started and possibly never will, unless we, the people of this colony, bring sufficient pressure on the government to make them realise what their responsibility is, not only to the classes, but to the masses of the labouring people of this colony.

f. *Garvey campaigns for election on a programme of social reforms*

Nembhard, *Report of an election speech*, January 1930

In campaigning, he was doing so in the interest of the entire island of Jamaica, in that its economical conditions were so poor that there was need for someone with the ability of a statesman to bring about legislation to relieve the bad conditions.

Great need existed for a minimum wage, an 8-hour working day, better housing conditions, government development of Crown lands, free high school education.

He was not preaching hate and prejudice, because he loved and regarded all the people in Jamaica. There were good white men and bad white men and good Negroes and bad Negroes.

16. Trade unions were organised soon after the First World War, but generally they were weak. Many workers were without bargaining strength and were poorly paid. Unions did not have the full protection of the law and were distrusted by the governments and the employers. Trade union leaders were often active in politics.

a. The wages of domestic servants and teachers compared

British Guiana Daily Chronicle, 13 July 1919

A glance at the Commissioner's Report for 1918 will show that there are seven assistants at present receiving between one and two dollars monthly, a truly magnificent sum for nearly thirty hours per week. Twenty odd enjoy a pittance of between two and three dollars a month, while the vast majority average about four dollars monthly. The new Code provides for the abolition of this disgraceful state of affairs for it lays down that no uncertified assistant shall receive less than five dollars a month. Even then the lot of this class of worker will still be worse than that of a domestic servant. A cook for instance receives often five dollars monthly, her food and shelter. This many give to their house servants, yet all the State has to offer to women who are responsible for the adequate instruction of our children is an amount not even as large as the wages of the ordinary domestic.

b. Carpenters, members of a union, ask for more pay

Circular letter to proprietors of houses and building contractors, 21 September 1919

We, the undersigned carpenters of the city of Georgetown are members of the British Guiana Labour Union, humbly crave your indulgence and ask your kind consideration of the following:—

That since the advent of the great war which has revolutionised the whole world and which has caused necessaries of life and tools to be increased in prices to about 250 per cent, we have been suffering immensely, and although there is at present an abatement of same yet the prices still remain high. We are unable to live on our present emoluments, and to eke out an existence under such circumstances is a miracle and can be better imagined than described, as the majority of us have our wives and children, mothers, fathers, and other dependants to support, also rents to pay. Every department of labour has applied for and received an increase in wages, and shorter working hours and we the carpenters have never before approached you in any way whatever, and in doing so now, we feel justified.

c. Cipriani sees a Volunteer Regiment as a threat to collective bargaining

Cipriani in the Legislative Council, 1930

There are no privates in this little army. It is a battalion of employers; a battalion made up of prominent cocoa planters and sugar planters. All of them are well-known gentlemen, and white men; and these men have been formed into that band for the purpose of quelling any attempt at industrial unrest. They have been given the privilege to use arms and ammunition without any licence being paid on these arms. Since 1919 they have been enjoying (not to say abusing) the privilege afforded them. Those gentlemen who form that 2nd Battalion—I don't suppose your Excellency has been let into this secret yet—are known as the *Vigilantes*, and those *Vigilantes* are for the purpose of being called out to put down industrial unrest, or, more simply put, a collective bargaining of Labour for a living wage. If tomorrow Labour bargained for a right wage, or attempted to bargain, or argued with their employers, the *Vigilantes* would be called out.

d. *Working men in Dominica urged to organise and campaign for the adult franchise*

Speech of Cipriani in Dominica, 1932

It is the inalienable right of every man to live in and on his country. Working men in this country, and in every part of the British West Indies only exist, they do not live, and it is only a question of time when as a working unit he must go down and disappear, unless he pulls himself together and demands his rights and privileges. And if you are to demand them, and get them there is no hope except in the formation of a Working men's Association in this island of yours. . . .

I put it to you this way, that when those who now lead you shall have gone, you must have something in your hands with which to fight, and the only weapon you can use with success and efficiency is adult franchise, which will give you the privilege of returning to the Legislature and administration of your colonies, those you know will represent your interests and take care of you. . . . I want you to realise the time has come to think for yourselves, do not let us think for you all the time. Discuss it in your sordid, miserable homes, homes which are a disgrace and blight upon our civilisation, and there try and see whether you cannot figure out this for yourselves, and realise that in adult franchise alone lies our salvation.

e. *Responsible government as well as trade unions is necessary to protect the living conditions of the workers*

West Indian speaker for the League of Coloured Peoples, London, 15 November 1938

The most urgent need of the working people throughout the West Indies is the improvement of their economic condition through an immediate increase in wages and the provision of machinery whereby they might protect the meagre right acquired.

Such machinery is all the more essential in view of fluctuation of prices and markets by reason of external influences. Failing that the existence of a West Indian worker must always remain precarious. . . .

If the final solution of the evil of low wages and consequent poverty, and consequent bad housing, and consequent ill health and malnutrition, and consequent backwardness, can only be solved by the initiative of the ordinary working man, then trade union organisation is by no means sufficient.

The voice of the oppressed should be heard in the highest council, and the governmental system should be saved from reaction by the election, in whole or in the greater part, of members of the legislature.

17. There were riots, with some loss of life, throughout the West Indies in the latter part of the nineteen-thirties. Afterwards the British Government sent a Royal Commission to investigate social and economic conditions in the West Indies. The evidence given by individuals and groups exposed the kind of life led by the poor and unemployed.

a. A riot described by the Governor of the Leewards

St. Johnston, *A Colonial Governor's Note Book*, 1936

On the twenty-ninth of January, while we were giving a big garden party at Government House at St. Kitts, where I happened to be on an inspection visit, there suddenly flared up a full-sized riot, in the unexpected way that these things happen in the West Indies.

The reaping season for the sugar-cane crop had started the day before, and although there had been the usual annual 'preliminary discussions' among the labourers as to the rate of wages, all had turned out peacefully to work. All, that is, except a few malcontents who still advocated the strike. I drove round the island an hour or two after this to see the state of things for myself. At that time all was apparently quiet. But proceeding in the opposite direction to me a dozen or so of the strikers enlisted a drummer at their head and started to march round the island, calling to their ranks the labourers from each estate as they passed. The mob swelled like a snowball, and finally, taking confidence in their numbers and getting excited, proceeded to excesses. At one estate they severely assaulted an elderly white planter who had always been particularly kind to his labourers, and at another place a planter had to defend himself from a bad fusillade of stones by using a shot-gun.

The mob then became unmanageable, and the magistrate and the head of the police came to Government House to ask me to call out the Defence Force. This was a very serious step to take, but I had to come to a quick decision, and after a few minutes' careful thought and many questions as to possibilities I signed the order. I also sent a wireless message out for a warship, though I knew that none could reach us for two days. And I ascertained that guards were being posted on the wireless station and at other vital points. Finally, I issued an order closing all the liquor shops at once. . . .

It was just as well that I took the decision to call out the armed troops to support the small body of police, as within an hour, and as dusk was approaching, the situation at the entrance to the town became grave.

The Riot Act was twice read, and the mob still refusing to disperse the only thing left to do was to order rifle-fire. Three men were killed and eight wounded, but regrettable as this was it undoubtedly saved the town and thousands of innocent people from the menace of burning to their houses and violence to their lives.

b. An ex-governor connects the riots with poor prices for sugar abroad and low wages at home

Olivier, *Speech in the House of Lords*, 23 February 1938

I desire to draw attention to matters to which I think this House and the country generally ought to have paid much more attention long ago—namely, the general situation in the West Indies which gives rise to these occasional riots. . . . All through the West Indies the same conditions exist as are the fundamental cause of the difficulties which have occurred in Trinidad. There have been what are called labour troubles in almost all West Indian colonies this year, in British Guiana, in Trinidad, in Barbados, in St. Vincent, St. Lucia, St. Kitts, and Jamaica, all arising from the same cause—namely, that the British public do not pay sufficient for their sugar to enable the West Indian industry to pay decent wages to the workers. That has been the case for a long time, and is going to be the case, I am afraid, for a good time longer. That state of things has been in force for a great many years.

c. The Colonial Secretary, Trinidad, claims that government, oil, and sugar could pay fair wages

Colonial Secretary, Trinidad, in the Legislative Council, July 1937

While we all deplore the loss of life and the sacrifice that these disturbances have entailed I feel that we are entering on a new era in the history of Trinidad, more particularly in regard to relations between government and industry on the one hand and labour on the other.

Almost a year ago today the Wages Advisory Board submitted their report to Government. . . . The grievances and hardships that prevailed in this colony were set out clearly in the report and yet the members of the Board were not able to suggest any real comprehensive remedy for those grievances. . . .

In the meantime the cost of living has risen and on the other hand Government and many industries in this colony have prospered. The result is that the situation which was serious at the time when the Wages Advisory Board reported has become aggravated.

In the past we have had to salve our consciences with humbug and we have had to satisfy labour with platitudes. Those days have gone by; we can no longer say to labour we recognise your hardships but we cannot afford to remedy them. We have got to look at the matter from a different aspect. Today Government is collecting large revenues and the oil companies are paying big dividends. Even sugar is now to a considerable extent more than paying its way. . . .

There can be no question today of these three employing groups, Government, the oil industry, and the sugar industry being able to pay a fair wage and to provide decent conditions for its labour.

d. *Wages too low for even bare subsistence*

Memo. of Nevis Agricultural and Commercial Society, October 1938

We find that the minimum requirements for a labourer amount to one shilling and threepence per diem, as shown below:—

Breakfast — Bread 2d., sugar 1d.

Dinner — Meal or flour 2d., potatoes 1d., meat or fish 2d., lard or butter 1d.

Supper — Rice 2d., peas 1d., meat or fish 2d., lard or butter 1d.

In the above estimate there is no provision made for house repair, clothes or for protective nourishing foods such as milk or eggs. Nor is allowance made for household necessities such as oil, matches, soap, starch, etc. or for church and society dues, provision for sickness, medical fees. . . .

The chief industry that gives employment for a period of a few days per week for two or three months in the year, is cotton. Sugar-cane cultivation provides very little employment under the present system. Men who are fortunate in getting employment earn one shilling, the women, sixpence per diem. It is therefore evident that even in the case of the employed income falls far short of bare, minimum subsistence.

e. *The extent of assistance to the unemployed*

(i) *Evidence of Secretary, Board of Supervision, Jamaica,* 11 November 1938

In Jamaica

Chairman: And there is no unemployment relief here?

Answer: No.

Chairman: Then how do they carry on under those conditions?

Answer: God only knows. I would like to make one qualification in regard to that. The only people who are not only sick and are given relief are women, and they are given relief because they have young children, and those are the only able-bodied section of the population who are given relief at the present time.

(ii) St. Johnston, *A Colonial Governor's Note Book*, 1936

In the Leewards. Relief operations continued, and thousands of out-of-work labourers were temporarily employed on the roads and on excavating reservoirs. We tried to avoid any actual semblance of a 'dole', as we knew that once that system came into vogue it would be very difficult to drop it again. Genuine cases of distress were, however, dealt with through the Board of Guardians and the clergy, though much sifting of the wheat from the tares was necessary. One hardly legible begging letter I received stated that the writer was 'a awfunt'. After enquiry it was discovered to be perfectly true, but the orphan happened to be over sixty years of age! I also had one or two anonymous letters threatening my life for not immediately distributing among them the money that, they stated, had been sent out by the English Parliament as a gift for them! It was difficult to explain to ignorant labourers the conditions attached by the 'Treasury' to the loan-in-aid, and that neither Imperial nor local moneys were intended as free gifts.

f. Labourers cannot afford medical attention

Evidence of a St. Kitts Unofficial Member, 27 December 1938

A labourer who earns 10d. or 1/- a day and living five or six miles away from the doctor has to pay six or seven shillings, and then there is medicine which comes to about two or three shillings, and that is ten shillings for his first visit. The doctor's diagnosis may be wrong and he has to be recalled, so that it costs the patient another ten shillings and that makes twenty shillings. How often could a labourer call a doctor? He calls him at the first or else when he sees death is coming in order to get a death certificate. They find it extremely hard.

g. Unofficial members claim that houses can be built only at the expense of the government

Memo. of St. Kitts Unofficial Members, 9 November 1938.

It will serve no useful purpose to describe the hovels in which most of the agricultural labourers and many of the domestic servants live, nor to moralise upon the consequences of living in such surroundings; it is sufficient to remark that they are a standing menace to the general health of the community, and that in these surroundings it is almost impossible to practise cleanliness and hygiene. These hovels should be replaced by structures in which the owners take some pride, but this can only be done if the State will assume the responsibility for erecting them, and will bear a large proportion of the cost.

h. A Jamaican trade union lists matters requiring laws to safeguard the interests of its members

Memo of Bustamante Trade Union, 18 November 1938

Amendment to *Law 37 of 1919 Related to Tradesmen's Unions:*—

  (i) Amendment to the law to legalise picketing.

  (ii) Insertion of a section to the law for the protection of unions and members thereof in the incidence of strikes.

Social legislation required for the following:—

  (i) Minimum wage.

  (ii) Maximum working hours for all workers.

  (iii) Sick leave with pay for weekly and monthly employees.

  (iv) Old age pension, health and unemployment insurances.

  (v) Public prosecution for poor persons.

  (vi) Protection for hourly and daily workers who by the nature of their work are apt to contract infectious or contagious diseases in places such as hospitals, sanitary departments of government.

18. Since the end of the Second World War West Indian governments have passed many laws to regulate working and living conditions. Social reform has also been an integral part of national plans, although it will take some time to eradicate poor standards in education, public health and housing.

a. Legislation in Barbados since 1938

Ten Year Plan for Barbados, 1946–56

An articulate public opinion is now ready to express grievances and to insist upon the reform of many of our social and political institutions, although unfortunately it is often not sufficiently informed to be able to understand the machinery of government and not sufficiently educated to be able to form an intelligent opinion as to the direction which the reforms should take.

This movement, which gained added impetus from the appointment and report of the West India Royal Commission, has already led to a substantial measure of social reform. The lowering of the franchise in terms of the acts passed in 1943 and 1944 resulted in a much greater representation in the House of Assembly of the lower and middle classes who now wield a powerful influence upon the social and economic life of the colony. The general trend of progress can be seen from such measures as the establishment of the Peasants' Loan Bank, the introduction of a school nutrition scheme, the fostering of labour organisations and the enactment of much social and labour legislation, such as *The Old Age Pension Act*, 1937; *The Trade Disputes (Arbitration and Enquiry) Act*, 1938; *The Trade Union Act*, 1939; *The Labour Department Act*, 1943; *The Workmen's Compensation Act*, 1943; *The Wages Board Act*, 1943; *The Education (Amendment) Act*, 1943; *The Shops Act*, 1945. The introduction into the Legislature of the Factory Bill in 1944 and the Housing and Town and Country Planning Bill in 1945, although they have not yet been passed, mark still further important steps forward.

b. Social reform as part of the Jamaican National Plan

National Plan for Jamaica, 1957–67

Within the framework of material and financial advance there are the necessary ingredients for a better basis for social conditions. This is therefore the Plan's second major emphasis.

The chief concerns here are with the laying of a good island-wide basis for health, sanitation, housing, and perhaps even more basic to effective social development, for education.

(i) *Health and Sanitation*. A healthy population will reduce the wastes which now occur due to incidence of disease, ignorance of health precautions and inadequate nutrition. The health programme is aimed at bringing preventive medicine to the people, thus reducing the need for hospitalisation; at large scale campaigns for eradication of debilitating diseases such as malaria, T.B. and yaws; at supplemental feeding for mothers and young children, and provision of midday meals for children in school; and education in good dietary habits. Important for these ends, as many diseases occur through use of polluted water, is the provision of safe, adequate and readily available water supplies throughout the island. There are big schemes to cover the densely populated areas and minor schemes for the provision of tanks in many smaller communities.

(ii) *Housing Assistance*. A major part of the Plan is for rural housing which is a logical continuation of the work of the organisation established to provide prefabricated homes for hurricane sufferers. The efficiency developed in that field is to be projected into rural housing schemes under which frames and roofs for rural housing units will be provided, with the labour for completing the house contributed by the owner/occupier; this will make it possible to build a comfortable small house for a very low cost. These will then be available either as part of a rural housing scheme or within the framework of the Farm Development, Land Settlement and other schemes. Without adequate housing, on or near the land to be worked, rural efficiency will suffer greatly.

At the same time the well established Owner/Occupier, Self-Help and Indigent Housing Schemes will be continued. Assistance will also be given in selected cases to private builders who are catering for middle income housing requirements.

(iii) *Education*. The spread of literacy and basic general education through the programme . . . will provide the vehicle for greater social, political and cultural awareness at all levels of society. This formal educational programme will be reinforced by the work of the various social welfare services, with programmes for civic and cultural education, and for training in group participation among adults in the backward areas.

The education proposals allied to the agriculture proposals form the core of the Plan. To provide an opportunity for every Jamaican child to have five years of elementary schooling is a major revolution in educational policy. From this decision flow many others which accept the need for a greater supply of teachers, a greater demand for secondary and higher education, which when met will in itself increase the supply of teachers, and the need to meet technical and vocational demands to a greater extent than heretofore.

c. Social services rival economic projects in bids for public money

Independence brochure of 'The Nation' Trinidad, 31 August 1962

The so-called 'revolution of rising expectations' and a rapidly rising population make it necessary that constant provision be made for expenditure on social capital so that there is always the problem of how much to spend on directly productive projects offering quick returns, *vis-à-vis* those with a larger gestation period and more social in nature.

This is a problem always faced by governments which have at all times to take cognisance of the welfare of the society or community and cannot think as the supposedly 'economic man' does merely in terms of maximising economic returns. Both types of investment social and economic are important if as one authority put it 'the main goal of economic policy should be to create a productive structure compatible with the new social principles and capable of supporting and perpetuating democracy'.

We as a nation have to think seriously about all these factors and try to guide and work for our country in such a manner that in time we may be able to shed the term under-developed as it is presently applied by breaking the barriers to economic growth.

7

Government and Politics

A. REPRESENTATIVE AND NON-REPRESENTATIVE
FORMS OF GOVERNMENT

1. Colonies were settled in the name of the King and he appointed Governors and other officials for the islands. In England he had the help of his Councillors in supervising English trade and plantations abroad. Appointments were often made for the King by these English Councillors but many of the people selected then sent deputies to do their work in the West Indies.

a. Charles I appoints Warner his Lieutenant over four islands

Letters Patent granted by Charles I, 13 September 1625

The said Thomas Warner hath lately discovered four several islands in the main ocean towards the continent of America, the one called the island of St. Christophers, one other the island of Nevis, one other the island of Barbados and the other the island of Montserrat which said islands are possessed and inhabited only by savage and heathen people and are not, nor at any time of the discovery were, in the possession or under the Government of any Christian Prince, State or Potentate. . . .

Know ye therefore that we, in consideration of the premises, and to the intent that the said Ralph Merifield and Thomas Warner may be encouraged and the better enabled to proceed in a work so likely to tend to the propagation of Christian Religion, the honour of us, and good of our people, do by these presents take as well the said islands as all the inhabitants there. . . . And all lands, goods and other things within the said islands, or any other neighbour islands inhabited or possessed, or hereafter to be inhabited or possessed, into our Royal protection.

And of our especial grace have given and granted to the said Thomas Warner during our pleasure, the custody of the aforesaid islands . . . together with full power and authority for us and in our name and as our

Lieutenant, to order and dispose of any lands or other things within the said islands; and to govern, rule and order all and singular persons which now are or hereafter shall be abiding in the said islands, as well our natural born subjects as the natives and savages, by such good and reasonable orders, articles and ordinances as shall be most requisite and needful at the discretion of him the said Thomas Warner.

And all such as shall disobey, to chastise, convert and punish according to their faults and demerits. And also with force and strong hand to repress and annoy all such as shall in hostile manner attempt to possess or invade the said islands. And generally to do all such acts as shall or may tend to the establishment of our Government settling a colony or plantation.

b. *The King appoints a new group of councillors to manage trade and plantations*

Act of the Privy Council, 1675

The Right Honourable the Lord Keeper of the Great Seal of England this day acquainted the Board by His Majesty's command that His Majesty, having been pleased to dissolve and extinguish his late Council of Trade and Foreign Plantations . . ., had thought fit to commit what was under their inspection and management to the committee of this Board appointed for matters relating to trade and his foreign plantations, viz. The Lord Treasurer, . . . *and twenty others.*

And H.M. did particularly order that the Lord Privy Seal, the Earl of Bridgewater, Earl of Carlisle, Earl of Craven, Viscount Fauconberg, Viscount Halifax, Lord Berkeley, Mr. Vice-Chamberlain, and Mr. Chancellor of the Exchequer should have the immediate care and intendancy of those affairs, in regard they had been formerly conversant and acquainted therewith . . .; and that their Lordships meet constantly at least once a week and make report to His Majesty in Council of their results and proceedings from time to time; and that they have power to send for all books, papers, and other writings concerning any of His Majesty's said plantations.

c. *The Provost-Marshal, Jamaica, names his deputy*

Duke of Newcastle to Governor of Jamaica, 1730

His Majesty having been graciously pleased to grant the office of Provost Marshal of Jamaica to Mr. Forbes who has been many years in my service, and for whom I have a particular regard, I must beg that you will be so good as to give him your assistance that he may enjoy the full benefit of that employment, in order to which you will be pleased to countenance Mr. Edmund Hyde, whom he has appointed his Deputy; which I shall acknowledge as a particular obligation.

d. *A governor complains of the way appointments are made*

Governor of Barbados to Lords of Trade and Plantations, July 1691

I must point out the inconvenience of granting out the offices of this island by patent in England. Every office of profit now is no sooner vacant than it is begged for by someone or other in England. Formerly, all offices relating to the island in general were given by the Governor, and the subordinate places by the officials above them; as the Provost Marshal by the judges, and so forth. I know that the King and your Lordships are strangers to the inconvenience of the present practice, and I must point out that it is a disservice to their Majesties, discouragement to Governors and prejudice to the islands.

First it lessens the authority of the government and brings it into contempt. Governors cannot reward merit or ensure the due execution of justice, since they cannot appoint persons whom they know to be qualified, and it is reasonable to suppose that a Governor on the spot can better judge of well qualified persons than people far away in England. Again, the best of the offices are granted to non-residents and enjoyed by three, four and even five farmers and sub-farmers. It must be mere chance if they are executed by qualified men, and it is not unreasonable to believe that such underlings will stoop to base and unworthy practices to make their market out of offices. The Governor has no check upon them.

2. Until the end of the eighteenth century each new British colony had a Council and a House of Assembly which, with the Governor, made laws for the colony. The colonists were anxious to claim their rights as Englishmen and were particularly aggressive in their claims to make their own laws when taxation was involved.

a. *Cromwell's commissioners ratify the form of government in Barbados*

Articles of Surrender, 11 January 1652

That the government of this island be by a Governor, Council, and Assembly, according to the ancient and usual custom here: that the Governor be appointed by the States of England, and from time to time received and obeyed here, the Council be by him chosen, and an Assembly by a free and voluntary election of the freeholders of the island in the several parishes.

b. *The King establishes an Assembly in Dominica*

Royal Proclamation, June 1775

We are desirous that a full and complete Legislature should be established within our said island of Dominica, upon a permanent and lasting foundation, and such regulations made touching the same as may contribute to the happiness, interest and satisfaction of all our good subjects within our said island of Dominica.

It is therefore our Royal will and pleasure that Writs for our said island of Dominica shall be issued in our name for the election of Representatives to serve in the lower House of Assembly for the said island of Dominica.

c. *The Assemblies and the English Government disagree on whether colonists have political and legal privileges by virtue of English birth or by special grant of the King*

(i) *Jamaican Assembly*, 1675

The claim made in Jamaica. Whereas the laws and statutes heretofore made and used in our native country, the Kingdom of England, for the public weal of the same, and all the liberties, immunities and privileges contained therein, have ever been in force, and are belonging unto all His Majesty's liege people within this island as their birthright, and that the same now are, ever were, and ever shall be deemed good and effectual in the law.

(ii) *Lords of Trade and Plantations*, 1679

The claim rejected in England. For as they cannot pretend to further privileges than have been granted to them either by charter, or some solemn act under your Great Seal; so having from the first beginning of that plantation been governed by such instructions as were given by your Majesty unto your Governor, according to the power which your Majesty had originally over them and which you have by no authentic act ever yet parted with; and having never had any other right to Assemblies than from the permission of the Governor and that only temporary and for probation, it is to be wondered how they should presume to provoke your Majesty by pretending a right to that which hath been allowed them merely out of favour . . .; when what your Majesty ordered for a temporary experiment to see what form would best suit with the safety and interest of the island shall be construed to be total resignation of the power inherent in your Majesty, and a devolution of it to themselves and their wills.

d. *No taxation without local consent*

(i) *Articles of Surrender*, January 1652

Barbados. That no taxes, customs, imposts, loans, or excise shall be laid, nor levy made on any inhabitants of this island without their consent in a General Assembly.

(ii) *Judgement of Lord Chief Justice Mansfield, in the case of Campbell* v. *Hall, 1774*

The Chief Justice of England declares that the King could not use his royal prerogative to tax Grenadians after he had promised, by a proclamation, to establish an Assembly. That by letters patent dated July 20, 1764, the King, by virtue of his prerogative, ordered the imposition of a duty of $4\frac{1}{2}$ per cent. on all commodities produced and exported from Grenada from and after September 29, 1764, such duty to take the place of all customs and import duties hitherto collected upon goods imported and exported into and out of the island under the authority of His Most Christian Majesty.

The general question that arises out of all these facts is whether the letters patent under the Great Seal bearing date July 20, 1764, are good and valid to abolish the French duties and in lieu thereof to impose the $4\frac{1}{2}$ per cent. duty above-mentioned. . . .

It has been contended . . . that though the King had sufficient power and authority before October 7, 1763, to do such legislative act, yet before the letters patent of July 20, 1764, he had divested himself of that authority. . . .

After full consideration we are of opinion, that before the letters patent of July 20, 1764, the King had precluded himself from the exercise of a legislative authority over the island of Grenada.

The first and material instrument is the proclamation of October 7, 1763. See what it is that the king there says, with what view, and how he engages himself and pledges his word. '*For the better security of the liberty and property of those who are or shall become inhabitants of our island of Grenada, we have declared by this our proclamation that we have commissioned our governor, as soon as the state and circumstances of the colony will admit, to call an assembly to enact laws.*' With what view is this made? It is to invite settlers and subjects. And why to invite? That they might think their properties more secure if the legislation was vested in an assembly than under a governor and council only.

Next, . . . the proclamation of March 20, 1764, invites them to come in as purchasers; . . . on April 9, 1764, . . . an actual commission is made out to the Governor to call an Assembly as soon as the state of the island would admit thereof. . . .

We therefore think that by the two proclamations and the commission to Governor Melville, the King had immediately and irrecoverably granted to all who were or should become inhabitants or who had, or should acquire property in the island of Grenada, or more generally to all whom it might concern, that the subordinate legislation over the island should be exercised by an assembly with the consent of the Governor and Council, in like manner as in other islands belonging to the King.

Therefore, the abolishing of the duties of the French King and the substituting of this tax in its stead . . . is void. . . . To use the words of Sir Philip Yorke and Sir Clement Wearge, 'It can only now be done, by the assembly of the island, or by an Act of Parliament of Great Britain.'

3. The colonial Assemblies harassed the Governors, the local Councillors and the officials, all of whom they regarded as the King's servants and a threat to their rights as Englishmen to control their own internal affairs.

a. Governors: the men and the work they were supposed to do contrasted by an 18th century critic

Long, *History of Jamaica,* 1774

The Governor is representative of the king in acts of legislature; generalissimo of all the military forces; vice-admiral for the conservation of the rights of Flotsam, Jetson, etc.; and president on trials for piracy; chancellor and keeper of the great seal of the island; judge of probate of wills and . . . in the ecclesiastical court; judge of appeal in the court of errors. . . . A combination of offices, which at first view seem to require such an accomplished education, such a comprehensive power of genius, judgement, memory, and experience, as are almost inconsistent with the limited period of mortal existence, or with the common faculties of the human mind.

What then are we to expect from those governors, whose education and profession have tended more to mislead than instruct them in the knowledge of these so very dissimilar functions. . . . From the commander of a brigade of foot; a gentleman is metamorphosed on a sudden into a grave judge of court. What is to be expected from such judges?

b. *The King allows Assemblies to pay the Governor, but not to use the salary to control him*

Instructions to the Governor of the Leewards, July 1733

Whereas it has been represented that the salary of £1200 sterling per an. which we have heretofore thought fit to allow out of the duty of $4\frac{1}{2}$ p.c. arising in our Leeward Islands for our Governor-in-Chief, is not at present sufficient for his support and the dignity of that our Government, we have taken the same into consideration and are graciously pleased to permit and allow that the respective Assemblies of our said Islands may by any act or acts settle upon you such sum or sums in addition to your salary of £1200 per an. as they shall think proper; . . . provided such sum or sums be settled on you and your successors, or at least on you during the whole time of your government there; and that the same be done by the first respective assemblies of our said islands after your arrival there before they proceed upon any other business.

c. *St. Kitts Assembly find a way to control the pay of officials*

St. Kitts official to Council of Trade and Plantations, 1734

There is another act passed, dated the 7th June, 1732, in St. Christophers, . . . for explaining an Act made in the eighth year of King George I, entitled *an Act for raising an impost on liquors*, which was originally given for support of the Government, and the contingent charges thereof; and out of this cash fund myself and all the rest of the public officers were constantly paid our established fees and salaries after they had been examined by the Governor and Council. Now this fund, by way of their explanation, is appropriated to the use of the forts and fortifications, purposely to take away the power of issuing money by the Governor and Council, and thereby divest the Governor and Council of means to pay the said officers; and all the officers are now actually and solely dependent upon the humour and caprice of the Assembly.

d. *The Assemblies harass Government officials by laws regulating offices and fees*

Attorney-General to the Council of Trade and Plantations, 6 August 1713

I am humbly of opinion that the *Act to prevent any one person from holding two or more offices of profit in Jamaica,* is not fit to have H.M. royal confirmation; it appearing to be designed only for a particular purpose, to deprive Mr. Rigby, Provost-Marshal under Mr. Baker, of the deputation of the office of Secretary, (held by him from Mr. Baker); . . . both the said offices are held, and always have been so by virtue of H.M. Letters Patent, and are properly to be regulated by H.M. directions, and are not incompatible to be held and executed by the same person. Besides, the Act . . . is unreasonable for that many single offices of that island are not sufficient for the maintenance of one person, and where they are not incompatible, there never was any law made before for restraining one person from having two.

e. *Jamaican Assembly refuses to pay for its own defence*

Council of Trade and Plantations to Mr. Secretary Stanhope, 17 February 1716

As for the Assembly of Jamaica, . . . it might have been hoped . . . they would have complied with what H.M. recommended to them . . . and that they would readily have agreed to the repaying what had been advanced by the Governor and Council for the subsisting the late Regiment . . . and the two independent companies now there, and that they would have made further provision for the said two companies. If they do not find some method for discharging this debt it may have very ill consequences, since it will throw the burthen of such debts, which are contracted for their own defence, and therefore ought to be supported by themselves, upon H.M. and because it will ruin the credit of the Government there in such a manner, that upon the most pressing and extraordinary occasions no man would venture to advance anything upon it. However till the Assembly can be brought to a due temper in this matter, there does not at present occur to us any other method than what the Governor has proposed for the discharge of that debt, viz: that H.M. be pleased to give particular order for its being paid out of the first and readiest of his revenue in that island.

f. The Assemblies attack the Governors and Councils to get exclusive control over the voting and spending of the public monies

(i) *Governor of Barbados to Council of Trade and Plantations*, 1712

In Barbados. The Council and Assembly have had a great dispute about the Excise Bill. I did all I could to accommodate the matter, but some here aim at nothing less than to make themselves an independent people, and to that end endeavour all they can to divest the administration here of all the Queen's power and authority and to lodge it in the Assembly. This project hath been a long time on foot and a great progress hath been made in it, for they have extorted so many powers from my predecessors that there is now hardly enough left to keep the peace, much less to maintain the decent respect and regard that is due the Queen's servant.

(ii) *Governor of Jamaica to Council of Trade and Plantations*, 1716

In Jamaica. Were I not able to assign particular instances in a strict literal sense of the Assemblies assuming the executive part of the government, the whole course of their proceedings might well justify that expression. . . . In particular, their order to muster the soldiers, and visit fortifications by their own authority; their appointing officers to collect the money raised by them and making large appointments out of it; their refusing to admit the Council to mend money bills or confer with them; their soliciting bill, in which the whole business of the government is put into the hands of a few of themselves to be transacted without the privity of the Governor and Council; their raising money by subscriptions to support that power here; with some extraordinary acts of oppression, which appear upon the minutes, are . . . instances which amount to an assuming in good measure the executive part of the government.

g. *Jamaican Assemblies find ways of doing no public business when they cannot have their way*

(i) *Memorial of Jamaica residents to Council of Trade in vindication of the Assembly of Jamaica,* 21 February 1716

Right claimed to adjourn without Governor's permission. It has been urged in Jamaica in disfavour of the island and probably reached your Lordships, that the Assembly dissolved in Feb., 1713, adjourned themselves for a month without his Lordship's leave. . . . It is humbly apprehended to be warranted by their charter of government whose constant language has successively directed that the laws and usage of the Assemblies of that island are to be assimilated to the laws and usage in England. For should it be the misfortune of the island to be lopped of that privilege, they become subject to the pleasure of a Governor, and in consequence are deprived of the freedom of Englishmen.

(ii) *Mr. Secretary Stanhope to the Council of Trade,* April 1717

Right denied. It seems reasonable that the Governor should be instructed to support the prerogative of the Crown, and to insist that the Assemblies have no right to adjourn themselves, otherwise than *de die in diem* except over Sundays, without leave of the Governor.

(iii) *Governor of Jamaica to Council of Trade,* 4 June 1733

Increasing the quorum for doing business. These two last sessions have proved very fruitless, the Council having made the necessary amendments to some bills and rejected others . . . (from the Assembly), which produced several indecent messages. . . . Thus nothing having been done to purpose in the Legislature for the defence or ease of the subject in a time of imminent danger, (the Assembly) applied again and again for a recess, resolved to do no more business this session, and for that purpose reduced the quorum to five members for adjourning, and increased that for doing business to twenty-five and so separated, which obliged me by the advice of the Council on Monday the 28th of May last to prorogue them to the third of July next.

h. Assemblies find ways to evade the review and disallowance of their laws by the King's Council in England

Council of Trade and Plantations to the House of Lords, 23 January 1734

All these colonies, however, by their several constitutions, have the power of making laws for their better government and support, provided they be not repugnant to the Laws of Great Britain, nor detrimental to their mother country; and these laws, when they have regularly passed the Council and Assembly of any province, and received the Governor's assent, become valid in that province, but remain repealable, nevertheless, by H.M. in Council upon just complaint; and do not acquire a perpetual force, unless they are confirmed by H.M. in Council. . . . All the governors of colonies, who act under the King's appointment, ought, within a reasonable time, to transmit home authentic copies of the several acts by them passed, that they may go through a proper examination; but they are sometimes negligent of their duty in this particular, and likewise pass temporary laws for so short continuance, that they have their full effect even before this Board can acquire due notice of them. Some attempts have been made to prevent this pernicious practice; but the annual support of government, in the respective colonies, making it necessary, that laws, for that purpose, should pass from year to year, the Assemblies have frequently endeavoured in those laws, as well as in others of longer duration, to enact propositions repugnant to the laws or interest of Great Britain, of which this Board have never failed to express their dislike to the Crown, when such laws have fallen under their consideration; and many laws have, from time to time been repealed on that account. But, as to such laws as do not directly fall within the above rule, against which no complaint is made, and where the Board are doubtful of the effect they may have; it has always been usual to let them lie by probationary, being still under the power of the Crown to be repealed, in case any inconvenience may arise from them. It has been usual, when a law has contained many just and necessary provisions for the benefit of the colony where it was passed, intermixed with some others liable to objection, to let it lie by, and give notice thereupon to the governor of the province, that it should be repealed, if he did not, within a reasonable time, procure a new law, not liable to the same objections, to be substituted in the place thereof.

4. The Assemblies also challenged the English Parliament whenever it made laws which were to be applied to the West Indies.

a. Barbados rejects the laws of trade made by the Commonwealth Parliament

Declaration of Governor, Council and Assembly, 18 February 1651

They allege that this island was first settled and inhabited at the charges, and by the especial order of the people of England, and therefore ought to be subject to the same nation. It is certain, that we all of us know very well, that we, the present inhabitants of this island, were and still be that people of England, who with great danger to our persons, and with great charge and trouble, have settled this island in its condition, and inhabited the same, and shall we therefore be subjected to the will and command of those that stay at home? Shall we be bound to the government and lordship of a Parliament in which we have no representatives, or persons chosen by us, for there to propound and consent to what might be needful to us, as also to oppose and dispute all that should tend to our disadvantage, and harm? In truth, this would be a slavery far exceeding all that the English nation hath suffered. . . .

And the Government here in subjection, is the nearest model of conformity to that under which our predecessors of the English nation have lived and flourished for above a thousand years. . . .

Wherefore, having rightly considered, we declare, that as we would not be wanting to us all honest means for the obtaining of a continuance of commerce, trade, and good correspondence with our country, so we will not alienate ourselves from those old heroic virtues of true Englishmen, to prostitute our freedom and privileges, to which we are born, to the will and opinion of anyone; neither do we think our number so contemptible, nor our resolution so weak, to be forced or persuaded to so ignoble a submission, and we cannot think, that there are any amongst us, who are so simple, and so unworthily minded, that they would not rather choose a noble death, than forsake their old liberties and privileges.

b. *Slave Registry Bill an infringement of the rights of colonial legislatures*

Resolutions of the Barbados Assembly, 17 January 1816

First. Resolved that this House having received from its agent in London the copy of a Slave Registry Bill lately introduced into the House of Commons, conceives itself most urgently called upon to protest against the infringement which this Bill attempts on the rights of our colonial legislature.

Third. Resolved that although the ostensible object of the Bill is to obtain a registry of slaves, it obviously proposes to attain that by imposing a tax upon every slave proprietor within the colony in manifest violation of that sound and just principle of the British Constitution that 'representation and taxation are inseparable'.

Fifth. Yet to evince the cordial desire which this House feels to co-operate in any measure deemed necessary for carrying into effect the Acts of the Imperial Parliament for abolishing the slave trade, it declares that it is most willing to adopt by an Act of the legislature of this island such parts of the Registry Bill as are compatible with the legitimate rights and local circumstances of the inhabitants of this island.

c. *Powers of House of Commons not superior to those of Houses of Assembly*

The Humble Petition of the Assembly of Jamaica, 12 December 1823

We, Your Majesty's dutiful and loyal subjects, the Assembly of Jamaica, have of late years frequently prayed Your Majesty to take our oppressed state into your Royal consideration. It is with pain that we once more remind Your Majesty of our grievances: . . .

Resolutions have been moved by one of Your Majesty's ministers and agreed to in the Lower House of Parliament, falsely assuming that the labouring population of this island are ill-treated and unhappy, and voluntarily pledging that House to interpose in their behalf with a view to their emancipation.

It is our duty humbly to represent to Your Majesty that we have taken no oath of allegiance to the Imperial Parliament, and that we cannot submit to the degradation of having our internal interests regulated by the Commons of Great Britain, whose powers within that realm are not superior to those which we, the Assembly, have ever exercised within the island of Jamaica.

Should Your Majesty's Parliament proceed in their attempt to subvert our constitution, and offer for the Royal assent any act that arrogates an authority over the interior of our island, we beseech Your Majesty to reject the act, and, by that timely interposition of Your Royal prerogative, to save us from utter ruin.

d. *The Imperial Government explains why it will use the authority of the Imperial Parliament*

Circular Despatch from the Secretary of State to West Indian Governors, 10 December 1831

Nothing has been further from the wish of those who have successively administered the affairs of this country since that period (1823) than to have recourse to any measures of a coercive character. The circular despatches which were written from year to year, repeating the expression of hopes which had been in no instance fulfilled, and of confidence which had not been justified, evince with what extreme reluctance the Ministers of the Crown have been compelled to relinquish the expectations which were originally entertained, that effectual measures for the improvement of the condition of the slaves would be at length spontaneously adopted by the colonial legislatures. The despatches have been written to point out in detail the defects of such laws as were enacted in alleged fulfilment of the wishes of His Majesty's Government to impress upon the several Councils and Assemblies the necessity which existed for satisfying the feelings entertained in this country in favour of the slaves, and the inadequacy of their legislation to effect that purpose. If His Majesty's present advisers have resolved to pursue no further this course of warning and entreaty, it is not that they are in any degree less anxious to conciliate the goodwill, whilst they consult the real interests of the colonist, but only because they feel that the language of admonition has been exhausted, and that any further attempt to produce an impression upon the legislatures by the same means alone, could add nothing to the respect of those bodies for the authority of the Crown, whilst it would be in vain to expect that it could contribute anything to the accomplishment of the object in view.

5. After 1815 Trinidad and St. Lucia were ceded to Britain, but Houses of Assembly were not established. They were ruled by Governors advised by a Council without further powers. The British Government rejected a petition for an Assembly from the white residents of Trinidad.

Lord Liverpool to Governor of Trinidad, November 1810

The question proposed for decision has no necessary reference to that state of things which has existed for so many years in the old West India islands, but may be stated to amount to this: whether in a new colony, in which the rights of the Crown and of Parliament must be admitted on all hands to be entire, it would be advisable to surrender those rights in whole or in part, and to establish a system of government analogous to that of the other West India islands?

Even if the circumstances of Trinidad were in all respects much more nearly the same with those of the other West India colonies than they unquestionably are, the determination of Government would probably be to negative such a proposition; but it so happens that the circumstances of the island of Trinidad are in many respects so materially different from those of all the other West India colonies, that supposing the system of government established in these islands to be the best which could be afforded them in their situation, it would not follow that the same system could be rendered applicable, either in justice or policy, to the island of Trinidad.

In all the other West India islands (with the exception of Dominica) . . . the white inhabitants form the great majority of the free people of the colony, and the political rights and privileges of all descriptions have been enjoyed exclusively by them. The class of free people of colour in these colonies, as far even as their numbers extend, has grown up gradually. They have thereby in some degree been reconciled to the middle situation which they occupy between the white inhabitants and the slaves. But in the island of Trinidad, the people of colour at this time form a very great majority of the free inhabitants of the island, and the question would arise, according to the proposed system, whether in establishing for the first time a popular government in that colony we shall exclude that class of people from all political rights and privileges? Such an exclusion we know would be regarded by them as a grievance, and it may be doubted how far it would be consistent with the spirit of the capitulation by which their privileges were to be secured and their situation certainly not deteriorated from that which they enjoyed under the Spanish Government.

In the second place, in most of the other West India islands, the great body of the proprietors and white inhabitants are British, or descendants from British families. To them the British Constitution and Laws have become familiar. They have been educated, or suppose themselves to be educated in the knowledge of them; and though the resemblance is certainly not great between the constitution as it is supposed to exist in our West

India islands and as it is enjoyed in Great Britain, the circumstances above referred to would in some degree account for the attachment of the inhabitants of the old West India islands to a system of government in which a popular assembly forms a prominent part. But in the island of Trinidad the white population consists of a mixture of people of all nations.

The greater part of them must be wholly ignorant of the British Constitution and unaccustomed to any form of government which bears any analogy to it. In the case of Trinidad therefore, amongst the most numerous class of white inhabitants there can be no material prejudice either of education or habit in favour of such a system; and the partial and exclusive principle on which it is proposed by the white inhabitants to be founded, whereby the largest proportion of the free people of the island would be excluded from all participation in its privileges, appears to defeat the object of it, and to constitute in point of justice and upon the very principles of the system itself a decided and insuperable objection against it.

... In addition to these considerations it is material to add that the abolition of the slave trade by Parliament imposes upon the Government the necessity of keeping within itself every power which may be material for rendering this measure effective.

It is essential for this purpose that in a new colony the Crown should not divest itself of the power of legislation, and that neither the Crown nor Parliament should be subject to the embarrassments which on such an occasion might perhaps arise from the conflicting views of the Imperial Parliament and a subordinate Legislature.

Under these circumstances you may consider it as a point determined, that it is not advisable to establish within the island of Trinidad any independent internal Legislature.

6. The assemblies were elected by a limited number of voters. Many free people were disqualified by lack of property or by their colour.

a. Qualifications for voting

Royal Proclamation, 21 June 1775

And it is our further will and pleasure, that every white man professing the Christian Religion, being a subject of Great Britain, and having attained the age of twenty-one years, and being seized of TEN ACRES OF LAND, fee-simple, fee-tail, or for life, or in right of a wife; or by any HOUSE, houses, storehouses, or other buildings, situate in any of the towns of the said island of Dominica, worth to be rented, if in Roseau or Portsmouth, twenty pounds current money per annum; and in any of the out-lying towns, ten pounds like money per annum; or who shall have twenty pounds per annum for life, out of, and charged on lands or tenements; shall be deemed a freeholder capable of voting for representatives of the said intended Assembly in any of the parishes in which freehold lies. . . . Provided that His Majesty's new adopted subjects thus made capable of electing, shall produce a certificate from the Captain-General or Commander-in-Chief of the island of Dominica, of their having taken the oaths of allegiance, abjuration, and supremacy.

b. Who were the most influential members in the Jamaican Assembly?

Governor of Jamaica to Lord Liverpool, 1810

The representative body (Assembly) is not composed of the principal landed proprietors of the island, very few of whom, comparatively speaking, are resident in it. But among the leading members (of the Assembly) are the agents or attornies, merely, of those proprietors; or of British merchants and mortgagees. And although they may themselves also be landholders they are nevertheless indebted for the principal sources both of their incomes and their consequence to the emoluments they acquire professionally, and the control they enjoy over the estates of others. It would be superfluous to point out how much influence may be derived from extensive concerns of this nature, and it will be sufficient to observe as one effect of such influence how little competition can be likely to arise upon the election of an Assembly from any reference to the political sentiments of the voters at large.

c. The free coloured in Jamaica are not allowed to vote until 1830 when all other disabilities are also removed

(i) *An Act to . . . ascertain who shall be deemed Mulattoes for the future*, 30 December 1780

Disqualification for voting. And for the better ascertaining who shall be deemed Mulattoes, within the intent and meaning of this Act; Be it further enacted by the Authority aforesaid, that no person who is not above three degrees removed in a lineal descent, from the Negro ancestor exclusive; except such as are now under any laws of this island, entitled to vote at elections, shall be allowed to vote or poll in elections; and no one shall be deemed a Mulatto, after the third generation, as aforesaid, but that they shall have all the privileges and immunities of His Majesty's white subjects of this island: provided, they are brought up in the Christian Religion.

(ii) *An Act to remove certain disabilities of persons of free condition*, 13 February 1830

Disqualification for voting removed. Whereas it is expedient to grant additional privileges to coloured and black persons of free condition . . . it is hereby enacted and ordained by the authority of the same, that all such persons of free condition, whether lawfully manumised or being the free-born subjects of his majesty, shall, from and after the first day of August next, be permitted to vote at any election for any person to serve in the assemblies of this island: provided he possess an estate of freehold, or a house in any of the towns of this island, such house being of the actual annual value of one hundred pounds . . . or else shall possess an estate of freehold in land and premises out of such towns, but in such parish where such election shall be held, of the actual annual value of fifty pounds.

(iii) *An Act to remove all disabilities of persons of free condition,* 21 December 1830

Civil equality with whites. Whereas two acts, passed in the eleventh year of the reign of his late majesty George the fourth . . . do not sufficiently remove the disabilities to which the free brown and black population of this island are subjected: And whereas it is expedient to grant additional privileges to such persons . . .

And be it further enacted . . . that, from and after the passing of this act, all the free brown and black population of this island shall be entitled to have and enjoy all the rights, privileges, immunities, and advantages whatsoever, to which they would have been entitled if born of and descended from white ancestors.

7. Emancipation made citizens of ex-slaves. Some observers doubted whether the Assemblies, long accustomed to considering only the interests of a few and still elected by a tiny number of voters, would change their habits when they had to make laws for all citizens. Criticism of the Assemblies came both from Englishmen and West Indians. But the British Government did not abolish Assemblies and a policy of conciliation seemed the only way of getting good work from them.

a. An English civil servant in favour of abolishing the Assemblies puts his views to the British Government

Memo. to the British Cabinet, January 1839

(i) *West Indian society could not support representative government.* What basis for a really representative system is to be found in the West Indian communities? The blacks have neither property nor knowledge and can't therefore have political power, or communicate it through any exercise of the rights of a constituency. Yet they are the mass of the people, and if there is any representation it ought to be their interests mainly that are represented. The coloured class have some property and such a portion of knowledge as may just enable them to possess political influence, but hardly make a good use of it; and though they have no goodwill to the whites, yet they are still worse affected towards the blacks. . . . They have naturally shown themselves disposed to make an alliance with the dominant and aristocratic class, and to join them in trampling upon the blacks to whom they feel it to be their shame and misfortune to be allied in blood.

(ii) *Can the assemblies deal with the problems created by emancipation?* The emergency now created brings under view of Government, the question whether the West Indian Assemblies be or be not, by their constitution and the nature of the societies for which they legislate, absolutely incompetent and unfit to deal with the new state of things and to provide for the peace and well-being of His Majesty's subjects in those parts.

b. A Grenadian editor criticises irregular attendance of councillors and assemblymen

Editorial, *Grenada Chronicle*, 25 April 1846

There was no meeting of the House of Assembly on Wednesday last in consequence of a sufficient number of members not attending. The House . . . stands adjourned to meet on Tuesday next. We do really hope that the members will be in their places punctually to the time on Tuesday, and continue to sit regularly, from day to day, until the business of the session is brought to a termination. It would be far preferable and decidedly more honest, in honourable members, if their private business clash with their public duties, to resign their seats, than, by retaining them, and not attending regularly, to retard the business of the country. We had, last week, to complain of the absence of the members of the Board of Council. The session commenced on Tuesday, the 14th, and it was only on the Thursday following, that a Board could be found and during that time there were no fewer than six bills and five messages from the Assembly to be sent up to them. Some of the members of the House think, we suppose, that it is now their turn to be absent, but this is manifesting an indifference to the public interest that we cannot otherwise than condemn.

c. Conciliation the basis of Metcalfe's policy in Jamaica

Comment by James Stephen, 1841

Here is a legislature which cannot be got rid of—which must exercise a most extensive authority for evil or for good—which may be kept in continued check by the superintending power rejecting its laws or which may be soothed, flattered and conciliated by an unhesitating acceptance of its enactments. They cannot be destroyed or much enfeebled. But they may be coerced or coaxed. Sir Chas. Metcalfe's recommendation is in favour of pursuing the latter course.

If one could always count on having governors like Sir Chas. Metcalfe—that is, masters of the arts of conciliation and disposed to use them—and if one could further count on a government in England strong enough to resist and silence the clamour which such a course of policy would provoke here, my belief is that Sir Chas. Metcalfe's plan would be the right one.

8. In the eighteen-fifties the old constitutions were reformed by the establishment of the Executive Committee. Without stable support in the Assemblies the Executive Committee found it difficult to work well.

a. The Governor's policy of conciliating the Jamaican Assembly is commended

Governor to Jamaican Assembly, 1854

A social revolution, unparalleled in extent and completeness in the annals of history, has taken place during the last quarter of a century with scarce any deviation from the previous routine of public business. What Jamaica stands pre-eminently in need of at the present stage of her political progress, is a strong executive administration, consisting of upright and intelligent men chosen from among her own citizens, to devote themselves to the exclusive study of her condition, charged with the sole responsibility in all matters of finance, and serving as an acknowledged medium of communication between the representative of the Crown, the Council, and the House of Assembly.

b. The Executive Committee established in Jamaica

An Act for the Better Government of this Island and for Raising Revenue in Support Thereof, April 1854

And be it further enacted, that it shall be lawful for the Governor . . . to nominate and appoint any person or persons not exceeding three in number, who shall be members of the Assembly for the time being, and in like manner to appoint one other person who shall be a member of the Legislative Council for the time being, to be members of and together to form and compose an executive committee for the assistance of the Governor in the general administration of the finances of this island, and in the execution of the duties hereby directed . . .

And be it enacted, that the duties of such executive committee shall be to assist the Governor in preparing the annual estimates, in levying and disbursing the public monies and in the general administration of the finances of the country . . . and in like manner it shall be the duty of the said executive committee and of every member thereof so required . . . to advise on, prepare and perfect all estimates, ways and means, messages, answers, bills and other proceedings which the Governor shall deem advisable to be submitted or communicated to either branch of the Legislature. . . .

The members of the executive committee shall in the Legislative Council and House of Assembly be the official organs of the Governor for all intercommunication between the Governor and such Houses respectively, and for the authoritative disclosure of the policy of the Government on all questions, political, financial and administrative. . . .

And be it enacted, that the right now existing in every member of the House of Assembly to propose a vote of money shall, from and after the appointment of the executive committee in manner herein provided . . .

cease and determine, and that it shall not be lawful during such period for the House of Assembly to originate or pass any vote, resolution or Bill for the imposition or appropriation of any tax or impost ... to or for any purpose, which shall not have been first recommended by a message of the Governor to the said House of Assembly, and by the executive committee for the time being under this Act appointed.

c. A member resigns to avoid votes of no confidence in an Executive Committee by the Assembly of Tobago

Minutes of Executive Committee, Tobago, 15 October 1860

The minutes of the last meeting were read and confirmed and the Administrator asked the Committee whether they had any remarks to make in regard to the notice of a vote of want of confidence in the present Executive Committee which had been given at the last meeting of the House of Assembly.

The Hon. Mr. Elliott stated that there was a strong feeling expressed against himself personally in consequence of his having accepted office in the present Executive Committee after having been a member of the previous one, and as he could not expect to command a majority in the House owing to its present temper, he deemed it advisable to tender his resignation to His Honour the Administrator.

The Hon. Mr. Gordon observed that having himself called on Mr. Elliott to form one of the Committee, he could not now with propriety desire that gentleman to resign office, although he was aware of the feeling of the House of Assembly towards him, but would leave him to adopt what course he chose to pursue in the matter.

The Hon. Mr. Elliott said he would not wish to peril Mr. Gordon's administration and would therefore advise him to try and procure another member of the Assembly in his place and that he Mr. Elliott would give his personal support to all the measures brought in by Mr. Gordon's administration in the House of Assembly as he was anxious that the business of the country should be proceeded with.

The Administrator in accepting Mr. Elliott's resignation thanked him for the zeal and ability he had displayed in discharging the responsible duties of a member of the Executive Committee.

d. Some Jamaican Assemblymen are disgusted by 'parties'

Member of Jamaica Assembly, 1865

There are certain gentlemen in this house who have made up their minds to one thing, and that is never again to be members of any party. I have found out that there is no such thing as good faith or consistency, and that the Executive Committee are ready, when the time arrives, to sacrifice their friends and to be on good terms with His Excellency the Governor. Their duty (those of no party) will be to do what they can for the public good to see what is best and most conducive to the public interest and to advocate that only.

9. From 1865 the Assemblies were either abolished, or their powers greatly weakened. These things were done by their own members, moved by one or more of the following reasons: fear that Negro voters would soon control the Assembly; dissatisfaction with the Executive Committee; belief that the Assemblies were beyond reform, and belief that government by Britain would be strong and efficient.

a. The charges against the West Indian Assemblies

Colonial Office Civil Servant to Secretary of State, July 1865

What they *are* guilty of are sins of omission, sins of neglect and mismanagement and refusals of money, for the education of the people, the administration of justice by paid magistrates, and the protection of property by a sufficient policy.

This has been enough in the circumstances of the Negro population in Jamaica at least, to produce a wretched state of depravity and degradation.

b. The Jamaican Assembly abolished

(i) *Member of Jamaica Assembly*, 1863

Wish for one man of strong will above 'party'. When I have witnessed what has taken place here, I could have wished in my heart for the sweeping away of the present system, and the establishment of a sort of paternal despotism. Yes, liberal as I am in my views, yet I freely confess that the wish has entered my heart, that some one man of strong hand and will, having at heart the best interests of the country and placed by his position above the miserable party influences, could be entrusted with the reins of government, to put the country fairly on the highway of progress and prosperity. I do not hesitate to say that the public good is being sacrificed to considerations of party success and personal aggrandisement while the schemes which are being enacted in this House are a positive disgrace to it.

(ii) *Jamaica Guardian*, 10 November 1865

Wish for a government to protect life and property. Jamaica is not the country for either a respectable coloured or white family to live in unless the government can safely protect life and property. To do these, we must have strong government and to have this, our present constitution must be greatly changed.

(iii) *Member of Jamaica Assembly*, November 1865

Total surrender is extravagant. I have no objection to giving the government whatever is necessary for the promotion of order, and the protection of life and property, but they ought not to be encouraged to indulge in habits of extravagance and waste of public money. Certain people in the House have become rebellion mad, and the government appear to be frightened out of their propriety and there is no end to their demands from the House. We have given them everything they want and now they are demanding a change in the Constitution in such a way as the country do not approve of. I can tell them that they will not get their Bill (cheers, loud). I can tell them that a reaction is setting in ... and the government will find that the proprietary and labouring classes of this country will not consent to indulge in extravagance.

(iv) *Colonial Standard*, 18 December 1865

Surrender the constitution to H.M.'s Government. In this emergency the proposal submitted to the country to surrender itself altogether, and unconditionally to the government of Her Majesty the Queen, is one that ought to be accepted without hesitation. There is not the slightest shade of a chance that the House of Assembly will ever be called to life again. Its doom is sealed from the very extravagances which the present session presented, and if we refuse the Queen's rule, we shall have to remain content with that of the bigots, the traitors, and the knaves who have already betrayed us. We should be subjected to the rule of an oligarchy, more obvious and mischievous, that in its constitution it would appear to derive its authority from the will of the people. The new proposals will interpose intermediaries between ourselves and the Queen's government unbiased and independent and disposed to apply equitable principles to the ruling of all classes. We should be saved from class legislation.

10. The essence of Crown colony government was that it gave to the British Government the power to make all laws for the colonies. West Indians were nominated as Unofficial Members to the Legislative Councils, but the Governor and his officials combined could outvote them.

a. The programme of Crown colony government for Jamaica

H.M. Instructions to Governor Grant, 1866

It will be proper that I should bring under your consideration some prominent features of the community you are to govern, and some of the more important questions which will present themselves on your assumption of the government.

The relief of the poor, the influence of the Church of England, and of other religious bodies, education and administration of justice by the magistracy—the police, the repression of praedial larceny, the unauthorised occupation of land, the introduction of capital and labour, taxation and official reform. . . .

Of all the reforms demanded by the state of society in Jamaica there is none of more urgent and immediate importance than the reform of a suspected and unsatisfactory administration of justice. . . . These objects will I think be best secured by the establishment of a sufficient number of stipendiary magistrates to deal with the Petty Sessions, administration of justice, so far as may be necessary, and to adjudicate also in cases of debt, trespass, and damages below a certain amount. It may not be necessary or expedient that the commissions of the present Justices of the Peace should be revoked. The principal evil . . . would seem to be that their decisions are open to a reasonable suspicion of partiality.

It is of great importance that the finances and public expenditure of the colony should be at the earliest moment subjected to a close examination, in order that it may be seen what economies and improvements can be effected, what reductions of unnecessary expense can be made, and what funds are forthcoming by a prudent system of taxation. Whether the taxes are the best that can be imposed, whether they are duly and equally collected, and whether their proceeds are regularly accounted for under a system of careful audit and examination.

b. What was expected of governors and officials?

(i) *Secretary of State to Governor of Jamaica*, August 1866

Governors. Her Majesty's Government has also the right to expect in those to whose charge such great trusts are committed, that . . . they will show themselves able to withstand the pressure of any one class, or idea, or interest, and that they will maintain that calmness and impartiality of judgement which should belong to the governor of an English colony.

(ii) *Secretary of State to Anti-Slavery Society*, 1877

Officials. The business of all the official members is to consider the interests of the peasantry very closely, and, without making themselves exclusively the representatives of those classes, to see that their interests do not suffer.

c. The Crown has ultimate powers but local interests cannot be silenced

Permanent Secretary, Colonial Office, 9 January 1866

In a country in which, for want of large educated constituencies, the Crown acting under control of Parliament and English public opinion, is the best or rather the only possible representative of the people, it is desirable, no doubt, that the power of the Crown should be a prevailing power: but it is not desirable that it should be paramount to the silencing of such local interests as can make themselves intelligently heard. There should be so much power of local resistance and obstruction as to compel the local, and even the Home Government, though possessed of adequate authority in the last resort, to be cautious and deliberate in the exercise of it. There should be security for any important question on which a difference of opinion exists, being fully canvassed and considered.

11. Barbados and British Guiana avoided constitutional changes at this time. Barbados never became a Crown colony, but the Assembly accepted an Executive Committee in 1881.

a. A Barbadian considers that extension of education would improve the quality of representative government

Editorial, *The Barbadian,* 11 October 1856

Admitting that in some of the islands there is much vulgarity and ignorance to be found in the House of Assembly and also that much jobbing and corruption is practised, a better remedy than sweeping them away, though not so immediate a one, would be the extension of education, of sound religious education, in the different islands. In 15 or 20 years this would begin to tell, and the people, having themselves more light, would send to represent them more enlightened men.

b. *A Barbadian claims that criticisms made of other West Indian Assemblies do not apply to Barbados*

Conrad Reeves in the House of Assembly, 9 February 1876

Our representation in the legislature is in the hands of the educated class of the country. We are not, like some other colonies, afflicted by absenteeism. It is not with us, as it is with some of our neighbours, that the proprietors of the soil are living in Europe, which necessitates the putting of all local power in the hands of an inferior class of men, mostly persons who have come from Europe to push their fortunes and leave as soon as their purpose is accomplished. The leading men in this country are persons whose ancestors for generations have lived and died here. These often send their sons to England for education, and are fitted by study and travel when they return to their country, to take an active and interested part in the management of its affairs, to fit them for which, indeed, they are sent away to be educated. . . . We are every day becoming more and more alive to the importance of fostering every institution promotive of social progress and individual advancement, and all classes of the country have the utmost confidence in its institutions, which are based and modelled upon those of the mother country (cheers).

c. *Executive Committee established in Barbados*

Governor of Barbados to Legislature, March 1881

By this enactment the practice of the House of Assembly has been in several respects assimilated to that in force in the mother country. . . . I venture to predict that the best results will follow from it. The responsibility of the Executive will be increased and more clearly defined, the transaction of public business will be expedited, the expenditure on public institutions will be more easily controlled, and the harmonious working of the three branches of the Legislature and therefore the safety of your constitution will be more surely secured.

12. Crown colony government was criticised. Here are some of the grounds of criticism.

a.

(i) *Henderson (Baptist Minister) to Espeut (a planter)*, 21 August 1876

Disappointment with the results. I did hope that the alteration in the form of government would have worked both for peace and prosperity. But it has done neither. It has benefited no one belonging to the colony; whilst it has wrought to the injury of the multitudes. It is killing our very manhood and making one of the most beautiful countries in the world a hateful place in which to live. But I must stop. It does not do for an Englishman as fond of liberty as I am, to remember how he is ruled.

(ii) *East (Principal of Calabar College) to Governor of Jamaica*, 6 October 1876

What other form will preserve the rights of all classes? I do not wish to convey to your Excellency the idea that we are so happy as to have no discontented persons among us. No doubt there are numbers who dislike theoretically the present form of government, but when these people are asked whether they would like to return to the old constitution, they repudiate the suggestion; and when asked to propose a form which under the existing circumstances would answer better than the present, they are wholly at a loss; and when further pressed, they are obliged to acknowledge that it would be impossible to frame a form which would not give paramount influence to the very class supposed to be inimical to the labouring classes . . . and that is fine, for the conservation of the rights of all classes, a government responsible to the Crown and amenable to the Parliament and the public opinion of the mother country, is the safest and best. This is my own conviction much as I love the representative institutions of my native land . . . I believe there was never more contentment among our people.

b. The efforts of Nominated Unofficials are barren

Rawle, *Open Letter to Nominated Unofficial Members*, Dominica, September 1921

I realize, gentlemen, that your position as Nominated Unofficials is one that bristles with difficulties. You are supposed to be the representatives of the taxpayers of the island, but are without a mandate from them, and without adequate means of ascertaining their views on any given subject....

Your efforts are at present barren. As an advocate of constitutional reform I seek to remove the cause of that sterility by the introduction to the Council of a certain number of elected members, in conjunction with whom you will, when unanimous, be able to neutralize the official vote.

c. Independent men refuse to be voting dummies

Wood Report, 1922

In regard to the five nominated non-official members (in Jamaica) who are expected to vote with the Governor, it is clear that it is becoming increasingly difficult to get the best men either to give so much of their time or to be content any longer to act as legislative dummies with votes which must be recorded automatically. Their sole power is the power of resignation when they disagree with the action of the Government and the Governor admitted that he had recently urged several men of independence and standing to accept nomination, but that in view of the present position they had declined.

13. Unofficial members could be elected in Jamaica from 1884. In 1891 the College of Electors in British Guiana was abolished and unofficial members elected directly. The Governors retained effective control.

a. New constitution in Jamaica

(i) *Secretary of State to Governor of Jamaica*, December 1883

In Jamaica the elected members are granted a right of veto in financial matters. The advance of education and the improved position of the Negro population have no doubt since 1866 largely increased the number of persons who would now possess and could intelligently exercise, such a franchise as that under which members of the Assembly were formerly elected. But Her Majesty's Government can find no sufficient ground for believing that the sudden and complete transfer of control over public affairs to a Council containing a large majority of unofficial members, most of them being elective, would secure the various interests which have to be regarded. A moderate step in advance will be preferable. . . .

In order that the voice thus given to the representatives of the people may be accompanied by a substantial power over finance, you will be guided by the following instruction, namely, that in questions involving the imposition of new taxes or the appropriation of public money for any other purpose than the payment of salaries already assigned to persons now employed on the fixed establishment of the colony, the vote of the official members shall as a general rule not be recorded against that of the unofficial members, if not less than six of the latter are present and agreed.

(ii) *Secretary of State to Governor of Jamaica*, 1884

Details of the new constitution explained. The new Council will consist of the Governor and four other *ex-officio* members, viz, the three officers who are *ex-officio* members of the existing Council (Senior Military Officer, Colonial Secretary, Attorney-General) and the Director of Public Works, not more than five members to be nominated by the Crown or provisionally by the Governor, and nine elected members. . . .

The power is reserved to Her Majesty or Her Representative of securing in case of necessity a control over its decisions by raising the number of nominated members to the prescribed maximum.

. . . I trust it will be rarely or never necessary for the Governor to exercise the power of over-riding the votes of the elected members, but it must be clearly understood that it is his duty to do so if in his opinion the public interest absolutely requires it. . . .

The qualifications of electors will be as follows:

That he has during the twelve calendar months preceding registration been an occupier or owner or tenant of a dwelling house, and has during the time of such occupation been rated in respect of the premises so occupied by him to all poor rates . . . and has during the twelve calendar months paid . . . public or parochial taxes or rates, or taxes and rates, to the amount of not less than one pound; or was possessed of any property in respect of which he has, during the preceding twelve calendar months, paid within the district, public or parochial taxes or rates, or taxes and rates, to the amount of not less than one pound and ten shillings.

. . . after the present year no one shall be registered as a voter for the first time without signing his name to the claim and adding the date of the signature in the presence of the registering officer or of a magistrate.

. . . the voting at elections of members of the Council shall be by ballot.

b. New constitution in British Guiana

(i) *Daily Chronicle*, 10 July 1889

A vote demanded for the intelligent and respectable in British Guiana. Is any one bold enough to stand up in this colony and say reform is not needed? In this democratic age when in every country of any importance the people have a voice in the election of their governors, we here have not even the semblance of Representative Government. . . . We should not wonder if soon we shall be nick-named across the water, 'The stick-in-the-mud colony'. Here we are with a government about as suitable to modern times as a wheelbarrow is for locomotion in comparison with the steam engine. 1889 and subjects of freedom-loving England, living under a 'Despotism sweetened by sugar!' . . . Surely the time has come when at least the intelligent and respectable and law-abiding portion of the community might be entrusted with the franchise. Make us feel that we are free men, by giving us a share in the duties and responsibilities of government.

(ii) *Berbice Gazette*, 29 November 1890

Criticism of the constitution of 1891 which gives the vote to owners of 3 acres or tenants of 6 acres of land or those with an income of $300 p.a., *to elect 8 unofficial members to the Court of Policy and 6 to the Combined Court.* The Reform Bill has at last been introduced in the Court of Policy. . . . In fact, so slight are the amendments proposed to the present constitution that it is hardly worth while making them at all. The number of members of the Court of Policy, it is true, is to be increased (to 16—eight officials and eight electives) but the qualification (for membership) being the possession of property of large value, there will practically be no difference in the class of persons eligible for the Legislature, as comparatively few persons unconnected with the planting industry hold property to the value of $7,500. This qualification is much too high and there ought also to be, as in the case of Financial Representatives, an income qualification (for membership), for the reason that there are in the colony many good and able men who do not own immovable property of any considerable value. The principle of direct representation on a reduced franchise has to a certain extent been recognized, but this concession is worthless without secret voting: and we would urge on the people not to be satisfied with any reform that does not give them the privilege of voting by ballot.

B. ATTEMPTS AT UNIFICATION IN THE NINETEENTH CENTURY

1. In the eighteen-thirties the British Government adopted the policy of reducing the number of separate governments in the West Indies whenever possible. This policy was not accepted by the West Indians who were in politics, and throughout the nineteenth century, although the British Government made attempts to execute its policy, little was accomplished.

a. The reasons for unifying Berbice, Demerara and Essequibo also apply to the other West Indian colonies

Secretary of State to Governor of British Guiana, 1831

But the still more decisive motive with Her Majesty's Government has been drawn from the conviction that the British colonies in the West Indies have been broken up into numerous separate communities, in a state of mutual independence on each other to a much greater extent than sound policy can justify. The evils resulting from the contracted dimensions of these colonial societies have long been, and are to this day, painfully experienced. In so narrow a sphere there is no room for the growth of that salutary public opinion which results from free discussion, and even from the most ardent controversy in larger societies. Every difference of private judgement on public affairs is thus exasperated by personal animosities and becomes the source of bitter feuds, in the pursuit of which all higher interests are neglected.

These remarks involve no peculiar reproach on the inhabitants of any peculiar colony, but rather on the system which has compressed within such narrow limits the range of their public duties and interests.

The legal and constitutional difficulties which impede any consolidation of colonial governments in the islands possessing representative assemblies, do not arise in the case of Demerara and Berbice, and the ministers of the Crown are persuaded that they could not advise a more useful exercise of the Royal Prerogative than in combining the whole body of inhabitants into one society, connected by common laws and institutions, as they are already connected by a community of origin, language, and rural economy.

b. The British Government appoints one governor for all the Leeward Islands and Dominica

Secretary of State to Governor of the Leewards, 11 February 1833

Amongst the many important subjects connected with His Majesty's West India colonies, to which the circumstances of the present times have called my attention, a prominent place has been occupied by the inconvenience resulting from the division of those possessions into so many distinct governments.

Were it likely to be acceptable to the respective islands it would not be difficult to show that advantages essential to their good government would be derivable from a more complete consolidation of their institutions than His Majesty has the power of effecting by his prerogative.

Not only the executive, but the legislative and judicial functions of several of the West Indian communities might be brought to centre in one assembly and in one court, with great benefit to the public interests. ....

The time has now arrived for reverting, as far as His Majesty's prerogative extends, to the principle of consolidation. A general union of the assemblies, and the erection of supreme tribunals administering justice throughout the whole range of islands, are measures to which, at present, I confine myself to stating, that though fully sensible of the great advantages they appear to promise, His Majesty has not authority to introduce them by the unaided exercise of his own prerogative. But the combination of the different governments in the person of the same officer is an arrangement clearly within the powers of the Crown, and has been effected by the commission which accompanies this despatch.

2. The Leeward Islands assemblies ignored the suggestions made by the British Government in 1833, and in 1838 successfully blocked an attempt by the Governor to establish a legislature common to them all. In 1871 such a legislature was established but without independent powers of taxation.

a. *The Governor advises the British Government not to press for a Treasury Department common to all the Leewards*

Governor of the Leewards to the Secretary of State, 27 September 1869

With reference to your Lordship's despatch, informing me that Her Majesty's Government desire to unite the colonies under this general Government into one colony, with one Governor, one Legislature, one Treasury and Audit Department, one Code of Laws, one Police Force, and one system for the administration of justice, and directing me to propose a scheme for arriving at this end, I have now the honour to submit to your Lordship the following suggestions.

The only point in the proposal of Her Majesty's Government which seems to me open to objection is the union of the Treasuries of the several islands. I will therefore deal with this subject before I proceed further.

It seems to me that this union would at present be impracticable. There exists so great a diversity between the financial conditions of the several islands, that the union could not be effected without great unfairness to the wealthier islands.

Take, for example, the cases of St. Kitts and Antigua. The former island has an overflowing Treasury—the latter has a debt of some £50,000. Further, it seems to me that the contruction of the machinery necessary to carry out such a union would be extremely difficult till the islands have been brought into closer connection with one another in other respects, and brought to some agreement as to the general principles of taxation and finance. At present the systems of the several islands are very different— one island (St. Kitts) deriving the whole of its revenue from indirect taxation, customs duties; another (Antigua) partly from this source, and partly from direct taxes of various kinds.

Moreover, for the present I do not think such a union or fusion of Treasuries is necessary. A common system of accounts and audit, and probably a common tariff of customs duties, would do all that is at present required to bring into a tolerably sound condition the finances of all the islands.

I am glad to think that we can dispense with this union for the present, for I must inform your Lordship that it is the part of the scheme which is the most vehemently attacked, especially in St. Kitts (upon which everything depends), and that it is the only part to which sensible men, who are generally very favourable to the scheme, object.

I would therefore respectfully advise your Lordship not to make shipwreck of a scheme which comprises so much that is practical and eminently advantageous to these islands, for the sake of this one point, however important it may seem to you.

I have little doubt that such a union will ultimately come, naturally, by the joint desire of the several islands, and when the necessity for it really arises.

In the meantime I would advise your Lordship to let it be distinctly understood that the power of enforcing such a union of Treasuries should not be given to the Federal Council, but reserved for the future joint consideration of the several local legislatures and the Imperial Government.

b. The Governor's advice is accepted

Secretary of State to Governor of the Leewards, 17 November 1869

I accept your recommendation, and you may consider that portion of my despatch, relating to the union of the several Treasuries, as withdrawn.

c. The benefits of federation to the Leewards are recited in order to induce Barbados and the Windwards to federate

Secretary of State to Governor of Barbados, 1 May 1873

It is impossible to peruse this record of the legislation which has been undertaken without perceiving that the colonies of the Leeward group have already entered upon a larger sphere of political and social action, than was accessible to them as small isolated communities, that many important requirements hitherto unattainable, except in an imperfect form, are being brought within reach of the inhabitants, and that in becoming members of a union, the islands now afford a more attractive field, not only to the capitalist, but to those who are prepared to devote themselves to public affairs.

I understand it has been questioned whether Federation in the Leeward Islands will not lead to increased expense rather than to economy. I should be much disappointed if this were to be the case. . . . But even if no saving were to result from this constitutional change, it would nevertheless be well worth making, for the sake of the increased efficiency that it is calculated to provide in the government of the islands, the administration of justice, and in other very important matters. . . .

In promoting the union of the Leeward Islands, and in desiring that the Windward Islands should follow the same course, Her Majesty's Government have not contemplated, unless possibly as a temporary measure, that Barbados and the other Windward Islands should form a Federation separate from that of the Leeward Islands; and in the 32nd section of the Leeward Islands Act, 1871, provision was expressly made for the admission of other West Indian islands into the union which at present comprises the Leeward Islands only.

Lastly, I have to point out that it is most desirable on general grounds affecting imperial as well as local interests that the Windward Islands should be included within a strong Federation. No one can dispute the advantages, for purposes of defence, of union between weak neighbouring communities.

3. In the eighteen-forties and fifties proposals similar to those put to the Leeward assemblies were made to the Windwards and Barbados. They too were ignored. A determined effort in the seventies was defeated in 1876 by the 'Confederation Riots' in Barbados.

a. The obstacles to a federation of the Windwards

Governor of Barbados to Secretary of State, 8 September 1871

In this government the position of affairs was: one only of the five islands was a Crown colony. In one other a single chamber had been in existence but a few months. In the other three double chambers exist, and the knowledge that the Duke of Buckingham (Secretary of State) had proposed a change here similar to that which had been initiated in the Leeward Islands, and the belief that I had been appointed to carry out the measures, had aroused a feeling of suspicion and jealousy in these islands, whose inhabitants were not then, and probably are not now, prepared to surrender their constitutions.

The reports of the hostility shown to the measure of Federation in two of the most important of the Leeward Islands found a sympathetic response here. . . .

There is one important difference between the Windward and Leeward Islands, viz. that arising out of the inequality of the population. The most populous island in the Windward Islands (Grenada, with 34,971 inhabitants) does not contain a fourth of the population of Barbados. One important consequence of these differences is, that Barbados would on this ground alone be entitled to nearly half as many councillors as all the other islands put together, while on those of production, trade or accumulated wealth it would be entitled to even a larger share. Your Lordship can scarcely be surprised that the minor islands do not feel disposed to place themselves so completely under the domination of Barbados, which has not acquired for itself a reputation of a generous and cosmopolitan spirit of legislation.

b. As a first step towards federation the Governor of Barbados proposes certain changes which would provide the Windwards with common services

Governor of Barbados to House of Assembly, 14 January 1876

1. That the Auditor of Barbados should be appointed Auditor-General of the Windward Islands, his salary and clerical staff being increased; such additional expense to fall entirely on the other islands.

2. That the power of transporting prisoners from Barbados to the other islands, and of receiving prisoners from the other islands here, should be secured to the Governor-in-Chief.

3. That the new lunatic asylum here should also be open for the reception of lunatics from the other islands.

4. That a similar arrangement should be made about a common lazaretto.

5. That there should be a Chief Justice of the Windward Islands, and a

remodelling of the judicial system based on the necessity of centralising it in Barbados.

6. That there should be a Police Force for the Windward Islands.

c. *House of Assembly, Barbados, rejects consolidation of administrative departments and refuses to be part of a federation*

House of Assembly to the Governor of Barbados, 22 February 1876

The House of Assembly advisedly do not express a definite opinion upon the six proposals, the adoption of which your Excellency thinks necessary to the efficient discharge by you of the onerous duties of your office as Governor-in-Chief of the Windward Islands. The House have carefully read the message, but it is not on the face of it clear beyond doubt ... whether the changes are intended to embrace all the Windward colonies, as a group, and be applicable to them all, as though they were one colony, brought under a common administrative system.

... Your Excellency's message is open to the construction that the changes proposed actually contemplate the amalgamation of the now several distinct classes of departments of each colony, ... into one department of each class, to be common to the 'Windward Islands' as one colony. ...

The House of Assembly in order to prevent any misunderstanding between your Excellency and themselves, would beg respectfully to say that they cannot consent to deal with your Excellency's proposals on the basis of changes consolidating or amalgamating the administrative departments of the 'Windward Islands' with a view to oneness of departments by the obliterating of the separate and individual departments of each colony as independent of every other.

The House of Assembly wish especially to bring before your Excellency that they have no intention to consent to become one of a political Federation of islands, in any shape or upon any conditions incident to such a Federation—or to merge the independent separate Legislature of this island, whether for local or general purposes of legislation, in a Federative Legislature, whether such Federation and Federative Legislature already exist or are to be brought into existence.

d. Reasons suggested for the change of planter opinion in St. Lucia, St. Vincent, Grenada and Tobago

Governor of Barbados to Secretary of State, 11 March 1876

In my predecessor's despatches respecting confederation, he refers more than once to the opposition he feared it might encounter in the other islands of the Windward group as well as in Barbados. . . .

Now that the question is before all the colonies of the Windward group, so far from giving it a reluctant consideration, they are, as a general rule, considering it with an evident desire to see it successfully accomplished. . . .

Two reasons account for the favourable change of opinion in these four islands. In the first place, the subject has become better understood. The fact that Confederation was the most natural means of giving an outlet to the surplus of Barbados labour has forced itself on the conviction of the planters of the other islands, who, by means of that surplus, can double the produce of those islands. That centralisation would lead to a cheaper and more efficient system in the great public institutions has also been generally felt.

In the second place, the elective element in the Legislatures of those islands has been of late entirely abolished. . . . Now that St. Vincent and Grenada are as pure Crown colonies as St. Lucia, the people look more to the direct influence and advantages of the Government in Chief.

e. Some Barbadian planters tell their workers that federation will mean the return of slavery

Governor of Barbados to Secretary of State, 11 March 1876

The very same reason that induces the planters in St. Vincent, Grenada,

Tobago and St. Lucia to welcome Confederation induces the planters in Barbados to oppose it.

At first, some of the planters who opposed Confederation told the people that it meant the return of slavery. . . .

When my six points were under discussion in the Assembly, it was reported to me by the Inspector-General of Police that certain managers of estates and some leading white shopkeepers were industriously repeating the same absurd stories about the return of slavery. One shopkeeper called the black porters and others who were in the street and said, 'If these six points pass today, I shall be able to buy you as slaves tomorrow at 12 o'clock.'

Other opponents of Confederation contented themselves with telling the people that it meant putting a poll-tax on every black man.

Since then a sound public opinion has been growing on the subject. The attempts to mislead the people have proved abortive; and even among the electoral body, restricted and exclusive as it is, there is now a strong feeling in favour of Confederation.

To sum up the state of the question at this moment in the Windward Islands, it is clear that the legislatures of four of the islands will ask for Confederation, and that in the fifth the vast majority of the people are also in favour of it.

f. A Barbadian sees federation as a way to make Barbados into a Crown colony

Conrad Reeves, *Speech in the House of Assembly*, May 1876

We have declined Confederation, because in the form which it takes in the case of the West India colonies it means, and can only mean, the surrender by us, in the long run, of our representative form of government which we have enjoyed for 250 years.

4. At the end of 1884 the British Government proposed the federation of St. Lucia, St. Vincent, Grenada and Tobago, with half the members of the federal legislature elected. The promise of elections was not strong enough to overcome resistance in the islands.

a. Grenadians object to a common Treasury
Editorial, *The Chronicle and Gazette*, Grenada, 31 January 1885

It is a foregone conclusion that the majority of the inhabitants will declare against any form of annexation with the other islands, unless, perhaps, it can be carried out on a principle which will prevent our prosperous island from being retarded by the backwardness or impecuniosity of the others. The principal objection, as far as we are able to gather, to confederation (or union) is raised on the ground of finances. The leaders of the people object . . . to a common or federal Treasury. . . . Confederation has been designed principally for the salvation, at the expense of this prosperous island, of others that are financially ruined.

b. A St. Lucian objects to the capital being in Grenada
Letter in 'The Voice of St. Lucia', 14 February 1885

But what is worse, our beautiful St. Lucia is to be classed as and sunk into, a Magisterial District, under Grenada.

Know you not that even with the sugar depression we are better off than our neighbours, aye, better off perhaps, all things considered, than the elected seat of government . . . with the exception of Barbados, St. Lucia stands foremost and claims priority over her sisters in the Windward group.

c. The Governor reports opposition in St. Vincent and Tobago
Governor of the Windwards to Secretary of State, 1 March 1885

I proceeded by the mail steamer of the 19th February to St. Vincent, . . . An enormous crowd was collected at the wharf and in its vicinity, and as I stepped into my carriage with Lady Robinson loud shouts of 'no confederation' were raised. These shouts were continued during the evening. . . . The mob stoned Mr. Gore and the Lt.-Governor as well as Captain Denton and Mr. Kingdom, the Acting Attorney-General.

On the following day at 12 o'clock, I addressed the Legislative Council. ... There were between 300 and 400 persons present. ... On the assurance of the Official and Unofficial Members that the feeling of the people was strongly against Confederation or Union, I accepted the Resolution which it was proposed to address to Your Lordship.

On the 23rd I proceeded to Tobago in Her Majesty's ship *Dido*. The people of this island ... were very quiet, orderly and hopeful.

Mr. Carrington ... whilst regretting the decision that the people had arrived at frankly admitted that the Unofficial Members gave undoubted expression to their views. In accordance therefore with Your Lordship's instructions I accepted a resolution to the effect that the people of Tobago did not desire to enter into Union or Federation with any of the other islands.

St. Lucia is even more strongly opposed to Union than Grenada and I conclude that no object would be gained by my meeting the Legislature of that island.

C. STAGES FROM IMPERIAL CONTROL TO SELF-GOVERNMENT IN THE TWENTIETH CENTURY

1. When colonies in which the elected members had some control over revenue and expenditure got into financial difficulties the British Government reasserted its powers of ultimate control through the Governor and his officials. This happened in Jamaica, Antigua, Dominica, British Guiana and British Honduras.

a. Dominica may only receive aid from Britain if she accepts a majority of officials in the legislature

Governor of Leewards to Dominica Legislative Assembly, May 1898

1. The Governor has the honour to inform the Legislative Assembly that he has received a despatch from the Secretary of State informing him that

a supplementary estimate amounting to £120,000 was recently voted by the House of Commons to cover deficits in the revenues of some of the West Indian islands including the whole of the Leeward Islands, and also for the purchase of lands in St. Vincent and the construction of roads in Dominica.

2. Dominica may thus benefit under this vote in aid of revenue, to the extent of £15,000.

6. The Secretary of State has, however, pointed out ... that where direct Imperial aid is given there should be Imperial control of the finances, and he has therefore stated in unmistakable terms that neither the money which has been voted in aid of Dominica nor any further assistance which may be offered to the West Indian colonies will be forthcoming, in so far as Dominica is concerned, unless and until the existing constitution is modified so as to give the Crown control of the finances by creating a majority of official members in the legislature.

7. The Secretary of State remarks that it will not be sufficient that there should be a majority of officials and nominated members combined, in as much as a nominated member is not required to give the Government constant and undeviating support. But, provided that an official majority is secured, the Secretary of State will not insist upon the abolition of the elective system, should the continuance of that system be preferred locally to nomination by the Governor, of representative members.

9. The Secretary of State contemplates that towards the deficit on the 31st of December 1897 £1,000 should be paid as a free grant from the £120,000 vote by the Imperial Parliament, and an additional £500 as an advance without interest; but no part of these moneys nor any other Imperial assistance will be available until the Presidency complies with the condition above referred to.

b. In Jamaica the governor and elected unofficials frustrate one another

Barbour Report to the Secretary of State, 1899

When ... either more revenue must be raised or expenditure must be reduced, the Government was in favour of increasing taxation, while the elected members of the Legislative Council pressed for reductions of expenditure. From the nature of the constitution the Government was practically unable to carry proposals for increased taxation in opposition to the votes of nine elected members, while the elected members could not in any satisfactory manner enforce reduction of expenditure. ... The only real responsibility for the finances rested on the Governor, but he could not enforce his policy except by filling up the Council with nominated members.... Such action on his part would be a very unpopular measure, would bring him into direct conflict with the elected members, would expose him to popular clamour, and it is not surprising that it was not exercised.

c. Divided responsibility for finance in British Guiana

(i) *Report of British Guiana Parliamentary Commission*, 1926

A Parliamentary Commission comments on British Guiana's financial administration. Hand-to-mouth finance and haphazard and ill-considered taxation are the inevitable outcome of a system under which the responsibility for the finances rests with a Government who cannot enforce their policy and the financial power with the elected members who have no real responsibility.

The practical consequences of this lack of ultimate control are chiefly to be seen in the financial system of the colony. This system is prejudicial to trade, inconducive to sound financial policy, and costly in that it prevents the colony's loans from being issued as trustee securities. We have referred elsewhere in greater detail to the vital importance of establishing a definite, far-sighted and consistent financial policy. At present the elected members are in the position of a minor who can overrule his own trustee. ...

It appears to us essential, as well on the ground of immediate financial exigencies as on that of future development, that the authorities finally responsible for the solvency and good government of the colony should have power in the last resort to carry into effect measures which they consider essential for its well-being.

(ii) *Report of British Guiana Local Commission*, 1927

A local commission advises that the Governor be given ultimate powers.
The preponderance of evidence was in favour of the abolition of the existing Court of Policy and Combined Court, and the substitution therefore of a single legislative body.

It is our opinion, and the opinion of every witness who came before us, that the introduction into the Legislature of such an element (nominated Unofficials) would be an improvement.

(The Governor) to reserve, for his own decision, any matter which he and the Secretary of State consider essential to the good government of the colony, but that this power should not be exercised without reference to the Secretary of State (should such be possible), and in any event the Governor's action in this respect should be reviewed by the Secretary of State at the earliest possible moment.

2. During the First World War there was a renewed demand for elected members in the colonies which had none. In Dominica, St. Lucia, Grenada and Trinidad elections took place in the nineteen-twenties. But the ultimate power remained with the British Government.

a. *'Marryshow appeals to Trinidadians to join Grenadians in a demand for a more dignified and responsible form of government'*

Letter from Marryshow, *Trinidad Guardian*, 16 October 1917

Sir, I want ... to make an appeal to representative public men of Trinidad for help. Grenada has cast the die, and will soon submit a most popular and influential petition to the King, praying for representative institutions of government for the colony. The whole colony, almost to a man, is behind the petition. ... It will be a delight to feel that Trinidad's needs are like unto ours, and that it is possible to count on her support in this matter. On this side, we feel we have been sheltered by the Crown colony government in times when we needed such care. We are grateful for the past. But we desire, not shelter, but advancement and progress. . . . Will Trinidad lend the force of her position to a movement for Representative Government? . . . The spiritual Great Britain which is at war against the system that keeps the German people under the heel of those who think for them, feel for them, act for them, will never refuse the prayer of her loyal subjects for a substantial measure of the right to govern themselves. It is all left to us, to make our application and show the justice of, and our worthiness for, the claim.

It should be no question as to who has taken the initiative. . . . This question of Representative Government concerns the majority of the islands. . . . Were it not a question touching the attainable ideals of the entire West Indies, were it not for the fact that it is necessary that we have representative institutions in these islands before we can even hope to have federation, I would have been the last person to address Trinidadians on their own business. But this is the business of every colony 'jointly and severally' and I speak not as a Grenadian to Trinidadians, but as a West Indian to West Indians. Believe me, it is with great earnestness that I make this serious appeal to leaders of public thought in your prosperous colony, to organise themselves for an island-wide movement, that if possible Trinidad might say in no uncertain voice that this West Indies must be a new West Indies in the new world that shall dawn as a result of the war, and that she is convinced such a new West Indies is dependent on a more dignified and respectable form of government which alone can justify our elevation to the inter-imperial citizenship of empire.

b. *Some Indians in Trinidad ask for communal representation*

Meeting at Couva Electric Theatre, 1 September 1921

The East Indian community of Trinidad and Tobago in public meeting assembled resolve as follows:

1st. That whereas a definite movement has been started for the promotion of Representative Government in and over the colony of Trinidad and Tobago which in the opinion of the East Indian community will be productive of the highest measure of prosperity to our island;

2nd. And whereas the East Indian community which forms one-third of the population of Trinidad and Tobago and has been hitherto instrumental in effecting the economic and industrial development of the colony, will naturally share in such a prosperity.

3rd. This meeting, therefore, pledges its whole-hearted support to the popular cause of Representative Government, on the distinct understanding that such a representation will procure for all people their full measure of proportional or communal representation to which they are entitled.

c. Major Wood (Under-Secretary of State) assesses the strength of the demand for representative government, and proposes a very gradual reduction of the official majority

Wood Report, 1922

(i) *The demand cannot be resisted completely.* Several reasons combine to make it likely that the common demand for a measure of representative government will in the long run prove irresistible. The wave of democratic sentiment has been powerfully stimulated by the war. Education is rapidly spreading, and tending to prōduce a coloured and black intelligentsia, of which the members are quick to absorb elements of knowledge requisite for entry into learned professions and return from travel abroad with minds emancipated and enlarged, ready to devote time and energy to propaganda among their own people. Local traditions of representative institutions reinforced these tendencies. In the British islands these go back to the early days of European settlement; in the present and former French islands they were first fostered by the ideas promulgated through the French Revolution, and are today sustained by the fact of direct reprèsentation in the French Parliament. A near neighbour, the United States, is seen to have bestowed free institutions upon Cuba and the Philippines, and lastly among

British colonies there is the present example of Jamaica with its powerful elective system and of Grenada about to enter upon the enjoyment of the first instalment of similar privileges.

(ii) *Allow elected members but retain ultimate control.* Given then on the one hand that the control of the Secretary of State must continue in effective form, and on the other that the movements towards elective representation must be met, it would seem clear that this can best be done by following existing precedents and including in the legislatures a certain number of members chosen by direct election.

... The main stages of such evolution may be briefly suggested:—

The first stages would be on the basis approved for Grenada by such adjustments of numbers as will, while leaving the official bloc in a clear majority, give place to 'Elected Members' by reducing the number of nominated officials.

The next stage would appear to be the adjustment of numbers with the effect of transferring the majority held by the Official 'Bloc' to the hands of the elected and nominated elements conjointly. Such a redistribution of numbers, under which, of course the nominated unofficial element would retain complete liberty of voting as it likes ... would at the same time afford reasonable likelihood that on grave matters the responsible element in the community represented by the nominated members would be found in support of the Government and thus furnish a majority if, on the most unfavourable hypothesis, the elected members were unanimous against it. In this connection it is worthy of note that it is desirable to establish definitely the liberty of nominated unofficial members in Jamaica to vote as they like. Only in this way is it possible to relieve nominated members of the stigma, which detracts so much from their usefulness both in the community and in debate, that they are mere dummies under the thumb of the Governor to whom it is useless to appeal by discussion or by argument.

(iii) *Maintain the confidence of capitalists in the stability of Trinidad's government.* Although the recent demand for a change in the constitution only came to a head in 1921, when meetings were first held in the colony to discuss the matter, the question had been raised so long ago as 1850, and in 1888 a Commission was appointed to consider it. But it is not the history of the question which creates the difficulty in Trinidad so much as the general conditions prevailing in the island. Trinidad is the one community which appeared largely to lack any homogeneous public opinion. Socially it is divided into all kinds of groups which have very few relations with one another. There is a considerable French Creole element largely engaged in cocoa-growing, French-speaking and preserving its own traditions. There is a Spanish element which is reinforced continually by intercourse with Venezuela. Above all, the colony possesses a very considerable East Indian element, roughly 130,000 people out of a total population of 360,000 largely illiterate, speaking some five or six different languages, and living a life of its own. And lastly, in addition to the African and coloured element, there is an appreciable number of Chinese, mostly engaged in the retail trade. With a population so constituted Trinidad is exceptionally cosmopolitan. It is the only one of the West Indian islands which contains mining enterprises on any substantial scale, and considerable capital has been embarked in asphalt and oil development by outside corporations. It is, accordingly, important that no action should be taken which would disturb the confidence felt by such capital in the stability of the local government.

d. A comment on the first elections in Trinidad

British Guiana Daily Chronicle, 31 March 1928

The experiment which however has the greatest fascination for us is that of Trinidad. That handsomely endowed, cosmopolitan and prosperous island had never enjoyed representative government under the British flag. . . . When therefore the great adventure was made it was not surprising that the reactionary press of the island should seek every subterfuge to prove that . . . the colony no more wanted elective principles than they wanted the moon. The figures of the recent polls have been seized upon to prove the indifference of the people. It is pointed out that out of a total of

21,794 registered voters, only some 7,000 recorded their votes; ergo 14,000 electors, or two-thirds, were indifferent to whether there was Crown colony government, nominated representatives, or any old thing. . . .

The real facts of the case however, are that 6,162 voters returned their representatives unopposed; so had no occasion to go to the polling booths. In other words only 15,632 electors must be regarded in relation to the seven thousand odd who went to the polls. Of these fifteen thousand 7,231 represented Port of Spain alone of whom no less than 4,163 voted; while we have seen it stated that over one thousand voters had to be turned away from the polls in Port of Spain owing to the crush, and the inadequate arrangements provided. We venture to think that 5,000 persons out of the electorate of 7,000 is a very creditable showing indeed. In the country constituencies there is nothing of which to be ashamed. In no part of the world is there ever anything like fifty per cent. poll in rural districts. . . . But after the two country constituents which sent in members unopposed are deducted, the country constituents of Trinidad still polled 2,827 votes. Trinidad, we think, has made a very handsome showing; and we would not venture to encourage those who think otherwise to try and take away the right of the Trinidadians to elect their representatives in the Legislative Council.

3. The electing of some members of the Legislative Councils did not satisfy West Indian critics of Crown colony government for very long. They wished elected members to control the policies of West Indian governments instead of the Governor and Secretary of State.

a. A petition from Jamaica for a greater responsibility in their own government

Petition of Members of the Legislative Council, March 1922

We approach . . . with a feeling of respectful confidence, . . . asking Your Majesty to take into consideration our earnest desire to be invested with a larger measure of political rights by an extension of the privileges of the representatives of the people, in granting them greater authority and responsibility in connection with a levying and appropriation of our revenues, and a larger share in the initiation and framing of our domestic legislation. . . .

We pray . . . to direct Your Majesty's attention to the composition of the Executive Council of the island on which the popular section of the Legislative Council is entirely unrepresented, and on which as a consequence the representatives of the people have no recognised voice, and therefore no direct means of offering advice or contributing opinions on matters affecting general legislation, and on the fiscal and financial policy of the government.

b. Cipriani claims Dominion Status for the West Indies

Cipriani in Legislative Council, Trinidad, 14 November 1930

The Wood Commission . . . in the face of very strong representation and very strong opposition by the Chamber of Commerce and other responsible associations, . . . accepted the principle of representative government. . . . That report made it clear that as time went on and the elected members proved their fitness for more representation and more power, it would be given to them. Time has gone on, and . . . nothing has been done. . . . We make the same claim that we again brought forward in 1930, namely, that the people of this colony have got the education, the ability, the civilisation, and the necessary culture to administer their own affairs.

. . . Crown colony rule may still be ideal for the primitive races and for peoples just emerged from slavery. Crown colony rule may be all well for the jungle and wilds of Africa, but it has outlived its usefulness in these colonies, and we, the peoples of these colonies, have got to stand shoulder to shoulder to oust it to get some other rule which gives more freedom, more liberty, and recognises the rights and privileges of a free people. It is all very well and good to talk of us as 'subject races'. I laugh that to scorn! We are free people of the British Empire. We are entitled to the same privileges and the same form of government and administration as our bigger sisters, the Dominions, and we have got to use everything in our power, strain every nerve, make every effort—I go further and say to make every sacrifice—to bring self-government and Dominion status to these beautiful colonies.

c. The voters of Grenada claim the right to control their own affairs within a self-governing West Indian Federation

Address to the Hon. T. A. Marryshow & G. Elmore Edwards, September 1932

In pursuance of the principle of the self-determination of peoples within the British Commonwealth of Nations and in exercise of our inherent and undoubted rights as free men, we the people of Grenada adopt and present these our claims as the instrument by which we and our successors shall be governed. And in support of our demands, we further present that our education, status and wealth justify us in determining in what manner our affairs shall be conducted and under what system we shall be governed in the future.

Whereas the said colony of Grenada forms part of what is generally known as the British Commonwealth of Nations, but there is still imposed upon us the status of a Crown-ruled section of the said Commonwealth of Nations with no rights, powers or privileges vested in the people of the said colony . . .

And whereas such effective control is now vested in a Governor and Commander-in-Chief and the inhabitants are thereby fettered and restricted in the enjoyment of their rights as free men:

And whereas it is necessary and desirable that this colony should as an intermediate step towards the realisation of Self-Government within a federal union of the British West Indian Islands, be governed under a constitution which preserves to the people the right to have an effective control in the government of themselves and their own affairs. . . .

BE IT THEREFORE RESOLVED:—

That there shall henceforth be established a government by the Crown represented by an Administrator for and on behalf of itself and the people of Grenada and that such government shall submit all matters appertaining to the conduct of the affairs of the colony for decision by a Legislative Assembly the majority of whose members shall be chosen by the people and whose function shall be to make laws and authorise the collection and disposal of all monies for the use of the colony and for any other purpose agreed upon by the members in session and generally to do all manner of things in the interest of peace, order and good and effective government of the colony. The duration of the Assembly shall be for a period of four years.

The Crown shall after consultation between its representative and the representatives chosen by the inhabitants, make the necessary provision for the constitution of an Executive Council.

d. Crown colony government stifles popular initiative
Report of Unofficial West Indian Conference, Dominica, 1932

Crown colony rule unquestionably stands today at the bar of public opinion throughout the Caribbean archipelago indicted on three major counts: firstly, that it is wasteful and inefficient; secondly, that it discriminates among the various sections of the population, and denies equal opportunities to those whom it governs, and whose happiness and advancement it should seek impartially to promote; and thirdly, that it is indifferent to public criticism and popular aspiration as expressed by the elected representatives of the people, so that instead of a fundamentally harmonious and fruitful co-operation between government and governed there exist in most of the West Indian islands two hostile camps; one displaying an arrogant and calculated contempt of popular desires and opinions, and the other a sullen and suspicious resentment of all the acts of government, a state of affairs, which, inevitably, reacts unfavourably on both camps to the detriment of the peace and progress of the community as a whole. But there is a more subtle, more impalpable and with all more pervasive evil attendant upon the Crown colony system. It is the stifling of popular initiative. Powerless to mould policy, still more powerless to act independently, paralysed by the subconscious fear of impending repression and thereby bereft of constructive thought, the West Indian has hitherto been inclined to dissipate his energies in acute and penetrating but embittered and essentially destructive criticism of the Government on which, nevertheless, he has waited for the initiation of all policies intended to benefit his people, and which he has expected to assume the full responsibility for all necessary decisions. His political life has been overshadowed by a government too omnipotent and too omnipresent, and has had little opportunity for independent growth.

e. A Governor comments on the claim for Dominion status
Governor of the Leewards, 1936

But some more educated West Indians began to talk darkly of the defects of Crown Colony Government, and their newspapers began to question why the living conditions of the people were not made better and what this system of government, 'with its overpaid imported Englishmen', was doing about it? After all, these things are a matter of opinion. They on their side felt that if the paternal system of government from the Colonial Office were abolished and they had 'Dominion Status' instead (this phrase was very much in the various newspapers of the Empire just then), they could administer their affairs just as well as 'the imported Englishmen' could. Whether this would be so or not the fact remains that nature and the world depression had combined to bring about a situation which must inevitably have been exactly as difficult, to say the least, for whatever body of men had to meet it. And the Dominion Status that they longed for would surely imply that they would have to foot the bill each time such an abnormal situation as this occurred, and no longer expect help from the English taxpayers.

f. Greater West Indian participation in government necessary for successful economic and social reforms
Moyne Report, 1939

Rightly or wrongly, a substantial body of public opinion in the West

Indies is convinced that far-reaching measures of social reconstruction depend, both for their initiation and their effective administration, upon greater participation of the people in the business of government. . . . An examination of the social and economic problems of the West Indies which, however exhaustive, took no account of this point of view, would therefore be regarded by some sections of public opinion in the Caribbean area as having failed in a primary purpose. Moreover, we are satisfied that the claim so often put before us that the people should have a larger voice in the management of their affairs represents a genuine sentiment and reflects a growing political consciousness which is sufficiently widespread to make it doubtful whether any schemes of social reform, however wisely conceived and efficiently conducted, would be completely successful unless they were accompanied by the largest measure of constitutional development which is thought to be judicious in existing circumstances.

4. After the Second World War, West Indians eager for self-government wished to remove non-elected members from Legislative Councils, to have a majority of elected members in Executive Councils and to reduce drastically, or abolish entirely, the power of the Governor. The last of these the British Government would not agree to in the 1940s, and they also insisted on seats for the three important members of the Civil Service. But by the end of the 1950s the British Government had conceded what had been clamoured for.

a. The Secretary of State rejects proposals to abolish the Governor's powers

Secretary of State to Governor of Jamaica, January 1942

I am unable to entertain any proposals which would have the effect of obscuring the vital distinction between responsible and representative government; the supreme executive authority of the Governor must therefore be preserved, and it is essential that he should have the necessary powers of 'certification' and of 'veto'.

b. The Executive Council

Jamaica (Constitution) Order in Council, 1944

Composition. The Executive Council shall consist of the Governor as Chairman, three Official Members, two persons not holding office of emolument under the Crown in Jamaica who ... are members of the Legislative Council, who shall be styled Nominated Members, and five persons who ... are Members of the House of Representatives, who shall be styled Elected Members.

The Official Members shall be the Colonial Secretary, the Attorney-General, and the Financial Secretary and Treasurer.

c. Composition and powers of this kind of Executive Council criticised

Minority Report of Dr. Solomon, Constitutional Reform Committee, Trinidad, February 1948

The seat of power in every constitution is the Government, however that Government may be comprised; and unless the people have a controlling voice in the Government they have no say in the control of their own affairs. An enlarged Legislature with a majority of elected members does not in any way compensate for the absence of a decisive elected majority in the Executive, which is the Government. ...

It is right that power should pass from the hands of a single individual (in this case the Governor) to a democratically elected body. To suggest that the Executive outlined above is in any way democratic in its formation is but to prostitute the truth, while the recommendation which says that the Executive should be responsible to the legislature is completely contradicted by the provisions which ensure that official members shall sit as of right and that the nominated element may not be excluded by vote.

Surely to have advocated such contradictions is to have crossed the border-line between compromise and political confusion.

To have made such an Executive the principal instrument of policy does not in these circumstances increase the degree of responsibility to be exercised by the people themselves through their elected representatives. . . .

In as much as the Executive is for all practical purposes to be the Government, it cannot be said that the people of the colony are being given any greater say in the Government. . . . The general impression is that there is a pronounced fear of accepting responsibility of any kind, leaving the balance of power just where it was before. . . . The desire has been, as far as possible, to base their ideas on the Jamaica constitution, without pausing to consider whether the conditions which obtain in Trinidad today are identical with those which obtained in Jamaica in 1944.

5. Full independence and dominion status have come to Jamaica, Trinidad, Barbados and British Guiana, renamed Guyana, in the nineteen-sixties.

a. A Jamaican view that public and private institutions have been preparing for independence for twenty years

Five-year Independence Plan, Jamaica 1963–1968

In August 1962, Jamaica became an independent country with Dominion Status within the British Commonwealth.

The past 15 to 20 years have seen the gradual development of the institutional framework essential to a country moving towards independence.

Since 1938 a two-party system of political representation has evolved.

Adult suffrage was granted in 1944. Jamaica has had many democratic elections since that year and the results of the ballot have been the sole determinant of political succession. What many other newly independent countries must discover in the future, Jamaica has so far proven to itself and to the world in the past 18 years, namely, that a small country can establish and maintain political stability through a democratic system of Parliamentary Government under the Rule of Law.

Jamaica's legal system, patterned closely on the British system and now underwritten in the Constitution which came into effect with Independence, provides full safeguards to persons and property and for the maintenance of law and order.

The civil service has been reorganised to bring it into line with the requirements of a developing community and to fit into the Ministerial system which came into full operation in 1957.

A variety of agencies and institutions have been established to deal with the requirements of an advancing community. These include special organisations for the promotion of development such as the Agricultural Development Corporation and the Industrial Development Corporation, the Tourist Board, and the financial institutions including the Central Bank and the Development Finance Corporation.

The machinery operated by the Government for dealing with industrial relations has developed considerable experience over the past 25 years.

In the private sector a strong trade union movement, active employers' organisations and associations such as the Chamber of Commerce and the Manufacturers' Association, the Jamaica Agricultural Society, and various agricultural commodity associations, look after their specific interests.

These changes along with political and economic development, form a foundation of growing stability but which is sufficiently flexible to adjust to the stresses and consequent changes demanded of an emerging and developing society.

Present-day Jamaica is a microcosm of the world, mixing many of its peoples, having many of its problems, some of its fortunes, and endeavouring to answer the question that must concern every country today, large or small, namely, can a small country achieve and maintain at once, parliamentary democracy, economic viability, and social justice.

b. The Barbadian Prime Minister pleads for a national culture in a small modern independent country

Preface, Barbados Independence Issue, 'New World', Dead Season 1966 and Croptime 1967

After over 300 years of British rule, Barbados has attained independence. To the people of Barbados this is a moment of great significance. For henceforth we will not be the subjects of any colonial power; rather we will be citizens of the land that gave us birth and sustenance, that fashioned our joys and our sorrows.

We in Barbados are part of a world-wide movement which in the post-war period has brought freedom to subject peoples in Africa, Asia, South America and the Caribbean. Like the peoples of these areas, we are waging a war against poverty and unemployment, and against all the accompanying social and cultural ills. In the face of manifold odds we are struggling to transform our economy from being colonist and backward looking, into one which is modern and progressive.

It is my sincere hope that independence will release in our people a sense of deep pride in their country, a feeling of being one people, and a self-confidence that we can overcome all obstacles that stand in the way of personal realisation and national development.

Our total commitment now and for the future is nothing less than the social and cultural upliftment of our nation. In this challenging task we must know who we are, whence we came, and where we are heading. A searching analysis of our heritage and traditions must be conducted if our cultural identity is to be established. Our novelists, poets and short-story writers have for some time now been holding a mirror up to our society and interpreting our customs, mores and personality traits. So far, something has been accomplished. I trust that our new political status will stimulate much greater activity in the arts.

May our people draw deeply on our cultural heritage. May we use independence not as an end in itself, but as a turning-point in time when we discovered new energies for a massive and successful assault on the problems facing a small community.

D. REGIONAL CO-OPERATION SUPERSEDES
FEDERAL GOVERNMENT

1. After World War I, the initiative passed from the British Government to West Indians in commerce and in politics. Their schemes were not greeted with enthusiasm. The British Government restricted itself to encouraging conferences of civil servants and unofficial Members of Legislative Councils on matters of common interest.

a. *The Federal League advocates united action through a 'Loose form of federation'*

Trinidad Guardian, Report of the meeting to form the West Indian Federal League, 7 October 1917

The meeting was unanimous in desiring the formation of a League to promote Federation. . . . Since the war the necessity for the establishment of some form of federation has become more urgent, having regard especially to provision for representation of the West Indies at the Imperial Parliament and the Imperial Conference at Westminster and elsewhere. It was obvious to all present that this could only be attained by a system of federation and that as separate units the West Indian colonies would remain a voiceless and unrepresented cypher in the British Empire. It was equally obvious that the matter was one calling for immediate action, otherwise the end of the war . . . would find the West Indies still a conglomeration of obscure units with no organised voice for themselves or their neighbours and probably represented at the Empire Council by the Colonial Office.

It was decided that every effort should be made to avoid this. There were also many other grounds on which a loose form of federation, based on material action in common interests could not fail to appeal to the common sense of the West Indies as being not only desirable, but practically unassailable in theory and practice. . . .

The necessity of strong and united action by the West Indies in such matters as, among many others, of Mail Steamship Contracts, where the interests of the West Indies may come into collision with that of very powerful countries, was touched upon, for it was noted that the action of the Associated Chambers of Commerce could only after all, be advisory, as contrasted with the definite power to be wielded by a West Indian Federal Council.

Unfortunately there exists a class in the larger colonies who associate the word federation with the curtailment of the undoubted right of each colony to legislate for itself in internal matters, tax for itself and spend its revenue for its own needs. It is necessary to disabuse the minds of these people that federation whatever it may have meant in the past, means none of these things nowadays. . . . The West Indian colonies, each retaining their own dearly valued independence may combine together on unobjectionable and desirable lines to deal with matters in which we are all equally interested, thus presenting to the world a strong concerted front in matters where our united interests are threatened or overlooked. . . . This must not be regarded as a purely political matter not affecting the everyday man obsessed in earning his living; commerce has invariably been dependent for its stability on political strength—it is not possible to regard commerce and politics as things apart.

b. A proposal for confederation by conference
Edward Davson to Secretary of State, 22 September 1920

Sir,—I venture to address you with reference to the closer union of the West Indian Colonies, including with these our mainland colonies of British Guiana and British Honduras. . . .

I have presided at two discussions in the West Indies, the last of these being at the meeting of the Associated Chambers in Barbados last February. I may state, that while I found the opinion of the delegates unanimously in favour of the continuous and increasing co-operation of the various colonies ... I found on the other hand a general reluctance on their part to commit themselves to, or even to discuss any definite scheme of political federation; and I gathered that this was not based on any hostility to the idea of unity, but was due to the practical difficulties entailed in the formation of any dominant Federal Council and to the fear that such a body might in some way interfere with the liberty of action of the respective colonies.

It may be said ... that the idea of co-operation is already developing itself. This is so; but such co-operation unless developed systematically cannot progress very far. Nor can one believe ... that the greatest good can be obtained from the West Indies if each unit is to be left to work out its destiny by itself. ...

The prospect of a Federal Council, under a Governor-General, creates but a lukewarm feeling in the West Indies and I now venture to propose an alternative scheme. ...

Conferences have from time to time been held in these colonies—conferences by medical officers on quarantine, by law officers on the formation of a West Indian Court of Appeal, by customs officers on the uniformity of tariffs, as well as the conferences promoted by the Associated Chambers of Commerce and by the Agricultural Department. These conferences have invariably been attended with success, and one is tempted to feel that, when any such system is successful, it is better to proceed by developing it than by experimenting in other and untried directions.

I propose that a Central Council be created of say, ten members, nominated by the Secretary of State and ... there would be certain branches or sections dealing with legal, medical, fiscal, educational, police, commercial and other questions. Each section would hold regular triennial meetings instead of as now, occasional ones, which would be attended respectively by the Attorneys-General, Surgeons-General, Collectors of Customs, Chief Educational Officers, Chiefs of Police and Chambers of Commerce representatives of the several colonies. ...

When any resolution calling for action resulted from such sectional conferences, it would be submitted to the Central Council. Should it meet with the unanimous approval of the Council, it would then be forwarded direct —and not via the Secretary of State—to each colony with a request that it might be considered by the local legislature. . . .

On the other hand, should a resolution be adopted only by a majority of the Council, it would be referred to the Secretary of State for his consideration, while, should it be rejected, it would fall to the ground. This procedure would grant a certain measure of autonomy to the West Indies when the desire for action on a certain matter was unanimous. . . .

If the approval of the various colonies to the scheme is to be obtained, they should be called upon to incur the minimum of expense through the idea of 'Federation by Conference'. . . . It is obvious, however, that the sectional conferences, as well as the Central Secretariat, would entail a certain though not considerable, expenditure of money. . . .

I trust, Sir, that you will pardon my submitting the above views for your consideration. I believe that such a scheme, a loose form of federation, is all that is needed or desired at the present stage of development, while the granting of such a measure of slightly increased self-government would undoubtedly be appreciated by the West Indian colonies.

c. *Lukewarm response to the invitation to attend a conference at Trinidad in January 1922*

Editorial, *Gleaner*, 22 December 1921

Jamaica gladly accepted the invitation to join in a conference on West Indian questions to be held in Trinidad in January next. Trinidad, British Guiana, the Bahamas, British Honduras and the Windward Islands have all declined the invitation. . . .

Jamaica . . . has been anxious for the formulation of some scheme that would bring the West Indies into closer working unity. She has through the Jamaica Imperial Association, suggested such a scheme to the other colonies, and these seemed to regard it favourably. When the moment came for action, however, most of the colonies declined to act. . . .

Thus collapses the first official effort put forth to bring the British West

Indies into closer touch with one another. . . . We think that our sister colonies have made a mistake. . . . Yet we for one will not allow present disappointment to prevent us from trying to convince the sister colonies that there is at the very least nothing to be risked by meeting, to deal with questions affecting us all. . . .

West Indians have not yet acquired a sense of the necessity of co-opera-tion. Yet the prospect is not at all dark. The Chambers of Commerce of the different colonies have been formed into an Associated Chamber of Commerce, which meets every three years to consider and pass resolutions on matters affecting the industrial and commercial welfare of the West Indies. One of these conferences has been held; another is scheduled to take place next year. . . . And if these unofficial conferences continue to be held, it must of a surety become apparent to the legislatures of the colonies that conferences such as that proposed by the Secretary of State for the Colonies might serve a useful purpose. We hope so; in the meantime we regret that there will be no meeting of West Indian delegates in January. For, so long as each colony decides to speak and to act alone, just so long must their action be weak and uncertain, and their voices of little weight in the United Kingdom, where, above everywhere else, they must desire to be heard.

2. The West Indians who were trying to organise trade unions saw in federation a means of improving the standard of living of the workers; since federation meant for them and for the politi-cians who criticised Crown colony government, the surest and quickest way to West Indian self-government.

a. A labour leader puts the case for federation and self-govern-ment to his colleagues

Cipriani, *Speech to British Guiana and West Indies Labour Conference*, January 1926

The Trinidad Working Men's Association moved the following resolution:

It is the opinion of the Conference that in the best interest of the people of British Guiana and the West Indies these colonies should be federated and granted some form of self-government, which will enable them to conduct their own affairs under a Colonial Parliament with Dominion Status.

Captain Cipriani (Trinidad) said that the question of federation was not entirely a labour question but it was a question which affected the life of every West Indian colony. . . .

It was quite true that there were many difficulties which presented themselves to the question of federation. One was the distance of ocean which divided each colony from the other. . . .

Insular prejudice was another difficulty and one which was a serious difficulty, but all the same in his mind it was not insurmountable.

Every West Indian island suffered from insular prejudice.

. . . but he would ask those present that day and those who represented labour and the labouring class, whether under all those forms of separate government it was not a fact that in each and every one there was similarity in this one point; that the under-dog never got a square deal. If they were satisfied that that was so then he put it to them that as representatives of labour it was their duty, it was their interest to strike out for some new form of constitution, and they could strike for no better constitution, no form in which they could hope to derive better benefits, no form in which they would look forward to greater prosperity and development of these colonies than the form he suggested under the name of federation, and if he said to them let their watchword be 'educate, co-operate and federate', then he thought he had put the case before them in its entirety. . . .

When all was said and done what was the form of government he advocated? What was meant by the federation which he was now urging them to adopt? What was meant by the form of government for which he was so earnestly pleading and asking their support? It meant plainly and simply and in few words that these colonies would be run by their own people and by their own Parliament.

b. A St. Lucian warns the Windwards against domination by Trinidad

Letter in 'The Voice of St. Lucia', 19 July 1932

I am in favour of West Indian federation because I feel it will simplify the form of government and reduce expenditure. At present the superstructure is too imposing and expensive for these impoverished islands, and any scheme, call it federation, or fetteration, or any other name that will simplify the machinery of government, is sure to meet with general approval. West Indian governors will soon hold their pow-wow in England out of earshot of the troubled scene. However, whatever may be their views on federation, in my view, the scheme that is immediately feasible and workable is a federation of the Windward and Leeward Islands, leaving out for the present Trinidad, Barbados and Jamaica until such time when it may be ripe to extend the scope of the fusion. To attempt more now is bound to be futile. Trinidad no doubt would like to be the top dog, with the rest of us, like little pups barking on the outside of the kennel just like Tobago, but that must not be. It must be an equal partnership or no partnership at all, with the Windward and Leeward Islands, no top dog principle is involved—it is a case of two impoverished groups seeking political and economic salvation by means of a union. One word more: the kind of federation envisaged presupposes representative institutions. If not, then our last state shall be worse than the first.

c. A speaker claims that the foundations of West Indian nationhood will be laid at the conference in Dominica in 1932

Rawle, Speech at West Indian Conference, Dominica, October 1932

Ladies and Gentlemen, it is fitting that as the first official act of the Conference we give a manifestation of our loyalty and devotion to the Crown. I shall therefore put a resolution to this meeting and ask you to adopt it unanimously, by all standing. This is the resolution:

'We the delegates from the British West Indian colonies of Trinidad, Barbados, Grenada, St. Vincent, St. Lucia and the Leeward Islands assembled at Dominica to discuss the question of federation and effective representation desire most humbly on behalf of the people of these colonies to express our deep and unswerving loyalty to the Person and Throne of His Most Gracious Majesty the King.'

The resolution was thereupon carried by acclamation.

Ladies and Gentlemen, today, Friday October the 28th, marks the opening of a new chapter of West Indian history—a chapter which we all fervently hope will record the emancipation of the West Indian peoples from their political and economic serfdom. We are fortunate indeed to be present at the opening of this epoch-making Conference. It is one that will lay the foundation stones of West Indian Nationality. It is one that we and our children will look back to, we hope, with the pride that comes from solid achievement. For myself I deem it a double honour to have the privilege of welcoming to Dominica on behalf of the people, the delegates who have gathered here tonight from all parts of the Eastern Caribbean. They have come to this Conference to assist in a common cause, with a common purpose, namely, to make an end once and for all, of the anachronism of Crown colony rule and to build upon sure and certain foundations a new West Indian Nationhood. Their presence is evidence of what I may term a new West Indian solidarity. It is evidence that the old prejudices of insularity are dying, prejudices that have kept us, West Indians, a people of common interest, of common stock, upbringing, tradition and ideas apart to our mutual detriment. The cancer of insular prejudice is disappearing before the awakening realisation of the common benefits of combination.

d. West Indian Trade Unions meeting in Congress declare themselves in favour of West Indian federation

Second Caribbean Labour Congress, Jamaica, September 1947

This Conference declares in favour of the establishment of a Federation of the British Caribbean Territories and of the immediate initiation of all the practical steps that must be taken to secure that end.

The Conference is convinced that the development of West Indian Nationhood, the evolution of our social and cultural standards, the expansion and stability of our economy, the orderly and vigorous development of our resources in human material and in land, the achievement of the individual and collective aspirations of our people and the creation of civilised standards of life whereby each and all may hope to enjoy life, liberty and the pursuit of happiness, can best and most fully be secured by the Federation of the territories concerned.

Note is taken of the fact that at all levels of activity, in trade and commerce, in the fields of production, in the Civil and other services, in Education and in social, labour and political organisations they are developing inter-relations between the territories which common interests and outlooks make possible and indeed dictate.

It is the conviction of Conference that these beginnings can only grow with speed and effectiveness within the framework of a political Federation and that there is no real barrier to Federation today which cannot be overcome by the united will and the combined statesmanship and leadership of the peoples of our lands.

3. Towards the end of World War II many political and professional groups advocated Federation. In response, the Secretary of State invited the legislatures to send delegates to a conference in Montego Bay in order 'to arrive at collective views for consideration by the individual governments'. Thus was set in train the series of meetings of committees and conferences which took place between 1947 and 1957. From their work came the Federation inaugurated in 1958.

a. The Legislative Council, Jamaica, decides to ask other West Indian governments how they feel about federation

Minutes of Legislative Council, Jamaica, 7 June 1944

Mr. Campbell moved—
Whereas successive Secretaries of State for the Colonies, including the

Right Honourable Colonel Stanley, have repeatedly asserted and emphasised the fact that it is the express intention and desire of His Majesty's Government in Great Britain to confer Dominion Status upon such component parts of the Colonial Empire that have reached the stage of political development as to warrant the grant of such status; And whereas it is desirable and essential for the fullest economic, social and political development of the British West Indies (including British Guiana and British Honduras) that a federation of all the islands and governments is a necessary pre-requisite to a grant by the Imperial Government of full Dominion Status to these islands and colonies:

Be it resolved that this Government take early steps to ascertain the desire and feelings of the governments and peoples of the other British West Indian islands (including British Guiana and British Honduras) on the question of federation with a view to a joint request to the Imperial Authorities to combine the various islands and colonies into a West Indian Federation:

And be it further resolved that a copy of this resolution be transmitted to the Right Honourable The Secretary of State for the Colonies.

Seconded by Dr. Anderson.

On the motion being put the Council divided as follows:—

Ayes—18.

Noes—1.

Passed in the affirmative.

b. *The Secretary of State announces British policy and invites West Indians to discuss federation*

Circular Despatch of Secretary of State to Governors of all West Indian Colonies, 14 March 1945

I have recently been considering the question of constitutional policy in relation to the Colonies of the Caribbean area. . . .

It will, I think, be generally agreed that under modern conditions it has become more difficult for very small units . . . to maintain full and complete independence in all aspects of Government. . . . Indeed the trend of post-war development, under the stimulus of greatly improved air communications, may well show a marked impulse towards a closer political and other association of those smaller territorial units which, through proximity or a common language, have mutual interests. I consider it important, therefore, that the more immediate purpose of developing self-governing institutions in the individual British Caribbean Colonies should keep in view the larger project of their political federation. . . .

For the reasons which I have set forth . . . and in view of the greater economy and efficiency in general of large-scale units of government under modern conditions, I consider that the aim of British policy should be the development of federation in the Caribbean at such time as the balance of opinion in the various Colonies is in favour of a change, and when the development of communications makes it administratively practicable. The ultimate aim of any federation which may be established would be full internal self-government within the British Commonwealth. . . .

I regard it as desirable that a lead should be given by His Majesty's Government in favour of the aim of federation, and that British policy should aim at the fostering of a sense of West Indian unity and of the removal of the present obstacles in the way of federation. In particular the fullest possible use should be made of every unifying influence, as circumstances permit, by the development of joint West Indian services, joint conferences, and through the organisation established under the Comptroller for Development and Welfare. It will be recognised that in recent years, and particularly during the war, there has been an increase in the matters which have been dealt with on a West Indian as opposed to a purely Colony basis, and that a yet wider field where such unified action could advantageously be taken is now open, e.g. in such matters as the establishment of a West Indian meteorological service, the adoption of the same quarantine code, the development of broadcasting and so forth. Further it is important that in considering the question of federation, attention should not be focused solely on political matters. There is scope for the development of unified action in the administrative and economic fields. . . .

With the aim of federation in view it is desirable that political developments in each Colony should be definitely related to the wider policy I have enunciated and should, as far as possible, follow similar lines. ...

I consider ... that the policy of His Majesty's Government in this matter should be announced and full opportunity given for public discussion of it. I would propose ... that this despatch should be published ... and ... an early opportunity could thereafter be taken to obtain the opinions of Colonial Legislatures by arranging for each of them to debate the issue of political federation in the West Indies. If all those Legislatures were then to declare themselves in favour of the aim of federation, the next step would be the consideration of the means whereby proposals could be drawn up for such closer association between West Indian Colonies as may prove immediately feasible. One possiblity is that a conference of West Indian delegates should be held at a later date, either in the West Indies or in London, to consider the formulation of proposals for that closer association.

c. *Some of the resolutions passed at the Montego Bay conference, September 1947*

Report of Conference, 1948

Resolution 1. That this Conference, recognising the desirability of a political federation of the British Caribbean territories, accepts the principle of a federation in which each constituent unit retains complete control over all matters except those specifically assigned to the federal government.

Resolution 2. That this Conference believes that an increasing measure of responsibility should be extended to the several units of the British Caribbean territories, whose political development must be pursued as an aim in itself, without prejudice and in no way subordinate to progress towards federation.

Resolution 3. That this Conference believes that the provision of adequate inter-Colonial and external shipping services and other communications is essential if progress is to be made towards federation, and recommends that in the meantime, and until a federal authority exists, a British Caribbean Shipping Committee should be set up. . . .

Resolution 4. Whereas progress toward federation will be accelerated by putting agriculture in the British Caribbean area on a more secure economic basis than now exists. *Resolved:*

That this Conference recommends that immediate steps be taken for the setting up of a central body of primary producers (representative of all British Caribbean Colonies) with a view to accelerating the development of agriculture throughout the area on a sound economic basis. . . .

Resolution 6. Resolved: That this Conference recommends:—

(1) the immediate constitution of a Standing Closer Association Committee. . . .

(2) that the terms of reference of the above Committee be to consider and make recommendations in relation to:—

   (*a*) the assimilation of

     (i) the fiscal, customs and tariff policy of the British territories in the Caribbean area . . .

     (ii) the legislation of such territories;

   (*b*) the unification of the currency of such territories;

   (*c*) the unification, so far as may be practicable, of the public services of such territories . . .

   (*d*) the form of a federal constitution and federal judiciary most likely to give effect to the aspirations of the people of such territories; and

   (*e*) the means of financing the operation of all federal services. . . .

Resolution 7. That this Conference recommends the appointment by the Secretary of State of a Commission to examine, in consultation with the Governments of the territories in the British Caribbean area, the question of the establishment of a Customs Union. . . .

Resolution 9. That this Conference recommends that the Governments of the British Caribbean territories should appoint a small regional committee to study and report upon matters of common economic significance, and to advise upon the merits of plans for economic development.

d. The British Caribbean Federation is set up

Report of the West Indies Constitutional Conference, 1961

A series of conferences beginning with the Montego Bay Conference of 1947 followed, in the course of which there gradually evolved a plan for a British Caribbean Federation. At the last of these conferences in London in February, 1956, Jamaica, Trinidad and Tobago, Barbados, the Leeward Islands Territories (less the British Virgin Islands) and the Windward Islands Territories—a total of ten Territories—decided finally that they would 'be bound together in federation'.

In the furtherance of this decision the British Caribbean Federation Act, 1956 provided for the establishment of the Federation of the West Indies and a subsequent Order in Council provided for a Federal Constitution. Under this Constitution there was to be a Governor-General who would preside over a Council of State comprising a Prime Minister and other Ministers; a Senate with two members from each Territory except Montserrat which had one; a House of Representatives of forty-five members distributed between the Territories on a weighted formula which took account of, but was not solely determined by, population; and a Federal Supreme Court. The legislative powers of the Federation were set out in an Exclusive Legislative List. Both the Federal and Territorial Legislatures were empowered to legislate for subjects on the Concurrent List but Federal Constitution affirmed the principles of freedom of religious worship and the greatest possible freedom of movement of persons and goods within the Federation and set out the aim of establishing as quickly as possible a Customs Union including internal free trade. Certain interim provisions of this constitution came into force on 3rd January, 1958 when the Rt. Hon. Lord Hailes, G.B.E., arrived in Trinidad to assume office as Governor-General of the Federation. The remainder of the constitution came into force on 22nd April, 1958 when the Federal Parliament was inaugurated in the presence of Her Royal Highness Princess Margaret.

4. In September 1961 Jamaicans voted in a referendum to leave the federation. Trinidad followed suit in January 1962. Attempts to maintain a new federation of the 'Little Eight' islands had broken down by 1965 when Barbados decided to seek independence on her own.

a. Professor Sir Arthur Lewis accepts that political federation is postponed indefinitely. New kinds of association must precede it

Lewis, *The Agony of the Eight*, 1965

Ultimately West Indians will come together again in political association, but only after the present generation of leaders is dead.

Jamaica is out for ever; should never have been in, since sentiment for federation was never strong in that island.

But it is the inescapable destiny of Trinidad, British Guiana and the other British islands to link their fortunes together.

No doubt it will begin with confederation, rather than federation; a common nationality, a common currency, and common representation abroad. Once established the links will grow like ivy. Associations should always start on a limited basis, and grow slowly with time.

The eight—or seven or six—must enter such an association as a unit, equal in numbers to the other units, and able to speak with a single voice.

The disparity in size between Jamaica and Trinidad on the one hand, and the eight on the other, was one of the obstacles to smooth working of the defunct West Indies Federation.

b. New association among the three independent countries and the new associated states of the Commonwealth Caribbean

Mordecai, *Preface to 'The West Indies Federation'*, 1968

The West Indian urge for closer association is having a strong revival. All the islands are now staunchly independent, the Leeward and Windward groups in the newfangled device of Associate Statehood, the three larger,

295

Jamaica, Trinidad and Tobago, and Barbados, each as single nations. But the search for common identity continues, although it would be wrong as yet to label this a popular movement. The turbulence of the Federal years has left the almost four million people on both sides of the Caribbean wary of anything resembling 'all that again'. The urge comes from their political leaders and the cognoscenti, spurred mainly by the economic dangers of separation and by their new responsibilities in a contracting world, so they take their stand a step ahead of 'the people', which is in itself a sign of advancing political sophistication.

Last year's meeting of the Commonwealth Parliamentary Association in Port of Spain, Trinidad, proclaimed the theme of Caribbean alliance in various fields. As I write, the University of the West Indies stages a regional conference to examine the technical basis for 'economic integration'. And in London a joint delegation of West Indian Ministers of Trade sternly presses Britain for safeguards if Britain succeeds in joining the European Common Market. The delegates go well prepared. Immediately Britain's application was announced, the Jamaican Prime Minister, Mr. Hugh Shearer, invited his eastern counterparts to design a joint strategy. This they promptly did and agreed as well upon a Caribbean Development Bank to mobilize capital resources regionally. Antigua, Barbados and Guyana are now about to be linked in a Free Trade area. Other islands including Jamaica are discussing a regional Free Trade area. Ministers and their key officials hurry between the islands conferring on regional development, agriculture trading blocs and flock of common problems. This follows on 'Summit' meetings rotating since 1964. Diverse conclusions can be drawn from the fact that Prime Ministers, Premiers and other visiting notables now find themselves far better known and more warmly welcomed than when all were brothers in Federation.

In this seeking of closer identity, the dialogue, the motions, and in some instances the personalities are the same as in the 1950's. The speeches sound like play-backs of recordings familiar when the Regional Economic Committee was the common workshop for union. Amity prevails. No trace remains of the jagged animosities and mutual distrusts which disfigured the break-up of the Federation only five years ago. West Indians do not nourish grudges long.

c. A free trade agreement between Guyana, Barbados, and Antigua is extended to create a Caribbean Free Trade Agreement

S. Ramphal's Speech to the Guyana National Assembly, 22 April 1968

The Bill which is before the House today ratifies the original CARIFTA Agreement which has already been adapted, debated and approved by this House as well as the Supplementary Agreement which was concluded to give effect to the decisions taken at the meeting of Ministers of Trade that was held here in Georgetown in February of this year. That meeting itself had acted in pursuance of resolutions taken at the meeting of Commonwealth Caribbean Heads of Government in October 1967. Between October and February an enormous amount of work was done in hammering out a free trade agreement that would be responsive to the interests of several member territories participating in it while serving the cause of the region as a whole. None of these efforts was more intensive than that which was concerned with the special interests of the smaller territories of the associated States.

None of us is so big or wealthy or developed that we can do otherwise than acknowledge that understanding of the problems that confront these small islands.

Eventually, at the Trade Ministers' meeting in Georgetown, we secured a consensus for transitional arrangements which go a very long way towards enabling the Free Trade Area Agreement to accelerate the development of these islands.

We know that some of these islands have misgivings still, but we feel that we should exhort them to proceed conscious of the fact that they do so in company with others of us who have a special regard for their particular needs.

d. *A Regional Secretariat and Development Bank complete three institutions for economic co-operation as the beginning of a long movement towards Commonwealth Caribbean unity*

S. Ramphal's speech to the Guyana Chamber of Commerce, 8 May 1968

The Free Trade Area Agreement is, of course, only a beginning and there is no cause for us to be complacent about ultimate success. Success will only come if we work hard to secure it. Already the last meeting of the Commonwealth Heads of Governments have taken important decisions towards economic integration. The studies that have been commissioned from the Economic Commission for Latin America and the University of the West Indies are going to be important features in ensuring progress. The Regional Secretariat that is now being established in Georgetown will have a vital role to play in organising these efforts and in ensuring that the dynamic which has now been injected into the regional movement continues without abatement. The establishment of the Regional Development Bank on the basis of the agreement which it is the Government's hope that we will achieve in another few days in Antigua, will complement the trading arrangements by providing regional and non-regional finance for practical works of development. These three institutions represent the beginning of a movement towards Commonwealth Caribbean unity whose ultimate forms we can only dimly discern.

Index